HOW TO SELL
LONG-TERM CARE INSURANCE

Your Guide to
Becoming a
Top Producer
in an Untapped
Market

Jeff Sadler

The
NATIONAL
UNDERWRITER
Company
PROFESSIONAL PUBLISHING GROUP

PO Box 14367 • Cincinnati, OH 45250-0367
1-800-543-0874 • www.nationalunderwriter.com

Cover and layout design: Jason T. Williams

ISBN: 0-87218-602-4

Library of Congress Control Number: 2001095530

1st Edition

Copyright © 2001
The National Underwriter Company
P.O. Box 14367, Cincinnati, Ohio 45250-0367

Printed in U. S. A.

DEDICATION

This book is dedicated to America's unsung heroes – the millions of family caregivers across our country; people like Sandy Primack, caring for his wife Joy, the victim of a brain-stem stroke, on a 24-hour basis while holding down a regular job. Their work is both admirable and inspirational.

Acknowledgements

Authors receive help in many forms before a book is finally published and I'm no different. This volume would not have been possible without the help and generosity, either intended or inadvertent, from the following people: Janet Strickland and Bob Hoffman for the many articles and ideas passed along during the course of a year; my fellow enthusiastic members of the National Association of Health Underwriters' Long-Term Care Working Group, under the capable direction of Diane Mahoney and, currently, Ross Schriftman, for their tireless analysis of all phases of this business; Eileen Sadler for listening and contributing her own thoughts on this issue; and Debbie Miner, the book's editor, for her own vision and dedication to making this the best possible book it could be.

TABLE OF CONTENTS

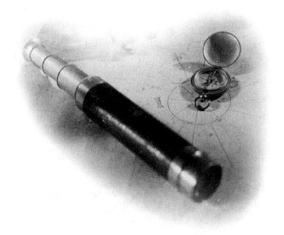

PART ONE:
THE LONG-TERM CARE NEED

"Experience is a great advantage. The problem is that when you get the experience, you're too old to do anything about it."

– Jimmy Connors

KEY CONCEPTS

1. Long-term care represents wealth protection, one of several components in a total financial plan.

2. There are three different groups of people to focus on for long-term care:

   - 65-and-over,

   - under-age-65, and

   - employers.

3. Planning in advance is critical.

4. Long-term care affects not just the person receiving care, but potentially many family members, friends and neighbors as well.

NEWS FROM THE
LONG-TERM CARE FRONT

Philadelphia, Pennsylvania: On December 13, 1994, Frank Gale sat down at his dining room table to write out the first check to pay for his mother's care in a nursing home – $5,266.13, covering one month and a few days of care. His mother, at 96, could no longer live on her own. The account balance before Gale subtracted the check he had just written was $58,000, mostly from the sale of his mother's small row house in Upper Darby. The nest egg she had slowly built up over the years by scrimping, saving, bargain-shopping and modest living would be gone in 11 months unless she died quickly.

On January 11, 1995, Frank Gale wrote a second check for $4,452.53 for the next month's care, reducing the account balance to around $48,000. Gale could think of a thousand other uses for that $58,000. Many Boomers today ponder those same thoughts.

It was not Frank Gale's first brush with long-term care. His wife Maria had previously cared for two elderly cousins, eventually placing them both in nursing homes. The cousins had nearly $300,000 in assets – at first. Maria spent it all on their care. She sold their house, their savings bonds, and their diamonds. Five years after they had first entered a nursing facility, the last of the cousins died in a home where 93% of the residents were indigent.

Frank Gale's mother Helen didn't die quickly. On November 6, 1995, he wrote the last check for $4,056.23. The nest egg was history. Helen Gale went on Medicaid, similar to two-thirds of Pennsylvania nursing home residents. Frank could not tell his mother any of this, as his mother was no longer mentally competent to understand it. It was just as well, he thought, as his mother would have been mortified to know that after nearly 100 years of supporting herself, she had now become a burden to society.

Frank and Maria Gale do not own, nor do they intend to buy long-term care insurance. The quotes were too expensive and after raising five children, they did not have the money to pay for it. They are not alone. Not one of the children who visit their relatives in the same facility had thought about this type of wealth protection. Their explanations are many: they can't afford it, they plan to move into a retirement community, they will take an overdose, or they will let Medicaid take over when their assets are exhausted.[1]

Somewhere, USA: "Dad had always been a proud, self-reliant man – a good provider to his three kids, all now grown and scattered around the country, raising families of their own. After Mom died a few years ago, he moved south where he bought a new home and enjoyed an active retirement. Then, last fall, Dad suffered a debilitating stroke. Because he was never one to talk about money, no one close to him knew how to provide for his lengthy and expensive convalescent care, who would manage his personal finances, or even what resources Dad could draw upon to meet basic living expenses. Hastily arranging a conference call to talk over the situation, his anxious sons and daughter came face to face with the question millions of Americans will almost inevitably confront – and dread: "What do we do now?"[2]

New York/Tallahassee: "My mother can still quote Dante but she can't remember she just asked three times in a row what day it is," says Iona Givens, a corporate lawyer in New York. Her mother, retired professor Azzurra Givens, is a widow who lives alone in Tallahassee, Florida. The struggle for Iona is how to help her mother, from a thousand miles away, maintain her independence. Her mother is battling failing eyesight and a fading memory, adding to the difficulty. She had been a professor at Florida State University, teaching French and Italian for more than 50 years. She retired in 1997 and in the three years since, lost her focus, became depressed, and ended up in a hospital and then a rehabilitation facility. Her daughter, an only child, worried about the next step until she found Home Instead, a national franchise that provides non-medical caregivers by the hour. This service enabled the retired professor to return to her apartment. A caregiver came every day to prepare meals, monitor her medication, and drive her to doctors' appointments and the supermarket. At a cost of $10-12/hour, Iona considered it a bargain. She also employs a maid service and pays \$15/month for an emergency-response bracelet. She is spending money, but is able to keep her mother in the residence she loves, close to the university and the senior center where she still teaches Italian. She phones every day, even if her mother doesn't always remember to pick up the phone.[3]

Massachusetts: "Adult children can be drawn into caregiving responsibilities that eventually overwhelm them." A 70-year-old woman moved in with her 40-year-old daughter and the mother was subsequently diagnosed with Alzheimer's disease. As a waitress, the daughter had some flexibility in her schedule and while her work was easier to juggle than most, she still lost a lot of hours. She started with six shifts and eventually went down to two. By the end, she was running on pure nervous energy. She worried about her mother, finances and her own sanity. Alzheimer's patients sometimes swear at you and she was taking a verbal battering from her mom. Finally, her doctor told her she was ruining her own health. Despite some financial security, the waitress scrambled and suffered nonetheless, giving up ten years of her life to care for her mother.[4]

The news from the front can be disheartening. So many missed opportunities to help families plan for the possibility of an illness or injury that will otherwise deplete hard-earned assets. Long-term care takes on many forms and shapes, affects a substantial number of lives in different ways, and yet the end-result is almost always the same – a devastating financial and emotional loss.

Is it as simple as just being prepared? Quite often, yes! While it is hard to predict the future, one thing is certain. If you wait until the long-term care event has happened, you are too late to do anything. Long-term care has far-reaching effects, potentially disrupting the lives of not only the people who need the care, but more important-ly, any number of family members who might have to participate in the caregiving process. The toll taken on caregivers is one only grad-ually coming to light today, but it can be the final motivating factor to get people to act *now* while everything is fine to prepare for a day when things are *not* fine.

While consumer publications run regular articles about long-term care, there is still an unwillingness to act on this knowledge. This has created a consumer educational gap that is a "threat to the financial well-being of everyone who mistakenly thinks long-term care [insurance] is a luxury rather than a necessity in the 21st century.[5] People will read about the waitress who likely took several years off her own life providing care for her mother, but not relate to it as something that could happen to them.

It is up to the financial services professionals of the world, not the media or anyone else, to motivate families to consider the long-term care issue. "Failure to discuss long-term care is causing American families to make unplanned sacrifices such as using children's college funds or foregoing job advancement," according to a recent national survey on long-term care by The National Council on Aging.[6] The person receiving the care has his or her own difficulties, but is now unable to deal with most issues. The other healthy family members left behind will be the ones confronting the problem and shelving their own future plans for the care of a loved one. These are the true losses on the front lines of long-term care today.

Ann Landers column, July 18, 2000

Dear Ann Landers:

Please tell your readers they should not only have life insurance, but nursing home insurance as well. Some long-term care is so expensive you have to sell your home and live in a rented room or with the kids to pay for it. When I found out the cost of caring for my husband, I worried about how I could afford it. Not everyone is lucky enough to die before they hit the floor. Most of us will need some kind of long-term care.

Nursing home insurance is not advertised the way life insurance is. I had to ask my insurance agent about it. Some policies will pay for nursing home care in your own home, ranging from $10 an hour to $125 for the day. All you have to do is call a nursing home and find out what it costs per day to understand the importance of this kind of insurance.

I feel blessed that I haven't required nursing care yet, but it could happen. The younger you are, the lower the payments. Urge your readers not to wait until it's too late. Tell them to get smart and get insurance.

– Beaverton, Oregon

Dear Beaverton: *You* told them, and I appreciate it because I didn't know that such insurance was available. Thanks for educating me as well as millions of others. What you have written is a godsend.

It's hard to believe Ann Landers needs a wake-up call about long-term care, but this is important publicity, at least in recognizing the potential problem. One of the problems with this kind of exposure is that the words "nursing home" are truly frightening to many today. Yet comprehensive long-term care insurance is so much more than that, providing reimbursement for care in virtually any setting. But many are put off by the nursing home reference as something that will not happen to them.

Nursing homes, currently clouded by accusations of neglect and abuse, are already in the midst of refocusing their patient care efforts. Primarily identified as the facility for long-term care, these places are altering their patient delivery to provide short-term convalescent care following a hospitalization. When the patient leaves the nursing facility, they will receive home health care or be transferred to an assisted living facility. Long-term care insurance is already ahead of this 21st Century trend, providing benefits in the complete array of long-term care arrangements.[7]

Be Prepared
The Boy Scouts have the right approach with their motto. But it is often difficult to get grown adults (some of them former Eagle Scouts, no doubt) to focus on what could happen to them if they ignore the future possible threat of long-term care. That's why long-term care remains today as the largest unfunded liability Americans

face, according to Ken Dychtwald, the author of the new longevity bible, *The Age Wave.*

Part of the problem lies in choosing the right motivator in a family. Sometimes it's the older person who is closer to potentially needing the care. In other families, it is the adult children concerned about their inheritances or in the time, effort, and cost it would take to be a personal caregiver. It is quite possible that this is a discussion no one in the family really wants to have. But if one delays this talk too long, it will probably be too late to help the long-term care situation that has just struck.

According to Ken Dychtwald, author of Age Wave, Boomers have different lifestyle expectations than their elders and are generally uncomfortable with aging. In order for Boomers to live the lifestyle they favor with recurring periods of work, education, retirement, marriage, parenting and elder care, they will require more financial planning.[8]

This is an opportunity for parents to play a role in their own financial future. As the elders, they are perhaps closest to needing this type of medical care. A chronic condition might leave them incapacitated and unable to make any future decisions themselves. This advanced planning has the benefit of including them in the discussion when they can still shape their own future.

Boomers, on the other hand, have much to lose if they forego advanced planning on behalf of their parents and themselves. Long distance plays a factor in getting this advanced planning to happen but that's where the financial advisor can bring families together. Contacting the individuals that will ultimately be affected by a long-term care experience is something that's easy for the advisor to do. The sale may be to the older adults, but the boomer kids may pay the premium in the interest of preserving those future assets. Regardless of the outcome, the opportunity to get everyone together will undoubtedly help you solve some of the financial needs of your prospects.

A Family Affair

As you can see, long-term care has far reaching implications. An elderly parent might need the care, but this will test the financial, physical and emotional limits of many other extended family members. The cost to a family is not just in terms of one life, or in the money laid out to pay for long-term care expenses. It is in the wages lost, the reduced Social Security benefits, the years off one's own life, the different and difficult retirement ahead for those that remain behind to pick up the pieces. It may be a strained marriage, estrangement from a sibling, and a whole different attitude from grandchildren towards their grandparents.

The idea that long-term care affects many people should be enough motivation to try and get them all together to plan ahead of time what will happen in the event of a long-term care need. This is easier said than done. When it comes to communicating about future planning and making decisions, neither parent nor child is especially strong in this regard. Parents hide financial information from their children and the kids go out of their way to avoid knowing about it. On the other hand, most are relieved when this is all worked out. There may be surprises revealed such as that parents have already looked into a facility they could go into should care be needed. They may be aware of the residence's costs and eager to look for a way to fund it, all to avoid being a burden on their own children.

"My client Carla's mother had a heart attack in her Arizona condo. Carla took time off work and flew down to be with her during the surgery. She stayed on for the opportunistic infection and later the pneumonia. It was a difficult month. Her mother had recently married a man who drove a Lincoln Continental, gambled, and liked rare steaks and bourbon. He made fun of Carla's vegeterianism, her casual clothes and even her Honda. The two of them stood across the room from each other in the ICU, trying, but barely able to maintain the illusion of civility. They hardly knew each other, and yet they had to make life-and-death decisions together about a person they both loved."[9]

Once people know what they want to do, actions can be taken, and the process of implementing a wealth protection strategy can be underway.

The Caregivers

"Age does not protect you from love, but love to some extent protects you from age."

– Jeanne Moreau

"My own descent into elder-care hell began in 1995, when my mother, then 69, was found to have Lou Gehrig's disease. It robbed her first of her speech (and boy she loved to talk!), then of movement of her limbs. My mom and I had lots of issues never resolved since my teenage years. But rather than get therapy, I decided to spend more time with her, taking months off from work to listen to old records, watch *Masterpiece Theater* videotapes and look at family pictures with her.... I learned things I had never known: that she had paid for my Catholic-school education by herself; that she was adored by her students, and that the attitudes I had so rebelled against came from a Southern upbringing that always required her to be a 'lady' — always. As my relationship with my Mom improved, my dad and I had knock-down-and-drag-outs over her treatment. He and the doctor wanted her in a hospital. She wanted to die at home. Dad wouldn't, couldn't pay for round-the-clock nurses. Part-time aides came and went, unable to take the hours and the unrelenting attention Mom needed. After she had a tracheotomy and required a tube down her throat, I had to learn how to apply suction to the tube when she felt saliva backing up. She died almost exactly a year later, on Labor Day weekend, 1996. During that year, I loathed my Dad at times and I'm sure he felt the same about me."[10]

It may be relatively easy to estimate the pure financial costs of long-term care. That may be enough to motivate some people to act. But it's not the whole story – not even close. A long-term care need is an emotional experience that can take a tremendous toll on individuals who must deal with the act of caregiving itself either by choice or, more likely, a failure to plan ahead.

As boomers in their 50s take on these caregiving chores, they'll face tough choices about their careers and finances. A 1999 study by the MetLife Mature Market Institute found that 84% of caregivers were forced to take an extended leave, reduce their hours, or quit their jobs altogether. Over their lifetimes, caregivers surveyed gave up an average $659,000 in lost wages, retirement contributions and other benefits.[11] Sure, these are dollar costs and there are a number of varying estimates of the monetary loss. But the emotional loss and the affect it has on the balance of the caregiver's life is the true cost here. How do you put a price on years of life given up as a result of the challenges of full-time caregiving; challenges taken on because there simply were no other options?

A study at the University of California, San Diego, found that people who rarely got a break from caring for an ailing loved one were more likely to become ill themselves. Also, the illnesses of these people lasted three times longer than of caregivers who were relieved more often from their responsibilities.

In a recent seminar I attended about Alzheimer's patients, I had a chance to talk to the physician who gave the talk. He said that the average lifespan of a full-time caregiver of an Alzheimer's patient following a period of full-time, hands-on caregiving was two years after the patient passes away. Two years! Is this a cost? Definitely!

Elder care demands is the other shoe dropping on American family life. The parents that raised today's Zoomers are now turning to those Zoomers for assistance themselves. As they've aged, these parents are finding that living on their own can be both challenging and dangerous. Today, many aging parents need housing help, and people born in the 1940s and 1950s are finding elder care as taxing as raising a family. And many of these people are doing both at the same time. Here, again, is another primary motivator to consider a long-term care plan to provide alternatives to going it alone.

My client Irena just returned from visiting her parents in a southwestern retirement community. She talked about how depressing it was, rows of identical suburban houses baking in a 110-degree heat. There was no one on the streets. Pollution and heat had kept everyone trapped in their air-conditioned homes, "waiting to die" as Irena put it. "My parent's lives have become their medical conditions," she told me. "It was the worst week of my life."[12]

"Taking care of an aging parent is always difficult, but it is even more difficult for employees who have to care for their parent in their own home, says Raymond Noe, co-author of a study and professor of management and human resources at Ohio State. "It essentially means that employees have a second shift of work when they get home."[13]

People with frail elders, and no long-term care insurance options, are faced with a difficult dilemma: should they drain family assets to pay for chronic care? "Or, if they quit working to provide care, how do they protect themselves from paying a high personal price? A 19th Century legal principle, the `family-member rule,' holds that family members shouldn't be paid for services to each other. It was based on extended-family households of the past, where members helped each other daily. At the heart of the issue is a cultural paradox: the notion that family members should care for each other out of love and duty is rooted deep in our definition of decency. Yet the way we measure worth in our society increasingly is economic. And because most men and women now are employed in their caregiving years, the financial stakes of caregiving have risen."[14]

Several long-term care policies today recognize that the family member may feel a certain amount of caregiving obligation and offer a benefit that not only pays for caregiver training of a family member, but then pays them for the care they provide. There may be an emotional toll still taken on the caregiver, but from a financial standpoint, there is at least some stress relief.

There are other more frightening consequences of elder care choices. A 67-year-old woman who was blind in one eye and had emphysema shot and critically wounded her daughter after overhearing talk of putting her in a nursing home. She also shot her daughter's boyfriend and was charged with two counts of attempted murder. She had been staying with her daughter for two months.[15]

The care we provide to others speaks to the values we have as a people and as a society. But we don't have to go it alone. Planning ahead may not always mean a long-term care insurance purchase, but it is one of the few options that can give a family choices, and spare the financial and emotional disaster caregiving can become. "The Dvoraks opted for private insurance because they didn't want to risk going on welfare – Medicaid – and they did not wish to be a family burden. 'I've seen how taking care of someone over the long haul creates a bitter hate, a situation where the caregiver basically wishes the person would die. I didn't want that to happen to my family.'"[17]

> Caring for elderly parents is increasingly becoming an issue in the workplace. Based on a survey of 1,400 seniors averaging 82 years of age, 40% rely on a working-age daughter or son for caregiving. That means employees have to change their work schedules – sometimes arriving later or leaving early, or taking time off – to care for their parents. Employers who offer financial or other assistance to these workers will find that the extra costs will be offset by more productive workers.[16]

Long-distance caregiving furnishes a different kind of stress for people. You may not be hands-on as a caregiver, but the stress related to *not* being there can exact its own price. "Sophia was desperate. Her 85-year old mother began calling every day from Illinois, demanding that her daughter leave her job and family in Washington, D.C., to fly 850 miles to take her to the grocery store, the next week to the dentist, and then to the podiatrist. Her mother, who was suffering from mild dementia but was physically well enough to live in her own home, rejected all other help, even from caring neighbors and a woman hired to provide transportation and companionship. Sophia's fears that her mother would set the house on fire or, given her forgetfulness and rebellious nature, would walk away into the night, were magnified by the distance separating them. When Sophia was able to visit, there were recriminations, guilt and frustration on both sides. Her mother ultimately required the full-time care of a nursing home and Sophia, though she still worried, no longer felt so overwhelmed.[18]

Nationally, the caregiving provided by informal, unpaid caregivers was worth $196 billion in 1997, primarily in care for older, chronically ill people. In California alone, it was nearly $23 billion. This is based on the number of hours people spent in informal, unpaid caregiving and an average of the minimum wage and the hourly wage for a home health care worker.[19]

How much more can we know about caregiving? The American Medical Association reports that elderly spouses strained by caring for an ailing husband or wife were 63% more likely to die earlier than other spouses. Health problems in elderly caregivers have been attributed to loss, prolonged distress, the physical demands of caregiving and the biological vulnerability of older people in general.[20] There is ample evidence that long-term care needs can result in both a financial and physical loss of immense proportions – not just to the individual needing the care, but to any number of extended family members, friends and neighbors who may get caught up in the process. All of these factors can help to motivate potential buyers of long-term care insurance.

KEY COMPONENT OF FINANCIAL PLANNING

Sales of long-term care insurance will not make great strides until long-term care insurance is commonly recognized as a key component of any complete financial plan. The easiest way to do this is to identify it as a wealth protection vehicle. It is a method of preserving assets and income. Of course, as we've noted, it also serves to relieve some of the emotional pain that accompanies this type of care – but as a financial piece of the puzzle, it fits squarely inside wealth protection planning.

Whether you are working with clients that are age 40 or age 90 or any point in between, before, or after, there are four essential elements of a financial plan that must be addressed. These four vital issues are:

1. *Wealth accumulation.* No matter what age you are, accumulation will be important. From the struggling late-par-

ent boomer to the eighty-five-year-old active senior, there will always be a concern about stretching the retirement dollar as far as it can conceivably go. Longevity can be our financial and physical enemy, and an enjoyable retirement will likely depend on how well we are able to manage our money before and after retiring. My own mother and mother-in-law worry about their finances, at ages 75 and 85, respectively. Their numbers look good on paper to me, but that doesn't keep them from worrying.

Four Essential Elements of a Financial Plan:

1. Wealth accumulation,
2. Wealth protection,
3. Wealth transfer, and
4. Wealth distribution.

2. *Wealth protection.* Most people only focus on the first goal of their financial plan – accumulation. But the money can go fast, when it is being spent on unforeseen expenses like long-term care. In the working years, disability income insurance can help protect assets and income by providing a source of dollars to help pay for normal monthly expenses like the mortgage, food and car payment. This, however, does nothing for payments to providers of long-term care services. A friend had a stroke at age 41 and, though she had enough disability income coverage to pay for the routine monthly expenses, there was not enough left over to pay for the needed physical and speech therapy visits. Where will this money come from? When this type of medical care is needed later in life, will there be enough money left to pay for it? Or will it be handled like the Gales' situation in Philadelphia, writing the checks for as long as they last, and then going on Medicaid? This is not a desirable financial planning result, so it makes sense to include long-term care coverage as a potential funding vehicle in the wealth protection portion of a total financial plan.

3.   *Wealth transfer.* Any complete financial plan will review
      the dynamics of succession planning. To whom will the
      money be left? One of the things on the minds of many
      Depression era-WW II veterans is that they leave one last
      legacy. This is a proud generation, a group of people sacri-
      ficing during most of their lives for the good of their fam-
      ilies. They are among the nation's wealthiest people today,
      and are enjoying the fruits of their labors. They want very
      much to pass on some of this money to their own children
      and grandchildren. This type of planning may involve
      wills, trusts, foundations and other vehicles of this nature.
      Wealth transfer is not only about what happens to the
      money after one dies. It is often, especially for the wealthi-
      er, about how to efficiently organize one's resources while
      one is still living. There are many ways this can be accom-
      plished and it will continue to be a fundamental concern
      as a person ages. This part of the financial plan hinges on
      how well the accumulation and protection phases have
      fared.

4.   *Wealth distribution.* Naturally, once money has been built
      up for retirement, there will come a day
      when one must begin withdrawing dol-
      lars from one's various financial pro-
      grams. There is a right and wrong way
      to do this, as these funds can erode due
      to carelessness through taxes, penalties,
      fees and other reductions. Since money
      has to be stretched to fit today's increas-
      ing longevity, it is very important to
      maximize the amounts that are already
      there and lose as little as possible in the process of using it.
      Annuities and life insurance can play a role in distribution
      planning.

> In a National Council on
> Aging survey, 93% of
> grandparents said they
> would not want their chil-
> dren to touch their grand-
> children's education funds.
> Yet, 50% of adult children
> said they would dip into
> these funds, and 12% have
> already done so.

   Long-term care needs fit nicely into this overall plan. This
involves a different approach than trying to sell long-term care as a

single need sale. It will be necessary to gather a complete set of financial data from an individual or couple in order to make recommendations about the individual's or couple's total needs. As part of this analysis, long-term care will either be needed – or not. Reviewing the net worth and cash flow of your clients with specific attention paid to the amount of liquid assets can help to make this determination.

The focus is no longer on nursing home care, as in the Ann Landers letter. Now, the perspective has shifted to long-term care insurance as a potential element of a larger, overall financial plan. This is a more understandable approach for people, as they can clearly see the role this type of coverage plays. An example of the type of information gathering form you should use appears in Figure 1.1.

The worksheet in Figure 1.1 will effectively calculate an individual's or couple's net worth. This is an important figure to have, as it is a strong indicator of whether a long-term care need exists or not. If long-term care insurance is to be a viable solution for handling these medical expenses in the future, net liquid assets (in addition to a home and car) for a couple should be at least **$100,000**. Liquid assets only include those items that can readily be turned into cash without a major loss in value (checking accounts, savings, stocks, bonds, etc.). Those couples with less than $100,000 will shortly spend down to Medicaid qualification since many states allow non-institutionalized spouses to keep as much as $87,000 in assets in 2001.

If the individual is single, then a lower guideline should be used and even more attention must be paid to cash flow to judge the ability to afford a long-term care insurance premium. In many states, individuals have to go into a financial free-fall to qualify for Medicaid. We saw what transpired for the Gale family – an entire depletion of assets. Each state has its own rules, and one should contact the state office that handles Medicaid applications to determine the minimal number of assets that can be kept. Thus, the single person may feel that they wish to protect their $50,000 liquid asset base and look to long-term care insurance to provide the funding needed to pay for long-term care expenses.

Figure 1.1

FINANCIAL WORKSHEET
Determine your net worth

Assets

Checking account balance	$_____
Savings account balance	_____
Home value	_____
Other real estate value	_____
Automobile(s)	_____
Other vehicles (boat, plane, etc.)	_____
Household furnishings and appliances	_____
Stocks (market value)	_____
Bonds (market value)	_____
Mutual funds (market value)	_____
Life insurance cash value	_____
Annuities (present value)	_____
Retirement equity (IRAs, 401(k), pension)	_____
Jewelry	_____
Other investments (collectibles)	_____
Loans owed to you	_____
Money owed to you	_____
Other assets	_____

Total Assets $_____

Liabilities

Current bills	$_____
Auto loan(s)	_____
Other vehicle loan(s)	_____
Home equity loan	_____
Other bank loan balances	_____
Credit card balances	_____
Real estate taxes owed	_____
Income taxes owed	_____
Other taxes owed	_____
Other debts	_____

Total Liabilities $_____

NET WORTH   (Assets minus liabilities) $_____

The net worth calculation can also reveal the source of liquid assets. This can be helpful once these vehicles are identified. For example, in a recent situation, completion of the net worth financial worksheet showed a collection of three Certificates of Deposit totaling $105,000. This was clearly the largest single asset the person owned, greater than the house valued at $88,000. There are a number of investments that may provide the same level of safety and yet offer more growth than a CD that, after taxes and inflation, is generally going backwards in terms of value. In this case, a recommendation to move a portion of that asset, say $50,000, to a single premium life insurance or annuity product that also contains long-term care protection might be advisable. In this way, there is still $55,000 in the "safe" CD, while the rest of that money is earning a potentially higher interest rate and is growing tax-deferred, while also furnishing the solution to the glaring need for long-term care protection.

The worksheet in Figure 1.2 applies to a determination of cash flow. This will reveal the amount of discretionary income one might use to pay a long-term care insurance premium. After calculating the income surplus, be sure it is ample enough to support long-term care insurance payments. The United Seniors Health Cooperative recommends that an individual spend no more than 7% of one's annual income on LTC premiums. If there is a strong need for protection, such as liquid assets greater than $100,000 for a couple or a reasonable amount to protect for a single individual, but little disposable income to fund the policy, you can always modify the LTC policy components (for example, the daily benefit amount, elimination period, benefit period, inflation protection) to help stay within budget.

Remember to center your long-term care presentation as part of an overall financial plan to individuals or couples. It is vital protection to ensure that future monetary and personal goals are met.

Figure 1.2

Determine your cash flow

Income
Take home pay $_____
Overtime   _____
Bonuses   _____
Interest   _____
Dividends   _____
Social Security   _____
Other income   _____

Total Cash Income $_____

Expenses
Mortgage or rent $_____
Credit card payments   _____
Automobile(s) payment   _____
Other loan payments   _____
Alimony, child support   _____
Food (incl. dining out)   _____
Insurance (auto, home, health, etc.)   _____
Utilities (heat, phone, electric, cable, etc.)   _____
Child care   _____
Elder care   _____
Personal care (clothing, cosmetics, hair)   _____
Medical bills not paid by insurance   _____
Education expenses   _____
Recreation (books, movies, etc.)   _____
Vacation   _____
Charity   _____
Savings   _____
Gifts   _____
Other expenses not listed   _____

Total Expenses $_____

**INCOME SURPLUS
OR DEFICIT** (Income minus expenses) $_____

The Longevity Risk

Pity the average gerontologist. How do you explain the logic of the aging process after reviewing the eating habits of 103-year-old Catherine McCaig, who discloses the dietary principle she has followed forever, as she chows down on a plate of deep-fried fish and chips: "I've always eaten whatever came along, as long as it wasn't moving."[21]

There is the age-old argument about whether longevity is influenced by one's environment or hereditary background. Conflicting studies have favored one over the other at various times. There is much evidence to support the lack of centenarian siblings, yet the aforementioned Catherine McCaig lives with her 94-year-old sister and they only recently lost their 94-year-old brother. The woman who set the modern longevity record at 122 years of age, Jeanne Calment of France, smoked most of her long life.

That's not to say that most people want to be age 100. An AARP survey indicated that 67% of those surveyed could skip the centenarian part. But even if people over the next few decades routinely made it to 90 years of age, that is a period of time in retirement nearly rivaling the time spent in employment.

> The number of people in America 100 years of age or older is calculated at 70,000 today, nearly double that of the centenarian population at the start of the 1990s. U.S. Census Bureau projections estimate 834,000 centenarians by the year 2050.[22]

The larger question is how will people fund these extra years. Let's say people retired between age 65 and 70, on average, and lived until age 90. This means paying for expenses for 20 to 25 years after stopping work. Are people prepared for this? Part of the planning process, of course, is to estimate the amount of money that one will need in retirement. First, one must identify the type of retirement people intend to have. Generally, many see their post-working years in two parts: busy and sedentary. The first part of having a lot of free time to oneself may be to spend more time traveling – going places one has always wanted to see, but never had the time to visit. From trips around the world to African safaris to scaling a difficult mountain in the Himalayas, these could be the stuff people dream about.

Once that urge is satisfied, then it's more likely a time to stay home and golf, play tennis, walk the beach, garden, take a class – things that may not be quite so costly. The longer one is able to maintain these parts of retirement, the more money will be needed. Just how much remains the ultimate financial planning question.

> According to an AARP Survey, 60% expect life to be better for the average 80-year-old in the 21st Century. Almost that many said they believe medical advances in this century could increase life expectancy to 120 years. [23]

But there is one more part that comes under the "Wealth Protection" heading: the medical period. The end of life is fraught with disease and health complications and, if there is money still available, this is often where it goes. This third part of retirement is not often discussed, let alone quantified. But these end-of-life medical expenses should be figured in with the active and sedentary years.

How best to quantify this risk? By asking questions about your client's retirement in your information gathering process, you can secure answers to help you make some financial estimates. Most people enjoy speculating about their retirement. Even the ones already retired still have plans and a need to determine how best to financially meet these goals. If it's a trip to the International Space Station, you can now put a multi-million dollar figure on this. Closer to home, that Winnebago has a cost, that Alaskan cruise, that trip to see the grandchildren each year – all can be quantified. Once done, and added in with the rent or mortgage and other ongoing routine expenses, the number becomes clearer.

> A 2000 Gallup Survey indicated that pain strikes old and young alike, but the frequency, severity and causes of pain change as people age. 75% of adults age 65 and older experience pain on a weekly basis, and suffer moderate to severe pain twice as long as younger Americans. [24]

The problem then becomes how to estimate the costs of medical care in those last few weeks, months or even years. This is more difficult to put a figure to, since there will be as many variations on it as there are people. Worse, the optimism about advances in medical cures and improvements in health technology has people believing there will be cures for cancer and Alzheimer's disease in this century. This leaves them reluctant to financially plan for chronic conditions that they believe are far less likely to occur in the future.

This optimistic attitude may make people feel that they will not have to worry about the costs of long-term care in the future. But, are they willing to gamble their life savings and a future inheritance for their grandchildren on it? Even if they acknowledge that these cures may avoid the medical costs, it is bound to increase longevity even further and the normal expenses of retirement must still be funded. Greater accumulations may be needed if all this comes to pass.

But, as any gerontologist will tell you, this is not an exact science by any stretch of the imagination. A consistent aging into one's 90s and 100s may bring forth a new host of aging diseases we don't even know about because not enough people have made it that far to develop a consistent theory. Better to work with the facts as we have them now. Financial plans can be – and usually are – adjusted in the future.

The Hidden Estate Tax

One of the hot talking points in Washington, D.C. are the significant changes made to the estate tax and its actual repeal in 2010 for one year. But even if the repeal becomes permanent, don't long-term care costs function in much the same way? Sure, no one calls the spending down of an estate to pay for these medical costs a tax. But that's only because it's not an official one. It certainly functions like a levy and, though it remains hidden,

$11.6 TRILLION

That's the estimate for the total value of estates to be passed on by parents to children 50 years and older from the years 1998 to 2017.[25]

it has a dramatic impact on the size of estates left (if any) to be passed on to children. We've all seen the charts that demonstrate the reductions in estate value for well-known celebrities from Elvis Presley to Miami Dolphins owner Joe Robbie, with the tag line "Estate Taxes Reduced the Amount of Money Left to Heirs by 68%!" In Joe Robbie's case, it cost his family the ownership of his beloved football team.

Could we construct something similar for the effect of long-term care costs on estates? The example below is an ongoing case, but it demonstrates that this type of chart is very feasible.

The Morgans placed their surviving parent into a nursing facility at age 84 in 1996. At that time, the size of the estate was $945,000, more than half of that liquid. The estate was able to earn some money on its liquid assets, at an average of 5% per year. Look at the effect each year that long-term care has on the size of the estate.

Estate size	Interest earned on liquid portion	LTC costs	Remaining estate size
$945,000	$25,500	$33,700 (8 mos.)	$936,800
$936,800	$25,090	$64,150	$897,740
$897,740	$23,137	$70,245	$850,632
$850,632	$20,782	$75,500	$795,914
$795,914	$18,046	$83,800	$730,160

So far, the estate is down 23% in less than five years, and the numbers aren't getting better. The size of the liquid estate is dwindling, down now near $300,000, reducing the amount of money the Morgans can earn to offset the ever-increasing long-term care costs. The patient is not doing well, but is not in imminent danger of passing away and, thus, the "hidden" estate tax will continue to subject the estate to further losses.

This is a common scenario and the family members have never felt so powerless as they watch the money slip away. Trying to do everything to make their parent comfortable, the Morgans (brother and sister) continue to write checks to the nursing facility, while attempting to manage the estate and its investment returns as best they can. There has already been talk about selling the house (a $400,000 value) now while they still have time to be patient and wait for a fair price.

Although some wealthy clients may be comfortable with the idea of spending thousands of dollars (and more) from their estates for long-term care, the children or other heirs who take over when the client becomes incapacitated may have different ideas. They will certainly question the financial planner as to why the long-term care need was never addressed.[26]

Long-Term Care as an Estate Planning Tool

"Experience is a revelation in the light of which we renounce our errors of youth for those of age."

– Ambrose Bierce

The importance of placing long-term care in the wealth protection end of the planning process has already been noted in this book. This incorporates a complete review of a client's current financial situation. This financial snapshot identifies where the individual is, making it easier to plot the future course of estate, financial, retirement, and tax planning. The planning process can never begin early enough, and, as people age, the years ahead become more critical in terms of thinking ahead. For many years, the focus of this planning was working towards a specific monthly benefit that one would live on in retirement. It was a time when defined benefit pension plans ruled, and also when people worked for the same employer for a long number of years and could focus on the one source of retirement income.

It's a different story for most people today. Workers do not stay at the same job for their entire careers. Defined benefit plans, so complex to administer, have yielded to the easier-to-budget defined contribution plans, and the direct intent is not so much to accumulate a large monthly retirement

According to Robert A. Esperti and Renno L. Peterson in their book Generations, "The definition of estate planning adopted by the National Network of Estate Planning Attorneys is: 'I want to control my property while I am alive and well, care for myself and my loved ones if I become disabled, and be able to give what I have to whom I want, the way I want, and when I want, and, if I can, I want to save every last tax dollar, attorney fee, and court cost possible.'"[27]

benefit as to build up a large lump-sum number, likely residing in several investment vehicles. Ultimately, the client will have to live on this large lump sum, generating a decent, livable lifetime income from these assets.

As retirement nears, there will be a change in priorities from wealth accumulation and protection to wealth transfer and distribution. One must finally work with the assets one has accumulated (and continues to) and decide on a future course. This will involve choices in housing and health care, and may involve selecting a retirement community where one can move between different levels of housing and care options depending on their personal needs, yet remain in the same subdivision. One can go from independent living to assisted living to skilled care, the cost of each altering as the level of care intensifies. This is long-term care planning worked into an overall estate plan. The cost of the care will have to be funded and it is here that a long-term care insurance plan can help furnish the dollars to handle this change in need.

This type of planning involves looking at both institutional and non-institutional care costs. Institutional care is provided in nursing homes and hospices. Non-institutional care involves home health care, home hospice, adult day care, respite care, and other similar forms of care. Four times as many Americans receive non-institutional long-term care versus institutional care.[28] Dollar estimates of these costs will be vital to the planning process.

In addition to planning for housing and health care (including long-term care), strategies will have to be developed for the many distribution options available in taking money out of the various vehicles to live on during retirement. What are the tax consequences? What will be the impact of federal income taxes, federal estate taxes (if any), and gift taxes, as well as state taxes? There is only a finite amount of money involved here that must be available to live on and to fund other needs like long-term care, so all of this planning is interwoven. Long-term care is a firm fixture in this overall process.

Planning concerns will be wide-spread, from health and emotional decisions to the more quantifiable financial choices. You will have taken a strong start by gathering the information for the financial fact sheets that will operate as a starting point for your planning.

Once this information is analyzed, it is easier to plan ahead. Whether the client is way ahead in wealth accumulation or far behind, a plan can be constructed with an eye on all four elements of the planning process: wealth accumulation, protection, transfer and distribution. Think of it all in the context of *wealth care*. Preserving what has already been done and what is currently happening with assets and income is one of the essential purposes of estate planning. Long-term care is about health care, certainly, but it is as much about wealth care. Protecting assets from both the known and unknown is the vital job of the planner.

> **Results of the Women's Retirement Confidence Survey:**
>
> • 88% of working women believe that people in the United States do not save enough money to live comfortably throughout retirement
>
> • 86% of women are confident they will have enough money for basic expenses in retirement, but fewer express confidence in having enough money to pay for medical expenses (64%) or long-term care (47%)
>
> *Source: Employee Benefit Research Institute* [29]

While long-term care insurance can be a part of this overall planning and provide both financial and emotional protection, it is not the only stop on this part of the planning road. There are other elements of this plan that complement the selection of long-term care insurance as the funding vehicle for these potential future treatment needs.

Planners also recommend that children and parents discuss emergency medical planning, transferring of money (if this is part of the plan) sooner rather than later, and the signing of both medical and financial durable power of attorney forms. Once an individual has entered a period of diminished capacity for whatever reason, it might be too late to enact some of these programs.

There are several things to consider. First, there is the financial durable power of attorney form. This document empowers a family member, close friend or a trusted advisor to make legally binding financial decisions when the individual cannot. Under a "springing" power of attorney, the person can stipulate under what conditions the power will be activated. Second, there is a medical durable power of attorney document, also referred to as a health care proxy. This enables a friend, advisor or family member to make medical decisions on the individual's behalf in case of incapacity, in accordance with his or her expressed wishes. Third, there is the alternative of conservatorship. This is a less flexible version of a power of attorney and can cost between 2,000 and $6,000 to establish. This less attractive option arises when an individual is incapable of handling his or her own affairs and members of the family cannot agree on essential issues of financial and care management. So the court intervenes and appoints a conservator, who must file reports with the court to secure approval of certain spending and transfers and the estate becomes public record. Finally, there is the issue of joint ownership. In many cases, this involves adding an adult child's name to bank and brokerage accounts, deeds or leases, effectively making the child a co-owner of the property. Of course, if the individual dies, the co-signer of the account will assume ownership of these assets, a potential problem if there are more siblings in the mix. It may also complicate the incapacitated individual's ability to qualify for Medicaid assistance. There

2001 Retirement Confidence Survey

Fewer U.S. workers were saving for retirement as the economy has sagged and confidence is eroding that they will have enough money to live comfortably. The survey also showed a sharp decline in confidence regarding the future. This diminished confidence is likely due to the stock market tumble, the shaky economy and rising unemployment in recent months. Growing public awareness of the high cost of prescription drugs and long-term care is also a factor.

"The decline in retirement confidence has occurred as public attention to the high cost of prescription drugs and long-term care has increased," say the authors of the survey, the Employee Benefit Research Institute. "Fifty percent of those who retire early say it is for a medical reason and confidence in having funds for medical or long-term care expenses is very low. [30]

are drawbacks to both conservatorship and joint ownership and both strategies should be examined carefully before making them a part of long-term care planning.[31]

Other elements of a complete estate plan can also come into play in the course of addressing the long-term care need. In the process of gifting, money can be repositioned to pay for a long-term care insurance policy. Annual gifts are a popular estate planning tool. Donors remove potentially estate-taxable dollars from their estate and pass it on to children or other beneficiaries to use now. Any donor is allowed up to $10,000 (as indexed) per year per person gift-tax free ($20,000 if from husband and wife donors). What if the child took a portion of that money and pre-funded a long-term care insurance policy? There are many options available today from insurers to pay policies up faster as well as an array of life insurance and annuity-based solutions. Parents remove chunks of money from their estates in a tax-favorable way; children now have the funds needed to pay long-term care premiums, and assets are protected for future inheritance by the next generation.[32]

These are some of the ways long-term care can be positioned as an estate planning tool. Centering it in the wealth protection strategy of an overall plan can link it more easily to other elements of the planning process and make it more understandable in its function as a vital funding vehicle in the care and handling of one's wealth.

THERE ARE POTENTIAL BUYERS

"It's a rare person who wants to hear what he doesn't want to hear."

– Dick Cavett

Martin and Susan Strouch are typical of a new breed of long-term care insurance buyers. They're in their 50s and have already taken steps to provide for care they might need in their old age. "Even if we live into our 80s, the total amount spent on premiums would probably not equal the cost of one year of long-term care," says

Martin, a dentist in Avon, CT. "I saw it as a way to round out our estate planning and protect our assets" because a few years in a nursing home could easily wipe out a lifetime of savings.[33]

There are people out there like the Strouches, who listen to the need for long-term care, review their own financial situation to see if the need pertains to them, and act on it if it does. We are barely scratching the surface of potential long-term care buyers, people who need wealth protection but who have not yet finished this part of their planning.

Figure 1.3, courtesy of the American Council of Life Insurance, illustrates the percentage of elderly and non-elderly by state that are potential LTC buyers.

Overall, in the USA, there are 70% of the non-elderly that are potential buyers of long-term care insurance protection and 31% of elderly buyers still to be convinced of the need for this form of coverage.[34] A married couple in Baltimore, Maryland, ages 70 and 65, have now converted from potential buyers to buyers. The husband's policy was rated up for high blood sugar, but he has an opportunity to reduce the extra cost if he maintains lower reading levels. His wife will have a permanent rating for her health conditions, but she was able to secure coverage. The annual premium combined for the two of them is $3,249. Although buying the coverage has put a pinch on their income, the couple is content. "It became the cost of long-term care insurance versus financial disaster for me and my wife," he says. "That's a big motivator."[35]

The Long-Term Care Triad

The 2000 U.S. Census advises us that there are now 76.9 million people age 50 and over, up 21% from 1990. This represents 27% of the total U.S. population, now set at 281 million Americans. Around 55% of those over age 50 are women.

Sure, boomers are contributing to these numbers in a substantial way. That 76 million group born between 1946 and 1964 will

Figure 1.3

State	% non-elderly who can afford	% elderly who can afford
Alabama	59%	27%
Alaska	80%	46%
Arizona	66%	31%
Arkansas	61%	25%
California	70%	38%
Colorado	80%	47%
Connecticut	78%	39%
Delaware	71%	27%
DC	67%	36%
Florida	63%	30%
Georgia	69%	27%
Hawaii	78%	40%
Idaho	70%	30%
Illinois	75%	35%
Indiana	73%	32%
Iowa	71%	32%
Kansas	68%	32%
Kentucky	61%	24%
Louisiana	60%	20%
Maine	69%	24%
Maryland	77%	42%
Massachusetts	75%	31%
Michigan	77%	29%
Minnesota	78%	21%
Mississippi	60%	28%
Missouri	73%	27%
Montana	63%	25%
Nebraska	70%	24%
Nevada	75%	35%
New Hampshire	78%	28%
New Jersey	78%	41%
New Mexico	55%	31%
New York	70%	30%
North Carolina	68%	30%
North Dakota	70%	20%
Ohio	74%	29%
Oklahoma	63%	24%
Oregon	72%	37%
Pennsylvania	73%	31%
Rhode Island	70%	35%
South Carolina	65%	19%
South Dakota	69%	18%
Tennessee	64%	29%
Texas	65%	29%
Utah	77%	29%
Vermont	72%	33%
Virginia	68%	40%
Washington	74%	37%
West Virginia	60%	18%
Wisconsin	82%	38%
Wyoming	68%	17%

bring these numbers to even greater heights by the time the 2010 census is completed. The "50-and-over" group represents an unlimited marketplace.

Many people have already written of this country's demographics. It is sufficient to now say there are nearly 100 million people to educate and work with that are in the age range of concern for a potential long-term care need.

Three prospect groups:

1. 65-and-over,

2. under-age 65, and

3. employers.

It is also appropriate to say that the age-65-and-over individual is a different breed than the under-age-65 person and that each has a different perspective on the need for long-term care. This book will address the two groups separately in Part One. Both are audiences for a financial review and each will be in a different position to address the long-term care need.

The employer is a relatively new audience for long-term care, but a strong one nonetheless. Employers who lived through the period where child care was a major employee concern are now experiencing a déjà vu of sorts. This time around it's not child care on the minds of most Boomers – it's elder care. Employers are losing their employees to the chores of caregiving and it is costing them valuable productivity. The National Alliance for Caregiving estimates that the current estimate of lost productivity due to workers caring for elderly relatives is $29 billion and rising. When the Health Insurance Portability and Accountability Act of 1996 was passed, clarifying the taxability of long-term care insurance, employers finally had a guideline to go by in formulating plans to add this coverage to their employee benefit portfolio.

More than 22 million households provide some level of support to a family member aged 50 or older, a 300% increase over the preceding decade, according to a September 2000 *Consumer Reports* study.

A recent Society for Human Resource Management study indicated that only 35% of employers had included long-term care in their employee benefit programs, so there is much work to do.[36] Much of the employer focus has been on providing resource and referral information for employees who suddenly have to deal with unexpected trouble in the form of a long-term care need. This is a tremendous growth opportunity for anyone willing to talk to employers about this need.

The Age-65-and-Over Prospect

Consider this: There are more Americans over the age of 65 today than at any time in our history. The Mature generation, born between 1909 and 1945, represent the vast majority of older Americans. They have become the nation's first distinct group of "senior citizens."

They are also the wealthiest of any generation in our brief history. They've struggled and saved, put in hard work and made sacrifices, and the result is a retirement beyond their wildest imagination. They are, in general, financially well-off and they travel and remain quite active. If you were expecting the sun and shuffleboard group, you've come to the wrong century.

But the wealth they've built up is at great risk. Medical concerns and chronic conditions can erode a strong asset and income base in a short time, as we've seen in previous examples. Planning is still vital for these individuals, from wealth protection to transfer and distribution issues. The flip side of longevity is outliving the resources so painstakingly put together.

Ken Dychtwald, author of *Age Power: How the 21st Century Will be Ruled by the New Old*, has some suggestions for working with the elderly prospect, suggesting that advisors adjust their goals and styles to those of their clients. This group, he says, appreciates self-sacrifice, appearances,

Profile: Woodie Sommers
Age 90, Sacramento, CA

He leaves his home four mornings a week, waves to his wife of 61 years and walks to his barber shop a half-mile away. "I do cadence walking, like I'm in the Army. It used to take me 10 minutes, now it's 12 to 14." He has been cutting hair since he first obtained his barber's license in 1933.[37]

fairness, loyalty and decency. These values can play out in various planning situations. In addressing self-sacrifice, advisors might suggest charitable planning that promotes education to the disadvantaged. In honoring their sense of loyalty, planners should not disparage the government. Elders love their country, no matter who's in charge in Washington, D.C.[38]

Long-term care needs should address these values. Many seniors want to leave an inheritance to their children and grandchildren, another example of their tendency towards self-sacrifice, loyalty and decency. Better to budget a few dollars, go without a few things, and protect the assets in place. Moreover, nothing is accomplished by running down the Medicare and Medicaid programs. They serve a certain purpose and Medicare has especially helped this group of senior citizens preserve the wealth they have. These programs are simply not the best alternatives to fund the long-term care need, as we shall see. This must be handled with the delicacy it requires for this audience.

Goal: Identify the age-65-and-over prospect's priorities

- *Stretching the retirement dollar as far as possible?*
- *Living independently for as long as one can?*
- *Leaving an inheritance to the children and/or grandchildren?*
- *Having the freedom to do as one chooses?*

For today's age-65-and-over prospect, long-term care insurance can represent freedom, independence and choice. Frank Gale's mother Helen did not really wish her last $58,000 to be spent on her nursing home care. She would have preferred a different result. Advanced planning and the proper placement of long-term care insurance would have allowed different choices to be made.

Age Is Just a Number

It is important to keep in mind that you are not dealing with the stereotypical senior any more. That person is long gone, replaced by a vibrant, healthy and active individual. My mother-in-law defines this new group by noting that, at age 85, she is not a senior citizen. Those are the people that are in their 90s. It's safe to say that she will adjust those numbers again the closer she gets to that new benchmark. In the meantime, she is busy with mah-jongg, dining out, crafts and movies. Her calendar is full.

This new mature American can be seen in large numbers in the town of Branson, Missouri, a music resort town that has become the new desired address for the retired. At nearly every theater and theme park in town, seniors can be found selling tickets in the box offices, ushering, greeting guests and selling assorted items in the town's many gift shops. Older Americans are now more concerned with neighborliness and work availability and good restaurants rather than the staples of old: golf courses, sunshine and senior centers.[39] These are your new long-term care prospects.

Working longer in some capacity will help generate extra income to stretch the dollar farther in those older years. If they are willing to continue working, it means they are likely healthy enough to qualify for long-term care insurance, assuming they have a need for this form of wealth protection.

> Even in America's youth-worship culture, a funny thing is going on at the workplace: older workers are in. Fewer older executives are content to walk off with gold watches – or even golden parachutes these days. Nearly 1 million more employees age 65 and older were in the workforce in 1998 compared with 1948, according to the Bureau of Labor Statistics.[40]

This is a different form of retirement planning than we've been accustomed to doing, but it may make the job that much easier. In 1999, there were about 3.9 million workers 65 and over, according to the Department of Labor.[41] These people are also leaders in business world. The CEO of Viacom, oversaw its merger with CBS at 76. John Glenn went into space at 77. This is not the image of the frail elderly many have had in the past. This age-65-and-over group of prospects is also healthier and more independent than many give them credit for. According to a study done by the MacArthur Foundation, only 5.2% of America's elderly live in nursing homes (down from 6.3% in 1982). Nearly 90% of seniors between ages 65 and 74 report no disability. Among 75-84 year-olds, 73% report no disability.[42]

> Profile: Elliott Carter, 91, NYC
>
> A two-time Pulitzer Prize winning composer, he is at his composition board every morning at 6:00 AM, working on his latest concerto, but his first loyalty is to, his wife of 61 years, doing the shopping, fixing her meals and assisting her on her walks.[43]

While this news is encouraging, the greater usage of long-term care comes from the nation's fastest growing population segment: the age 85+ group. This is where financial and medical worries converge in a major way. This is still a "no-man's land" of retirement living and the place most elderly fear – the time when finances are dwindling and health care costs are increasing. It's not always a rational fear, but it must be addressed.

In 1982, I had the opportunity to meet and spend time with a retired disability income salesperson from Rochester, New York. Ernie and his wife had moved to Winter Park, Florida in 1959, soon after he had retired from sales life. Our weekly conversations usually ended up the same – discussing his overriding concern that he and his wife would run out of money. He never planned on them both spending 23 years in retirement (and counting). His health was going downhill and he paid for a private duty nurse to tend to his own needs every day, as his wife was too frail to do it, although healthy enough herself. He saw the money going faster because of his health needs, but mostly he saw his long-time plans crumbling around him. Ernie had long believed he would outlive his spouse and she would never have to worry about a thing. He had always handled the finances and didn't know how to tell her their money was running out.

I would help Ernie once a month with his finances. He had spent a lot of money, but from what I could estimate his costs to be, he and his wife were still several years away from a welfare need. Ernie died a couple of years later, but his wife never had to learn much about finances. She too had fallen ill and joined Ernie some 90 days after his death. They had both spent thousands in out-of-pocket medical costs, victims (in Ernie's mind anyway) of living too long. Long-term care insurance was not much to talk about back then, but other than that Ernie had done an excellent job organizing his family's finances. But he was, after all, a financial planner himself.

> In her research of people age 65 and over, a Duke University gerontologist said she had come across an interesting paradox. Some 85% of them had told her their finances were fine, though not great, a higher percentage than among younger adults. But in asking them the additional question about whether they have enough to last, 80% were afraid the money would run out.[44]

According to the Census Bureau, there are over 35 million age-65-and-over adults in this country. There are some that work, many that are active, many that are healthy, and some that are not well at all. The number of chronically disabled older Americans was at about 7 million in 1999.[45] This represents an actual improvement even as the numbers of older adults increases. Many worry about having enough money. These worries can be eased, however, with a little bit of constructive financial planning. While these mature adults control a substantial portion of the country's wealth, they know little about whether they have enough, how long it will last, etc. By putting down the net worth and cash flow of these individuals, this unknown will become more visible and a set of priorities can be established for the future. Just by putting the (relatively) simple calculations down on paper, you can lift an enormous burden from your clients' shoulders. In quantifying the financial mystery of retirement, you can re-establish priorities for them going forward. Where they are financially will dictate where they should concentrate their resources. Whether it's wealth accumulation, protection, transfer or distribution, the plan is on paper and everyone in the family can see it. Long-term care insurance may well be a part of this new program, in addition to key forms like durable financial and medical powers of attorney. The age-65-

> The American Association of Retirement Communities estimates the average retired couple brings more than $250,000 in assets, has an annual retirement income of $30,000 and an average economic impact of $71,600, equal to nearly four new minimum wage jobs.[46] The essential question for financial planners and their clients to answer is, "Will this be enough?"

and-over prospect, even those well into retirement, would likely welcome all the planning assistance you're willing to give.

You will not work alone. There will be needs for estate planning/elder law attorneys, CPAs and even bank trust officers in addition to possible family members. But a well-educated and strong financial advisor can be the point person on the team, gathering data and making recommendations, calling on other experts along the way. The age-65-and-over prospect has always looked up to authority figures and trusted in experts. If you can earn that confidence, this is the market for you to work and prosper in.

> According to the Society of Actuaries, a 65-year-old non-smoking female would average 18.3 more healthy years and 5.7 unhealthy ones. (Males, age 65: 16.6 healthy, 4.9 unhealthy). How will these sick years be funded?

I Want a New Drug

"By the time we've made it, we've had it."

– Malcolm Forbes

Prescription drugs are a flashpoint for government debate these days. Inevitably, Medicare will be adjusted to absorb some of these costs, adding a greater burden to government revenues. Prescription drugs drove health care spending in 1999, accounting for 9.4% of the $1.2 trillion in total spending for all health care, according to the Health Care Financing Administration. Prescription drugs continued to lead all other health care services in spending growth. An increase in the number of prescriptions filled, a larger number of new, high-priced drugs in the marketplace, higher prices for existing drugs, and an increase in direct-to-consumer advertising expenditures also contributed to the higher spending growth rate for drugs.[47]

These continued price increases for prescriptions is haunting the elderly's finances. Medicare does very little in the way of paying for this health service today and the Medicare managed care plans that did offer this reimbursement have seen their bottom lines expand beyond acceptable levels. Drugs are often good – helping people maintain their conditions, avoiding costly surgeries, even keeping people independent and on their own longer. But, when combined with long-term care costs (also not reimbursed in a major way by Medicare), the financial position of many older Americans has been altered dramatically – for the worse.

What compounds the problem is that elderly people with chronic diseases, the classic long-term care cases, are particularly hard hit when it comes to out-of-pocket spending for drugs. In a claims-based analysis of drug use and spending by the elderly published in the March/April 2000 edition of *Health Affairs*, mean total spending on prescription drugs by persons with chronic diseases who filled at least one prescription in 1998 ranged from $1,600 to more than $3,000 and was 50%-200% higher than the mean spending for all persons in the survey. The chronic conditions that were monitored for prescription spending were: acid-peptic disease, osteoporosis, cancer, depression, arthritis, diabetes, asthma and pulmonary disease, hyperlipidemia, and cardiovascular disease.[49]

It's only a small group of drugs that are really driving prescription costs through the roof. Typically, sales of the most popular drugs, such as Vioxx for

Those elderly who have no close relatives and need outside help to manage their daily finances have several choices of strategy.[48]

- *Bank trust officers: skilled but expensive, could charge up to $2,500 annually to manage an account*
- *Stockbrokers: some are offering limited-service trust arrangements*
- *Professional guardians: elders can file for voluntary guardianship and not wait for the courts to declare them incompetent*
- *Care managers: can include financial planners, accountants and social workers to pay monthly bills, file medical insurance forms, arrange health care and sell property. Fees: $25-45/hour*
- *Non-profit assistance: check the local Area Agency on Aging or a Consumer Credit Counseling service for financial help*

For the fifth year in a row, all medicines bought in drug stores, retail stores and supermarkets rose sharply, growing 13% or more each year since 1996. This does not account for mail-order drugs or those administered in a nursing home that are also on the rise according to government estimates.[50]

arthritis inflammations and the anti-ulcer drug Prilosec, were responsible for half the $20.8 billion rise in prescription drug spending from 1999 to 2000, according to the National Institute for Health Care Management.[51] These drugs treat chronic conditions and make even the wealthier seniors financially vulnerable going into their long-term care future.

The Under-Age-65 Prospect

The youngest of the Baby Boom generation is now at least 36-37 years of age. Many are buying bifocals to read the fine print today, understanding better now what their parents experienced. They were parents late, savers even later, the first widespread "sandwich generation" and now have turned their attention towards their financial futures.

What's in store for these prospects? Every financial study you review comes to the same conclusion: This is a group that is way behind in its financial planning. Of the four main components of a sound financial plan, their top priority is of wealth accumulation. Yet this 2001 Strong Capital Management Survey gives us data we've all seen before:

- 32% of workers say they will have $100,000 or less in savings by age 65,

- 17% will have saved between $100,000 and $250,000, and

- 34% will have put away more than $250,000.

What would out-of-pocket medical costs do to these assets?

Boomers have changed virtually every societal institution on their charge through the life cycle. Today's older adult has already changed our perspective of retirement and of the aged, but it's safe to say the Boomers will also further re-define the "retirement" marketplace. Already, there are indications that this 76-million strong generation is having an impact on the older years as we perceive them.

THE ZOOMERS

AARP changed its name. It was called the American Association of Retired Persons, but now they just use the initials. Their monthly periodical *Modern Maturity* wouldn't do for today's new age 50+ adult, either. Would this up-and-coming generation, zooming into retirement with fast and far reaching agendas be interested in a periodical with near-80-year-old actress and frequent game show panelist Betty White on the cover? AARP didn't take the chance. They created an entirely new, *second* publication called *My Generation.* So, instead of Betty White, the newest AARP members saw 50-something actress Susan Sarandon on the cover of the feature article "Great Sex – What's Age Got to Do With It?"

The term "Zoomers" is attributed to the Del Webb Corporation, Arizona-based developers of the Sun City chain.

Joining AARP is considered by many to be a rite of passage for those nearing retirement. But if retirement is being constantly re-defined, so, too did AARP need re-defining. The future of this powerful organization depended on it. The jury's still out, but more people turning age 50 are joining.

Zoomers are among the first to experience something else – what some demographers call the first wave of longevity. Many have seen their parents live long enough to experience the hardship of a long-term care need. They have been witness to the liquidation of assets to pay the medical expenses associated

> **Top 5 Fears of the New Millennium**
>
> 1. Not being able to pay medical bills,
> 2. Social Security going bust,
> 3. Caring for elderly parents,
> 4. Not amassing an inheritance to pass on to children, and
> 5. Stock market crashing.[52]

with this need. They have seen their parents in a role reversal – now dependent on the care and responsibility of their children. The question is will Zoomers benefit from this knowledge and avoid repeating their parents' lack of planning? There are a number of positive factors that point towards some hope. These include the following: (1) their "better late than never" arrival into the realm of financial planning; (2) a willingness to listen to experts in fields in which they themselves have little confidence; and (3) a crusade for their children to enjoy all of the things they didn't and avoid putting them in caregiver roles. It is too early to say whether this will translate into proper financial planning by this group, including incorporating long-term care insurance into wealth protection plans.

The majority of long-term care today is family-based, leaving much of the financial and emotional expenses resting on the wide shoulders of adult children. As noted earlier, one in four families is providing care to elderly relatives or friends. Usually, sandwiched adults somehow have to divide their energy four ways – their children, their spouse, their parents and themselves. Add work, too, if this person is trying to maintain employment while caregiving.

This exhausting effort is taking its toll. Zoomers are closing in on their retirement years. They are realizing that they will have to put a significant amount of money away to enjoy their retirement years. Of course, many Zoomers have an entirely different view of what their retirement will look like.

Retire This

AARP already eliminated the word "retirement" from their vaunted association. Many Zoomers believe they will be working well into what has heretofore been assumed to be retirement time – age 65. They may change jobs and focus, but they will likely still be working in some capacity. Until recently, Zoomers' identity was largely tied up in work. Becoming parents themselves has changed that perspective some, but there is still a great deal of satisfaction to come from working. Perhaps they will corner the market for consultants in the future. Maybe they will pursue their favorite vocations – art, photography, writing – and try to turn it into a revenue stream. In any event, financial planning for the future will likely be counting employment wages or 1099 earnings as an income source.

Not that the nation doesn't need it. Every individual in America is aware of the increasing dependency ratio between non-workers and workers. Just keeping Zoomers in the workforce longer can have a positive impact on productivity, a critical measurement of a country's economic state.

Results of the Women's Retirement Confidence Survey:

- women are less likely than men to be confident of their ability to pay for long-term care (12% versus 21%)
- only 18% of women are confident that they will have enough money in retirement to pay medical expenses (versus 31% of men)

Source: Employee Benefits Research Institute[53]

In any event, the age-65-and-over years will look very different for the Zoomer. Many Americans say they plan to keep working in some capacity after they retire but want to work fewer hours, be their own boss, or switch to a career they find more personally rewarding, even if it pays less.[54]

One thing is relatively certain, though: Zoomers may not be able to outrun eventual poor health. As Susan Sontag says, "Everyone who is born holds dual citizenship, in the kingdom of the well and in the kingdom of the sick."

" A wasted youth is better by far than a wise and productive old age."

– Meat Loaf,
from the album *Bat out of Hell II*

Zoomers will face enormous financial pressures in the coming years. Ahead of many of them are their children's col-

American Council of Life Insurers Voters Survey[55]

- The majority of voters were concerned about achieving a comfortable standard of living in retirement.
- 88% said Congress should pass laws encouraging small businesses to offer pension and retirement plans.
- 82% said Congress should pass laws allowing employees to increase the amount they can contribute to 401(k) plans.
- 76% support the idea of the government providing tax incentives to encourage people to buy long-term care insurance.

lege education, their parents' financial and long-term care needs, plus their own future. There is a great need for financial planning to enable this generation to live as they have been accustomed. Many plan to downsize some after the children leave, and a majority do not plan to move after their primary working years are through. The mass exodus of retirees to Florida and Arizona may subside at last.

> *Zoomers tend "to view themselves as about 15 years younger than they actually are. That makes them fun to be around, but a bad mindset when it comes to financial planning."*[56]

Demands on income are high. Zoomers are very concerned about "Wealth Care" going forward. Congress may give them all the incentives they need, from higher pre-tax retirement contributions to expanded deductions for long-term care premiums. But they will still have to plan all of this out. Your information gathering process starts with the net worth and cash flow worksheets. From there, the priorities can be set – how best to accumulate and protect money already saved and future dollars to be set aside.

How well financial planners perform this task may well dictate what kind of 21st Century we have. The coming decades will be strewn with mature adults, trying to stretch their money as far as possible. It will be up to planners, advisors and insurance agents to make "Wealth Care" a reality.

FUZZY MATH

What a difference a year can make. In mid-2000, with the stock market continuing its running with the bulls, many workers were boasting of high retirement fund balances and of retiring early from the rat race to pursue the more esoteric pleasures of life. But, as has happened to the Zoomers before, the financial train derailed before it reached the station. By mid-2001, account totals were down, early retirement dreams were put on hold and there were darker clouds on the eternal optimists' horizons.

Add to this bitter dose of reality the delusion that many Zoomers have about how long-term care is paid for in retirement. In an American Health Care Association study, four out of five Zoomers interviewed did not know how long-term care is paid for and 25% said they were unwilling to consider paying for any additional insurance to cover these costs. While 41% were willing to pay between $1 and $49 per month for long-term care insurance, in most cases this is well below the actual costs of these policies.[58]

This is consistent with a U.S. Bancorp Piper Jaffray study that showed that only 20% of Zoomers were planning to use long-term care insurance to pay for this type of medical expense, even though they were aware of studies indicating more than twice that many will likely need this type of care. In addition, 71.7% of them envisioned staying in their homes regardless of health conditions and the treatment they might need later in life.[59] It is apparent they did not realize around-the-clock home nursing care already costs more than $120,000 a year in many parts of the country.[60]

What will happen to the Boomers when they really get old? "Will they accept age as gracefully as the GI Generation that survived the Depression and fought World War II? Or will there be an emotional and psychological train wreck at the junction of Delusion and Reality?"[57]

Even informed people can spend a lot of money on care. A year of nursing home care will cost, on average, $56,000 according to the AARP, who also noted the average stay is still around 2.5 years, meaning a possible funding need of $140,000 for this medical contingency.[61]

But, for Zoomers especially, medical and nursing home bills aren't the only costs to be faced. A MetLife study in 1999 concluded that a working person obliged to provide care and financial assistance to an elderly relative can lose up to $650,000 in lifetime earnings by

2001 Annual Retirement Confidence Survey[62]

- The percentage of workers believing they would have enough money to live comfortably during their retirement years: *down 9%*
- Workers that are confident they will have enough money to pay for basic expenses during retirement: *down 6%*
- Workers who believe that they will be financially prepared for medical expenses during retirement: *down 8%*
- Workers who believe that they will be financially prepared for long-term care costs during retirement: *down 7%*

Source: Employee Benefit Research Institute

Long-term care cost projections by year 2030

- Nursing home: $44,100/yr. increasing to $190,600/yr.
- Assisted living facility: $25,300/yr. increasing to $109,300
- Home health aides: $61/visit increasing to $260/visit
- Adult day care: $50/day increasing to $220/day

Source: American Council of Life Insurers

passing up promotions, leaving work early or going part-time.[63] The reduced contributions to Social Security as a result will also directly impact the person's own retirement benefit.

Many analysts feel that Zoomers are better off financially than their parents were when they reached 50. The near-decade long market run has certainly helped, even if those heady days have yielded to harder realities. But great disparities exist between the poorest and richest Zoomers. Many delayed child-rearing and are only now saving up for their child's college tuition. After getting divorced nine years ago, and with her children out of the house, a Maryland woman needed something to fill up her newfound time and shore up her financial situation. She went back to school and after eight years, graduated with a bachelor's degree in information services technology from the College of Southern Maryland. "I'm 50, a baby boomer, and I look back proudly on that time when I grew up," she said. "But this is a totally different situation to where I'd expected I'd be at this point in my life."[64]

If long-term care costs are confusing to Zoomers, the whole retirement nest egg thing has them baffled even more. Reports that it will take $1 million or more to retire makes matters much worse, says The National Center for Women and Retirement Research. Zoomers hear the $1 million figure and go into a sort of "financial paralysis." They know what they have ahead of them in terms of other financial commitments and it's almost inconceivable that this amount of money can be put aside in

> According to the U.S. Census Bureau, the wealthiest Americans are between the ages of 70 and 74, followed by those in the age 65-69 bracket.[65]

time enough to actually enjoy it. The high rate of divorce among Zoomers only compounds the problem. Those on their second or third marriages often have children even later in life. When that happens, it is very likely one could be signing over their Social Security checks to help pay for the kid's college tuition.[66]

To illustrate the impact of financing long-term care costs, a correlation can be drawn between the costs of care in a hospital versus a nursing facility. For those age 65 and over, the average cost of hospital care is $750/day with the average stay being 7.8 days. Thus, the total average cost is $5,850 with an average of $330 paid out of pocket because the majority of this type of health care is paid for by the patient's primary health insurance, Medicare or an HMO.[68]

Contrast that with the average cost of a nursing facility, noted earlier as $56,000 annually with an average stay of 2.5 years. That's a total cost of $140,000. What kind of help does someone get with that expense? In Florida in the year

> "Bob was so healthy, so alive when we married. We thought we could start all over again. Now look what's happened. We never worried about money. My first husband left enough for me to live on and hand down to the children. Now the nursing home has eaten up Bob's money and I'll have to dig into what John left me. What will be left for the girls? They'll have nothing that their father left for them. If I had known this might happen ... I might not have married again. We heard about long-term care insurance. We didn't do anything. It would have been a lot more important than that stupid prenuptial agreement."[67]

2000, Medicare paid for 13% of the costs of care delivered in a nursing home.[69] Even though there are limits, let's say that reimbursed $18,200. That leaves $121,800 (87%) to be funded elsewhere. That's a far cry from the $330 out-of-pocket hospital cost, a mere 5.6% to be paid by the patient. This is why long-term care is often referred to as a financial black hole.

Much of the $121,800 will be paid out of pocket unless and until the money runs out and the individual is eligible for Medicaid. But the Medicaid story is another of struggles with the bottom line.

States are already in a serious budget crunch with this program. The January 2001 state-of-the-state address delivered by Governor Bob Taft of Ohio listed as a challenge for his state the cuts in spending at the state and federal levels for long-term care. The recent Medicare cuts at the federal level resulted in a funding crisis for long-term care providers with nearly 1,700 bankruptcies nationwide and 59 in Ohio. It was noted that any reduction in spending at the state (Medicaid) or federal level (both Medicaid and Medicare) fails to recognize the need for dollars to attract and retain professional workers to provide long-term care services, along with a rapid growth of those needing this care.[70]

According to the American Council of Life Insurers, elderly nursing home expenditures will increase in total, from $61 billion annually to $330 billion by the year 2030. Some individual state increases are noted below:[71]

Florida: . . . .514% increase
Georgia 657%
Oregon 655%
New Jersey 338%
Illinois 550%
Nevada 1389%

Ohio isn't the only state grappling with long-term care costs and reduced third-party payments. In Florida, Medicaid covers only 88 cents of every dollar spent to run a nursing home. Figures for the Florida Association of Homes for the Aged show facilities lose $15.74 per patient per day. Eighty-two percent of homes last year didn't get enough from Medicaid to cover expenses, compared with 54% a decade ago.[72] In Minnesota in March 2001, hundreds of long-term care advocates rallied on the steps of the State Capitol to protest Governor Jesse Ventura's new budget. They noted that decreased Medicaid state funding would create a half-million-day gap in nursing home care as soon as 2003, the gap being the difference between the total number of days in nursing homes needed by older

Minnesotans and the nursing home beds that will be available.[73] Counting on government resources as part of your financial plan would seem to make little sense as budget woes have forced cutbacks even in the better revenue years of late.

It's not just the younger generations that have the cost of long-term care to tuck somewhere in their financial plan. Those that are age 65 and over have already run into the wall of medical costs. There has been ample publicity about long-term care over the last few years, but that problem pales in comparison to the ink devoted to the out-of-pocket costs for those dependent on prescription drugs. These are all medical costs, and the difficulty in paying for one is definitely going to impact the ability to pay for the other.

DEFINING LONG-TERM CARE EXPENSES

Since the mid-1980s, the percentage of older Americans in nursing homes has declined, according to a report from Brandeis University. The report indicates that the percentage of Americans age 65 and older residing in nursing homes fell from 4.6% in 1985 to 4.2% a decade later, with the sharpest decline among those 85 and older. If the 1985 rate had held, the number of elders in American nursing homes in 1995 – 1.4 million – would have been closer to 1.7 million.

"Nursing homes are no longer as prominent among long-term care options as they were a decade ago," the report's author says. "While nursing homes were the dominant care option as recently as the early 1990s, new options that provide lower-level care such as adult day care and assisted living have grown in prominence. Nursing homes have become more narrowly specialized, catering to those needing the greatest assistance."[74]

Defining long-term care expenses means identifying the type of assistance that is necessary and where this care will be administered. For many years, long-term care was associated with nursing homes, but as evidenced by the information above, this is only a small part of the long-term care story. Care is more often administered in another setting – the home, at an adult day care center, an assisted living facility and others. Understanding the various possible locations for receipt of long-term care treatment is part of estimating the financial costs of long-term care as one plans ahead for the future.

Nursing homes have long had a negative image, and this has been magnified in recent months by tales of nursing home neglect and abuse. These facilities were already in the midst of seeking a new identity, and had started filling a primary role as a place where Medicare-discharged hospital patients went to receive further care before ultimately being sent home. Their current mission has been to act as the last stop for individuals who have spent most of their income and assets and qualified for Medicaid. Two major problems are redirecting these facilities from this traditional course. First, the Medicaid program is looking to alternative ways to treat beneficiaries in need of long-term care help and are turning to home care and other options instead of a nursing home. Second, Medicaid, as noted earlier, reimburses the lowest amount of any third party payors of long-term care expenses. This hardly helps nursing facilities meet their bottom lines, forcing them to pay less to staff or to hire fewer highly skilled workers, resulting in higher employee turnover, providing opportunities for more stories of neglect and poor care, raising premiums for liability coverage for the facility that are difficult to pay because of the low Medicaid reimbursements, and creating a vicious cycle that continues to haunt these residences that will still have an important role to play in long-term care's future.

Where are the missing elders? That was the title of a recent study conducted by the National Center for Health Statistics. They found that the proportion of people age 65 and over that were staying overnight in a nursing home had declined by 8.2% in a recent ten-

Percentage of nursing home residents by limitations, 1997	
Limitations	**%**
Need help –	
3 or more ADLs	.83%
with dementia	.42%
without dementia	.41%
Need help with	
1-2 ADLs	.14%
with dementia	.5%
without dementia	.9%
Need no help	
with ADLs	.3%
with dementia	.5%
without dementia	.2%

Source: Agency for Health Care Policy and Research [75]

year period.[76] They put forth five reasons for the decline in the use of nursing homes despite the increase in the older age population.

First, was there a prevailing decline in disability rates? Evidence indicated that the rate of disability had reduced significantly over that ten-year period, with the percentage of age-65-and-over people experiencing at least one difficulty in performing an instrumental or physical activity of daily living (ADL) falling to 21.3%. Second, were nursing facilities serving higher-need patients at the expense of lower-need ones? Over the ten-year period, the nursing home residents were a bit more likely to have specific disabilities and, as a result, these facilities offered more hours of patient care per patient day than had been the case ten years earlier. Third, the supply of beds available in a nursing facility has simply not kept pace with the rise in elderly population. In the ten-year period reviewed, only 147,000 beds were added to the nation's supply of nursing facility beds where 271,000 should have been based on the increase in elderly population. Fourth, by the end of this ten-year period, more elders with disabilities were receiving health and personal care at home than ever before. Medicare certainly experienced dramatic increases until the Balanced Budget Amendment cutbacks in 1997. Finally, some elders with disabilities who would have been nursing home residents at the beginning of the ten-year study had sought other care settings by the end of the study. Assisted living, independent housing that provides access to disability care, has been hailed as a "new paradigm" for elders with disability. The results of these studies show that long-term care is being used widely – just less and less in a nursing home setting.[77]

Average length of stay of nursing home residents 65 years of age and over [78]			
		YEARS	
	Both Sexes	Males	Females
Avg. length of stay	2.3	1.9	2.4
ages 65-74	2.9	2.5	3.2
ages 75-84	2.4	1.9	2.5
ages 85 +	1.9	1.4	2.1

Source: U.S. Census Bureau

In December 1999, the government put in place tough new rules to crack down on nursing homes with repeated violations. Homes that were found to cause harm, through abuse or neglect, to even a single resident in two or more inspections can immediately be fined up to $10,000 and have their Medicare and Medicaid payments suspended.[79]

Still, the local nursing home costs in your area are going to be important to ascertain in order to properly assess all the potential long-term care costs that an individual might face. Try as we might, predicting the course of a long-term care situation is nearly impossible. So much depends on the type of care needed, the resources available and the possible family caregivers that may become involved. That's far too many variables to make any substantively accurate predictions about the likely setting and amount of long-term care that will be necessary. The best way to evaluate the possible long-term care residences is to check them out yourself. There are a number of items to look for as evidenced by the checklist in Figure 1.4.

Once you have a list of various facilities in the area that you are pleased with, be it nursing home, assisted living facility, adult congregate residence or adult day care center, you can note the costs that you've obtained and average them to determine what the potential expenses might be for any of your clients who might ultimately be staying in any of these residences. It will give you a monetary range to fund and your clients a better feel for the cost. The Cost Calculator Worksheet in Figure 1.5 will prove helpful in gathering the price data associated with these facilities.

Blue Bell, PA: A leader in serving the medical needs of mature Americans says that for longer and happier life spans, his prescription is providing a full range of health care services at **home.** The founder and former President of the Delaware Valley Geriatric Society is convinced that bringing health care services into homes or apartments

Figure 1.4

CHOOSING A FACILITY[80]

- Tour and compare as many facilities as possible.

- Get a feeling for how staff members relate to the residents.

- Talk to residents about how they like the place.

- Check to ensure that the facility has a license in good standing. You should contact the state office responsible for regulating these facilities for that information.

- Find out exactly what services are available.

- Get a documented list of rates, financial arrangements and any extra charges that might be added on, as well as refund policies.

- Ask how long the administrator has been with the facility and whether there is a staff training program.

- Share a typical meal with the residents or at least observe a meal setting.

- Ask for copies of the contract and facility rules to bring home and review on your own.

- Make repeat visits to the most promising of the facilities, showing up at various times of the day to observe what's happening.

- Make sure that the facility is a residence where you would place your own family member, relative or yourself.

---

not only enhances medical prospects and quality of life but also provides important economic side effects. He noted that the overwhelming preference of older citizens to stay in their own homes is also a desirable remedy for today's challenging health care costs. He also said that desirable health maintenance among the elderly, accompanied by ongoing home-based care, can affect great savings in expensive hospital and nursing home treatments.[81]

Home is where the savings are – and also the familiar surroundings. Medical advances have made it possible to bring almost all types of treatments into the home and, if one is not in serious need of constant skilled care, this is the most likely setting for an individual in need of long-term care. Comprehensive long-term care insur-

Figure 1.5

COST CALCULATOR WORKSHEET
For Nursing and Assisted Living Facilities

	Included in Base daily rate	Cost
Entrance or Membership Fee	_____	$ _____
Daily or Monthly Benefit Rate	_____	_____

Additional Services

Meals		
Regular	_____	_____
Special dietary	_____	_____
Room service	_____	_____
Guest meals	_____	_____
Extra (snacks)	_____	_____
Housekeeping	_____	_____
Laundry		
Linens	_____	_____
Personal clothes	_____	_____
Extras		
Furnished unit	_____	_____
Cable TV	_____	_____
Refrigerator	_____	_____
Utilities/Water	_____	_____
Microwave	_____	_____
Carpeting	_____	_____
Special bathroom fixtures	_____	_____
Telephone	_____	_____
Other	_____	_____
Transportation		
Scheduled	_____	_____
Unscheduled	_____	_____
Other	_____	_____
Recreational and Personal Services		
Beauty/barber shop	_____	_____
Shopping help	_____	_____
Medication supervision	_____	_____
Toiletries	_____	_____
Other	_____	_____

TOTAL (Base + Additional)　　　　Daily　$ _____

　　　　　　　　　　　　　　　　　　Monthly　$ _____

Figure 1.5 (continued)
EXPLANATIONS

Note: The cost calculator is intended for broad use with most types of senior housing. There will be many lines that won't be needed depending on the residence. For ease of use, as many anticipated expenses as possible have been listed to help with financial planning.

Costs: The first thing one must do is determine the likely locality for any type of long-term care. Locality means two things: in what area and what type of housing. The area can best be determined by the family – where would the individual(s) go if care was necessary? Would they stay where they are presently living? Or relocate to be closer to family and a stronger support system? Once determined, one can contact the local Area Agency on Aging in the locale where care will be sought for resource information about various facilities.

Types of Housing: There are many choices today for the long-term care patient. In addition to nursing facilities of various levels of care and assisted living facilities (the fastest growing type of senior housing), there is adult day care (similar to child care centers), home care, continuing care retirement communities (CCRCs), adult congregate living facilities (apartments, board and care homes) and government-subsidized housing for low income individuals.

Entrance or Membership Fee: Some facilities charge an entry fee. For an assisted living facility, for example, this could be one month's rent ($2,000 - $5,000). For CCRCs, the fees could range into the tens of thousands. These are most often one-time assessments.

Daily Benefit Rate: Nursing facilities and adult day care centers generally charge on a daily rate. Assisted living facilities and CCRCs most likely charge on a monthly basis. This worksheet is constructed for either calculation.

Rate Structure: Assisted living facilities use different types of rate structures from a flat rate (plus extras) to a bundled rate (inclusive of several services) to a tiered rate representing several different levels of care required.

The Extras: This is often the great unknown and the overlooked part of estimating long-term care costs. Always ask about any extra charges and get a price breakdown in writing. Daily benefit rates in many nursing homes do not include regular linen laundry service, for example, and may charge more for special dietary needs and hair styling. The more you know up front, the better to properly estimate cost and the amount of coverage needed in a long-term care insurance policy.

Rate increases: Most facilities raise their rates each year. This underscores the importance of inflation protection in a long-term care insurance policy. Find out the past price hike history to judge what the future might hold in terms of costs.

*According to Ken Dychtwald,
author of The Age Wave, here
are some of the entrepreneur-
ial and investment opportunities for the future:*

• *Home care services:
  Increasingly, people want
  to be cared for in their
  own homes instead of
  costlier, more regimented,
  less congenial nursing
  homes, making investment
  in home and home care
  services timely.*

• *Adult day care: There will
  also be tremendous opportunities for services that
  pick up people at their
  homes early in the day,
  deliver them to places
  where they can get care
  and recreation during the
  day, and deposit them
  back at home at the end of
  the day.*

• *Retirement housing: More
  and more retirees want to
  move to college towns that
  offer stimulating neighbors, plentiful intellectual
  and recreational opportunities and outstanding
  medical services like
  Gainesville, Florida and
  Columbus, Ohio.[82]*

ance policies address this need and provide funding for assistance rendered in a
home setting.

There is some concern that once the
elderly can pay for home care through private insurance, that the informal (and
valuable) caregiving provided by family
members, neighbors and relatives would
simply stop being rendered. In-depth
reviews by LifePlans, Inc. revealed, however, that informal caregivers continue to
provide care. The availability of the professional home care services helped informal caregivers spend less time on cleaning
and other "drudge work" and more on
talking, reading out loud, and simply
enjoying a loved one's company. Most
agreed that the privately funded home
care benefits were essential to keeping
people in their own homes.[83]

In addition to a home setting, the
other up and coming choice for a place to
obtain long-term care services is an **assisted living facility**. It's not exactly a nursing
home, more of an apartment with access
to nursing home-like services. There are
housekeeping services, transportation,
meals and other types of personal care, all
included in the monthly rate.

With the number of people who will
need help with activities of daily living
(ADLs) projected to increase by 51% in
the next 20 years, it is no wonder assisted
living facilities (ALFs) are in growth

According to the Assisted Living Federation of America, the most common needs of its residents are: [84]

ADL care need	% Residents
Bathing assistance	.60%
Medication dispensing	.59%
Medication reminders	.50%
Dressing assistance	.44%
Toileting assistance	.32%
Mobility assistance	.15%
Eating assistance	.10%

Other characteristics:

Cognitive impairments	.47%
Using wheelchair	.38%
Received home care	.27%

mode. Since 1998, the number of licensed facilities has increased 30%. Today, more than 500,000 people live in ALFs, where the average age is 84. The price of care can exceed $4,000 per month and should not be considered a cheaper substitute for a nursing home. An ALF does not offer the type of supervision or skilled care services that a nursing facility will, instead giving the resident more autonomy and freedom that can be a positive factor in the decision to select an ALF over a nursing home. [85]

In a sense, assisted living facilities are still searching for an identity. They are a lower cost alternative, but the assumption is that the individual is not as needy as one for whom a nursing facility would be a better choice. These residences are more expensive than an apartment, but there is a variety of services available that one can access as one wishes. Marriott and Hyatt have staked big dollars in investing in these ALFs as the homes of the future. It's less impersonal than a nursing facility, and this is some-

A recent American Nursing Home Credentialing Center survey indicated that 85% of Americans would be more confident in selecting a long-term care facility if they knew it had met rigorous quality standards. In addition, 87% would be more confident in the nursing care they received if they knew their nurse was a board-certified specialist. Only 34% knew that board certification for nurses was available. [86]

thing that has attracted people looking for this type of living arrangement.

Suburbs Struggle to Keep Seniors

WEST WINDSOR, N.J., March 11, 2001 – Fred and Mary Froehlich love the Cape Cod house that Fred built with his own hands 46 years ago, when West Windsor was a blue-collar farming community and not the vast plain of expensive houses it has become. They love the way their five grown children still come home for family gatherings. What they do not love are the taxes, $6,000 a year, which happens to be the same as Mary's Social Security benefits. So, like a lot of suburban retirees, Fred Froehlich is trying to persuade his wife to move, in their case to a spot in Delaware where taxes are a tenth of what they are here.

Mayor Carole Carson wants to keep the Froehlichs. She's done the math and knows what it means when retirees move out and a new generation of families with children moves in. It means more children swelling enrollment at schools, more garbage to pick up, more cars on the road, and more services in general. Since it costs an average of $9,599 a year to send a child to public school locally, even with state aid, one new child in the Froehlich household would completely offset the taxes the Froehlichs pay.

Mayor Carson does not want to lose the Froehlichs. And, like other communities around the country, West Windsor is scrambling to find ways to keep as many elderly residents as possible. An aging population is already changing what suburbia in this country looks like. She notes that seniors are a tremendous asset, both in terms of the values they stand for and the low cost they generally represent to a community. So she is leading a statewide drive to encourage seniors to stay in their homes by reducing the punishing level of property taxation.

The waning appeal of Sunbelt retirement communities is giving way to a new suburban phenomenon called the "naturally occurring retirement community" (NORC). Discounted public transportation, free medical screenings and the opportunity to audit college courses for a nominal fee are some of the incentives to keep seniors, rather than lose them to a targeted retirement area.[87]

These NORCs may yield new potential for a long-term care setting. It may well keep people in their own homes, or communities may decide to bring in a Marriott or Hyatt or Sunrise to build an ALF locally when the ability to live in one's own home becomes too overwhelming. Know that local communities are dealing with this issue now and how well they do at retaining retirees may dictate the array of long-term settings in the future.

Finally, the last stages of illness can result in the need for hospice care. This is often the last choice that can be made by or on behalf of the patient. Most long-term care policies provide reimbursements for hospice care. While the nation's health care system continues to make strides with regard to the major diseases, the cures are slow in coming. While there is a great optimism that solutions are close at hand, the truth is we are significantly better at pain relief than we are at slowing or reversing the disease. This is where a hospice program is vital. There are hospice facilities and there are programs that can be done at home. The individual maintains some control in the last few months, weeks and days of life. Not only does hospice prepare the patient, it has grief counseling for the family members who will ultimately be left behind. Many counties offer hospice programs and you can contact them for cost and setting options. You should also review the policy for the hospice benefits that are payable, usually the same as would be available for a nursing home or assisted living facility.

Comprehensive long-term care policies cover just about all of the types of care and settings in which this treatment might be provided. Some insurers have indicated that their policy covers care in settings that are still being formulated.

As the country continues to age, there will be an increase in the range in

At 75, Alzada Davis was suffering from cancer that had metastasized into her bones and experimental aggressive chemotherapy had not only failed but left her completely debilitated and unresponsive. Believing death was imminent, doctors had her admitted to a hospice. Family members were told it was a matter of hours or days, but refused to believe it. The family sat with her until one day she mouthed that she was hungry. The son told an incredulous nurse that his mother wanted chicken. After initially trying to explain to the son that his mother couldn't eat, she got the chicken and the long road to recovery had begun. She was discharged from the hospice and went to her son's home where hospice took over in their home program. Slowly, she improved until hospice was discharged and home health care had taken over. The course of long-term care is not always a predictable one.[88]

types of facilities that will provide long-term care. Take the case of Marie Black and her son Ralph. Marie is a skeletal woman of 106 years with skin so thin that a nurse's touch can leave a bruise on her arm. She never leaves her bed. Sitting up is painful. Her eyesight is gone, blinded by macular degeneration, an affliction that now affects her 77-year-old son Ralph. Ralph lives with his wife Helen on the seventh floor of Westminster Towers in Orlando, Florida, just an elevator ride and a short walk from Marie's nursing home room. They live in the independent-living section of the Towers, with the idea that as they age, they will move in to the facility's assisted living quarters and ultimately to the nursing home wing his mother is in.[89] Perhaps this type of multi-purpose housing is the future.

Key Product Elements
"Things are only impossible until they're not."
— Jean-Luc Picard, Star Trek,
The Next Generation

Long-term care insurance is not just another product to sell to make a profit on. You will need to invest some time in each client. You will need to spend the same time on your own financial program, seeing if, why and how long-term care fits. Long-term care covers a potentially damaging risk – one that is as much emotional as it is financial. You don't have to be older to market this product; younger agents can do quite well if they truly believe in the need for this wealth protection vehicle.

Four key design components of a comprehensive long-term care insurance program:

1. *Daily Benefit Amount,*
2. *Elimination Period,*
3. *Benefit Period, and*
4. *Inflation Protection.*

Once you've identified a need for long-term care (sufficient assets or projected assets to protect and sufficient cash flow to budget a premium outlay for the coverage) there will be four key areas that you need to understand.

DAILY BENEFIT AMOUNT

This is the specific daily amount that you would purchase based on where long-term care expenses will be incurred. As you can see from Figure 1.6, part of a 2000 MetLife Mature Market Institute Study, the costs vary considerably.

The average nursing home rates are usually the highest facility costs one would have to handle and the other services usually fall below those numbers. Exceptions would be the need for highly skilled care personal visits or around-the-clock home health care. In addition to the nursing home area daily rates, the 2000 MetLife Mature Market Institute Study also published the typical average home health care aide hourly rates to give you an indication of the expense involved with this generally custodial type of care (see Figure 1.7).

ELIMINATION PERIOD

This is the number of days before any benefits are payable after the onset of a claim. The longer the elimination period, the lower the cost. Surprisingly, there is a not a substantial difference between no elimination period (also called -0- days) where benefit eligibility begins on the first day of a claim and, say, a 90-day elimination period. Considering the difference in self-insuring between those two points ($100/day for 90 days is $9,000 out-of-pocket before benefits begin), carefully check all of the lower elimination periods – 0, 15, 20, 30 – to compare to higher periods – 60, 90, 100. Usually the selection here is based on the affordability of the plan, but there are more significant premium differences at the benefit period level.

BENEFIT PERIOD

We noted earlier that the average length of stay for a nursing home is 27 months. Assisted living facility average stays would certainly seem to range higher since the resident isn't likely to be as ill. I suggest a minimum benefit period of 4 years, or higher based on affordability of premium. Here, especially in one's mid-60s to early 70s, you can find some substantive differences in premium by electing a shorter benefit period and hoping it will be sufficient. The life-

Figure 1.6

AVERAGE DAILY NURSING HOME RATES[90]

Albany, NY $200	Miami, FL 123
Atlanta, GA 110	Middlesex City, NJ 195
Baltimore, MD.............. 163	Milwaukee, WI 179
Battle Creek, MI 195	Minneapolis, MN 106
Birmingham, AL 105	Nashville, TN 135
Boston, MA 278	New Brunswick, NJ 161
Bristol County, VA 199	New Haven, CT 227
Buffalo, NY 193	New Orleans, LA 97
Charleston, SC 108	New York City 295
Chattanooga, TN 136	Newark, DE 139
Cherry Hill, NJ 193	Newark, NJ 228
Chicago North 165	No. Metro Atlanta, GA 131
Chicago South 138	Oakland, CA 157
Cincinnati, OH 127	Oklahoma City, OK. 134
Cleveland, OH 200	Omaha, NE 149
Columbia, SC 120	Orlando, FL 125
Columbus, OH 162	Pensacola, FL 123
Dallas, TX 149	Philadelphia, PA 163
Dayton, OH 162	Phoenix, AZ.................. 152
Denver, CO 141	Pittsburgh, PA 181
Des Moines, IA 102	Portland, ME 192
Detroit, MI................. 113	Portland, OR 144
Dover, NH 200	Providence, RI 160
Fairfax County, VA 172	Provo, UT 135
Flint, MI................... 134	Raleigh, NC 120
Florence, AL 108	Richmond, VA 147
Fort Wayne, IN 137	Rochester, NY 187
Gary, IN 98	Salt Lake City, UT 135
Grand Rapids, MI............ 154	San Antonio, TX 114
Greensboro, NC.............. 132	San Diego, CA 149
Hartford, CT 210	San Francisco, CA 169
Hibbing, MN 90	Savannah, GA 103
Houston, TX 111	Seattle, WA.................. 174
Huntsville, AL 113	Springfield, MA 181
Indianapolis, IN 161	Stamford, CT 286
Internat'l Falls, MN 91	St. Louis, MO 138
Jacksonville, FL 150	Summit, NJ 242
Kansas City, KS 117	Syracuse, NY 196
Las Vegas, NV 133	Tampa, FL 128
Lehigh Valley, PA 167	Toledo, OH 128
Long Beach, CA.............. 138	Trenton, NJ 195
Los Angeles, CA.............. 122	Tucson, AZ.................. 149
Macon, GA 98	Washington, DC 165
Maryland (D.C. area) 173	Winston-Salem, NC 137

Figure 1.7

AVERAGE HOME HEALTH
CARE AID HOURLY RATE[91]

Alameda, CA	$19	Mercer County, NJ	$16
Allegheny, PA	16	Miami, FL	14
Atlanta, GA	15	Milwaukee, WI	17
Baltimore, MD	15	Minneapolis, MN	19
Battle Creek, MI	15	Monroe County, NY	17
Birmingham, AL	14	Nashville, TN	14
Boston, MA	19	New Castle, DE	20
Chattanooga, TN	15	New Orleans, LA	13
Chicago, IL	17	New York City, NY	14
Cleveland, OH	17	Oklahoma City, OK	14
Columbia, SC	13	Omaha, NE	16
Columbus, OH	16	Onandaga, NY	15
Dallas, TX	15	Orlando, FL	15
Danbury, CT	21	Pensacola, FL	14
Dayton, OH	16	Philadelphia, PA	14
Denver, CO	22	Phoenix, AZ	17
Des Moines, IA	18	Providence, RI	15
Detroit, MI	17	Raleigh, NC	15
Essex, NJ	16	Richmond, VA	13
Ft. Wayne, IN	17	San Antonio, TX	12
Gary, IN	16	San Francisco, CA	17
Grand Rapids, MI	16	Savannah, GA	12
Hartford, CT	24	Seattle, WA	19
Hibbing, MN	14	St. Louis, MO	19
Houston, TX	16	Stamford, CT	19
Indianapolis, IN	17	Tampa, FL	16
Jacksonville, FL	14	Toledo, OH	15
Kansas City, KS	16	Tucson, AZ	15
Lansing, MI	16	Washington, DC	16
Las Vegas, NV	18	Winston-Salem, NC	14
Los Angeles, CA	17		

time benefit period is always option #1 if the individual can afford it. Companies also typically market 5- or 6-year benefit periods, too.

INFLATION

The younger the buyer, the more critical this coverage becomes. We already know that health care costs increase rapidly each year, greater usually than the rate of inflation. There are three choices – compounded inflation coverage, simple inflation coverage, or no coverage. A younger buyer (under age 60) should seriously consider the compounded rider. It's not drastically expensive yet at those ages and it may be some time before you need to utilize the benefits. The mid-range buyer (age 60-70) should look at simple inflation coverage. It's much less expensive at those ages than compounded and since the need for care may be closer, the compounded rider might not offer that much more in benefits. Finally, for the buyer over age 70, he or she should weight the cost of the simple inflation benefit versus simply buying a higher daily benefit amount (like $185 when area rates are around $130) and trust that this higher benefit level will be adequate come claim time. Much depends on the ability to pay the premium.

ATTENTION FINANCIAL ADVISORS:
LONG-TERM CARE
PLANNING BEGINS AT HOME

"Never put off until tomorrow what you can do the day after tomorrow."

– Mark Twain

There are many financial advisors who do not practice what they preach. Long-term care is more a product advisors recommend for others rather than examine it for their own wealth protection. This is similar to doctors who smoke, all the while reciting to you the harmful effects of such a habit.

Why? It likely has something to do with the perception that long-term care is more of a retirement vehicle and requires little attention until one nears that magic age where he or she can slow down from the hectic pace of full-time work. But this ignores the purpose of long-term care coverage. It is intended as a protection of wealth that has either been built or is in the process of building. It is a financial tool that has less to do with age than simple mathematics.

Let's look at this from a dollars and sense standpoint. A 45-year-old has a stroke. As a result, there is permanent nerve damage. This person did not die but is severely disabled, requiring substantial amounts of physical therapy. A disability income policy owned by the victim helps to pay basic monthly expenses to replace the income lost due to the inability to work. But what pays for the physical and speech therapy visits at $175/hour? The medical insurance had short-term provisions for such treatment and covers the care for the first few months. Less than 18 months into the care, the policy benefits run out. How is this care now paid for? The disability income policy is barely covering the necessities – rent, food, clothing and basic utilities. Does one forego the therapy even though it is helping the patient improve? This is not the optimum solution, but discontinuance of treatment that is helping the person is the only *financial* alternative available.

A long-term care expense is a separate cost, apart from the traditional programs that address reimbursement of other medical costs, and those like disability insurance that provide dollars needed to maintain one's standard of living. The argument that long-term care can function like a financial black hole doesn't hold only for those of Medicare age. Sure, we know Medicare wasn't designed to cover long-term care expenses, but *neither was major medical insurance.* The same financial crisis long-term care creates for the elderly can have the same effect on the under-age 65 individ-

Despite the fact that the overwhelming majority of financial planners believe that long-term care plays an important role in a well-rounded financial plan, most Americans have given little or no thought to how they will pay for their own long-term care in years to come. According to an American Council of Life Insurers survey:

- 72% of planners recommend long-term care insurance to their clients "very often" or "somewhat often"
- Only 13% of Americans surveyed, however, have actually taken the steps to buy the coverage on themselves.[92]

Prospects, prospects and more prospects!

The 2000 U.S. Census tells us that the median age in this country is now 35.3 years, the highest it has ever been. This is fueled by growth in the over-age-85 population sector with a 38% surge over the last decade. This is surpassed only by the 49% rise in the number of people age 45 to 54.[93]

ual. It's no different! So the planners out there that are heartily recommending this coverage to others should remember to first examine their own financial plan to see how this "black hole" is being addressed for their own family.

What's the problem? It's simple, I think. The lack of market penetration can be viewed as an extension of many planners' own disbelief that the product is ultimately necessary, especially at younger ages like people in their 40s and 50s. If you have truly assessed your own need, seen the financial and emotional reasons for the product in your own financial program, then it is that much easier to both believe in the product and carry that conviction to the interview with a prospective client. People can tell whether you believe in what you are saying. In addition, a number of prospects will ask you if you own the policy yourself. What do you say to them? If you really believed in the need for this financial planning tool, they wouldn't have to ask you that question. They'd already understand how much you think of the idea.

A Florida long-term care specialist recently wrote in an article, "State of the art LTC product design? No problem, we're there. Major top-rated carriers already on board or waiting in the wings? No problem, we're there. Sufficient actuarial data to keep the carriers and their clients safe and secure? No problem, we're there. So for the last time I ask, what's the problem? The current problem is very simple; we have not done an adequate job of

*penetrating the marketplace. For example, Florida is
number one in the nation for LTC sales (10% of all
sales) and we have only reached approximately 7%
of the target market.... Make sure your house is in
order by examining your own family's situation
first. Then look around you.*[94]

At this point, as we conclude Part One, you have hopefully been convinced of the need and will keep reading to see what to do next. Long-term care can be a significant financial and emotional problem in this country unless valid funding sources are sought and put in place. After starting with your own financial plan, you are now ready to work with others who may have a need for this type of financial assistance should long-term care services be needed in the future.

Footnotes

1. Michael Vitez, "The High Cost of Living Longer," *The Philadelphia Inquirer*, November 20, 2000 (as reprinted on the philly.com web site).

2. "Family Matters," *Consumer Reports* (September, 2000), p. 64.

3. Mary Beth Franklin, "Caring Across the Miles," *Kiplinger's Personal Finance* (November, 2000), pp. 86, 88.

4. Eva Marer, "An Ounce of Prevention," *Financial Planning* (February, 2000), pp. 108, 110.

5. Conrad F. Meier, "Long-Term Care and the Four Urban Legends," *Broker News*, Florida Edition (February, 2001), p. 6.

6. "Long-Term Care Generation Gap," Business Wire, March 23, 1999.

7. Eunice Krieger, "The Future of LTC is Linked to Health Care," *National Underwriter*, Life & Health/Financial Services Edition, August 6, 1999, p. 12.

8. Carole Ann King, "Meeting the Changing Needs of the Aging," *National Underwriter*, Life & Health/Financial Services, May 15, 2000, p. 4.

9. Mary Pipher, Ph.D., *Another Country* (New York:Riverhead Books, 1999), p. 7.

10. Cathy Booth, "Taking Care of Our Aging Parents," *Time*, August 30, 1999, pp. 48, 50.

11. Sandra Block, "50 not so Nifty for Baby Boomers," *USA Today*, September 20, 2000, pp. 1B, 2B.

12. Mary Pipher, Ph.D., *Another Country* (New York:Riverhead Books, 1999), p. 18.

13. Tiffini Theisen, "Workers Suffer in Silence While Caring for Parents," *Orlando Sentinel*, March 28, 2001, p. E4.

14. Sue Shellenbarger, "Caregivers Raise Questions about Pay for Efforts," *Daytona Beach Sunday News-Journal*, January 28, 2001, p. 2E.

15. "Daughter Shot Over Nursing Home," *Associated Press*, March 11, 1999.

16.   Joyce M. Rosenberg, "The Lighter Side of Business," *Associated Press*, May 28, 1999.

17.   "LTC Bullet: AOK Article on LTC in AZ," *Center for Long-Term Care Financing* newsletter, September 14, 1999.

18.   Linda Greider, "Caring for Parents from Faraway," *AARP Bulletin* (October, 1999), p. 14.

19.   "Mother's Day 1999 Finds 63% of Mothers of Small Children in the Workforce; Caregiving Still Goes Largely Unrecognized," *PR Newswire*, May 3, 1999.

20.   Brenda C. Coleman, "Study Eyes Strain of Caregiving," *Associated Press*, December 15, 1999.

21.   "Living Like a Centenarian," *Fortune*, July 5, 1999, p. 152.

22.   "Aging Population Demands Interest of Funders," a news alert from *Health Resources*, www.healthrespubs.com, June 12, 2000.

23.   Will Lester, "Survey: Most Say No on Living to 100," *Associated Press*, May 25, 1999.

24.   "Four of 10 Americans Suffer Pain Daily, Gallup Survey Shows," *PR Newswire*, April 6, 2000.

25.   Diane Harris, "Where There's a Will," *My Generation* (May-June, 2001), p. 32.

26.   Allison Bell, "LTC Coverage an Issue Even for Wealthy," *National Underwriter*, Life & Health/Financial Services Edition, November 1, 1999, p. 4.

27.   David W. Arey, "Shifting Paradigms on Retirement Distribution Planning," *Journal of Financial Service Professionals* (July, 2000), p. 8.

28.   Gerald A. Mischke and Conrad S. Ciccotello, "Long-Term Care Trends and Demographics: Implications for Financial Planning," *Journal of Financial Service Professionals* (September, 2000), p. 54.

29.   "Latest EBRI Report: Education Key to Working Women's Retirement Prospects," *PR Newswire*, February 23, 2001.

30.   "Fewer Americans Saving for Retirement," *Daytona Beach News-Journal*, May 11, 2001, p. 2A.

31.   "Family Matters," *Consumer Reports* (September, 2000), p. 64, 65.

32.   "Tax-Free Gifts can Fund Parents' Long-Term Care," *Florida Broker News* (February, 2001), p. 17.

33.   Mary Beth Franklin, "Paying Today for Tomorrow's Care," *Kiplinger's Personal Finance* (November, 2000), p. 114.

34.   "Potential Market for LTC Insurance by State, "Who Will Pay for the Baby Boomers' Long-Term Care Needs? Survey, *American Council of Life Insurance* News Release, January 14, 1999.

35.   Chuck Jones, "Grave Concerns about Long-Term Care," *Life Association News* (October, 1999), pp. 72, 74.

36.   Chart entitiled "Health-Related Benefits, % of Companies Offering," *Employee Benefit Plan Review* (December, 2000), p. 15.

37.   Roy Hoffman, "Working Past 90: The Barber", *Fortune*, November 13, 2000, p. 384.

38.   Carole Ann King, "Meeting the Changing Needs of the Aging," *National Underwriter*, Life & Health/Financial Services Edition, May 15, 2000, p. 4, 20.

39.   Doug Johnson, "Seniors Buck Sun and Shuffleboard," *Associated Press*, January 12, 2001.

40.   Bruce Horovitz, "Age Just a Number for Some Leaders," *USA Today*, September 10, 1999, p. 2B.

41. Stephanie Armour, "Some Seniors Find Life's too Busy to Go into Retirement," *USA Today*, September 1, 2000, pp. 1B, 2B.

42. Robert M. Goldberg, "The 'Gerontocracy' Won't Swallow Clinton's Drug Plan," *Wall Street Journal*, June 28, 1999, p. A-26.

43. Roy Hoffman, "Working Past 90: The Composer," *Fortune*, November 13, 2000, p. 366.

44. Ron Panko, "A Lifetime Contract," *Best's Review* (May 2001), pp. 95, 96.

45. Paul Recer, "Elderly Americans Seem to Thrive," *Associated Press*, May 7, 2001.

46. Estes Thompson, "Retirees Drive Carolina Economy," *Associated Press*, May 31, 2000.

47. Mary Jane Fisher, "Prescription Drugs Continue to Drive Spending," *National Underwriter*, Life & Health/Financial Services Edition, April 9, 2001, pp. 46, 48.

48. Thomas S. Brown, "Elderly Should Plan for Financial Help," *Daytona Beach News-Journal*, June 21, 1999, p. 6A.

49. Earl P. Steinberg, et al., "Beyond Survey Data: A Claims-Based Analysis of Drug Use and Spending by the Elderly," *Health Affairs* (March-April, 2000), p. 198, 204.

50. Anjetta McQueen, "Prescription Drug Prices Driven Up," *Associated Press*, May 8, 2001.

51. Anjetta McQueen, "Prescription Drug Prices Driven Up," *Associated Press*, May 8, 2001.

52. Stephen M. Pollan and Mark Levine, *Turning No Into Yes: Six Steps to Solving Your Financial Problems (So You Can Stop Worrying)* (New York: HarperBusiness, 2000).

53. Kate Ligare, "Ensuring Financial Security and Choice Through Long-Term Care Insurance," *Health Insurance Underwriter* (March 2001), pp. 10, 11.

54. Christine Dugas, "Retirees Get Younger Every Day, Thanks to Smart Planning," *USA Today*, September 11, 2000, pp. 1B, 2B.

55. "ACLI Survey: Voters Say Retirement Security Key Election Issue," *PR Newswire*, September 2, 2000.

56. Sandra Block, "50 not so Nifty for Baby Boomers," *USA Today*, September 20, 2000, pp. 1B, 2B.

57. Fred Brock, "Aging Baby Boomers Refuse to Retire Quietly at the Beach," *Daytona Beach Sunday News-Journal*, December 24, 2000, p. 2E.

58. "Survey Finds Boomers Headed for Financial Disaster in Golden Years," *PR Newswire*, April 7, 1999.

59. "Retirement Survey Shows Vast Majority of Baby Boomers Have Misconceptions About Paying for Long-Term Care," *Business Wire*, June 1, 1999.

60. Allison Bell, "LTC Coverage an Issue Even for Wealthy," *National Underwriter*, Life & Health/Financial Services Edition, November 1, 1999, p. 4.

61. Lisa Lipman, "Boomers not Planning for Parents," *Associated Press*, February 7, 2001.

62. "Americans Confidence in Retirement Planning Down From 2000," *PR Newswire*, May 10, 2001.

63. Kevin Noblet, "Aging Parents' Finances in Focus," *Associated Press*, April 11, 2001.

64. Genaro C. Armas, "Baby Boomers Better Off Than Parents," *Associated Press*, August 3, 2001.

65. "Numbers," *Business 2.0*, December 26, 2000, p. 129.

66. Sandra Block, "50 not so Nifty for Baby Boomers," *USA Today*, September 20, 2000, pp. 1B, 2B.

67. Richard L. Birch, "Looking for LTC Gold? Try the Second Marriage Market," *National Underwriter*, Life & Health/Financial Services Edition, March 19, 2001, p. 31.

68. Glen A. Levit, "A Quick Look at Long-Term Care Demographics," *Health Insurance Underwriter* (April, 1999), p. 39.

69. Diane C. Lade, "Money Remains Root of Nursing Homes' Woes," *Orlando Sentinel*, March 6, 2001, p. A1.

70. "Seniors, Long-Term Care Need Additional Attention," *PR Newswire*, January 24, 2001.

71. "Elderly Nursing Home Expenditures by State (1995 – 2030), "Who Will Pay for the Baby Boomers' Long-Term Care Needs? Survey, *American Council of Life Insurance* News Release, January 14, 1999..

72. Diane C. Lade, "Money Remains Root of Nursing Homes' Woes," *Orlando Sentinel*, March 6, 2001, pp. A1, A14.

73. "Long-Term Care Advocates Rally to Send SOS for Minnesota's Seniors," *PR Newswire*, March 6, 2001.

74. "Percentage of Americans in Nursing Home Decreases," *Florida Broker News* (April, 2000), p. 22.

75. "Percentage of Nursing Home Residents by Limitations," from data assembled by *Agency for Health Care Policy and Research*, as reprinted on efmoody.com web site.

76. Christine E. Bishop, "Where are the Missing Elders?" *Health Affairs* (July/August, 1999), p. 146, 147.

77. *Ibid*, pp. 150-152.

78. Tom Rieske, Sr., "Nursing Home Stays Decline!" *Health Line* (January, 1999), p. 10.

79. Karen Gullo, "Clinton Urges Nursing Home Probes," *Associated Press*, January 14, 2000.

80. Donna Callea, "A Time to Every Purpose," *Daytona Beach Sunday News-Journal*, January 21, 2001, p. 1A, 10A.

81. "Geriatric Society Founder Says Care at Home is Best Medicine," *PR Newswire*, May 28, 1999.

82. Marshall Loeb, "Cashing in on the Aging Population," *CBS MarketWatch.com*, February 23, 2000.

83. Allison Bell, "Study Finds LTC Plans Enhance Family Care," *National Underwriter*, Life & Health/Financial Services Edition, September 6, 1999, p. 5.

84. "Senior Housing Facts," *Long Term Care Sales and Marketing Insight*, December 2000, p. 10.

85. "Is Assisted Living the Right Choice?" *Consumer Reports* (January, 2001), p. 26.

86. "Americans Support Rigorous Standards for Nursing Care," *PR Newswire*, May 6, 1999.

87. Iver Peterson, "Suburbs Struggle to Keep Seniors," *Fort Lauderdale Sun Sentinel*, March 11, 2001, pp. 1G, 3G.

88. Tom Berson, "Hospice Patients Live with Death Every Day," *Daytona Beach Sunday News-Journal*, November 28, 1999, pp. 1B, 8B.

89. Jeff Kunerth, "As Boomers Age, Florida Faces Elderly Explosion," *Orlando Sentinel*, March 7, 2001, p. A1.

90. "Nursing Home Costs Average $153 Per Day in U.S.; Costs Vary Widely From Region to Region," *Business Wire*, July 24, 2000.

91. *Ibid*.

92. M. Christian Murray, "Planners Recommend LTC, But Public Lags," *National Underwriter*, Life & Health/Financial Services Edition, May 24, 1999, p. 8.

93. Genaro C. Armas, "Census: Elderly Population Rises," *Associated Press*, May 15, 2001.

94. Peter S. Gelbwaks, "Millennium Madness," *Health Insurance Underwriter* (March, 2000), p. 41.

PART TWO:
WORKING WITH A CLIENT

"The really frightening thing about middle age is the knowledge that you'll grow out of it."
                                        – Doris Day

KEY CONCEPTS

1. Sales presentations should be adapted to a particular audience.

2. There are three distinct prospect groups: age-65-and-over, under-age-65, and employers.

3. Medicare and Medicaid are generally not viable options to fund long-term care needs.

4. Plan design is a function of budget and selecting the coverage that will likely benefit the insured best.

GETTING STARTED
Five Steps to Jump-Starting Your Work in the Long-Term Care Market

1. Recognize that there are at least three different types of prospects out there. First, there is the age-65-and-older prospect, whose health and finances may see some rocky stages just ahead. Next, the under-age-65 prospect is looking towards retirement and in various stages of pre-retirement planning. Finally, there is the employer client facing the next big business disruption – eldercare. There are also segmentations of these markets, with married couples versus singles and caregivers/health workers who may see the need more quickly.

2. Develop a sound presentation for each of the aforementioned prospects. With the age-65-and-over market, the key focus is on asset protection and ensuring the money will last them through retirement. With the under-age-65 prospect, long-term care is an estate planning tool and the major wealth protection vehicle. For the employer, there is the opportunity through group long-term care, either true group or voluntary, to cover not only the employee but the extended family members who might otherwise call on the employee for caregiving help.

3. Review your current client list. Have you talked with any of these individuals about wealth protection? This is not a cold call sale. If you have done any type of financial planning for clients, they are your best beginning opportunity. This way you will have some of the information you need to identify whether a long-term care situation will create some financial difficulties. When are the next annual reviews? If you have several coming up, this is a good chance to speak about this vital coverage.

4. Do your homework first! Research local long-term care facilities and costs, so that you are in a position of knowledge to both answer questions and make recommendations. This includes reviewing products and companies that are on the market. The better the preparation, the better the results.

5. Carry out the steps listed above. Market penetration on this product is exceptionally low, mostly because not enough financial advisors are actively explaining this need to clients. For many prospects, the sale can be made in the education part of the presentation – identifying the need. But if you never speak those words, you will never get confirmation from clients that they would like to solve this problem.

"We Don't Need No Education"

It is important to remember that we live in the information age. The under-age-65 prospects have spent hours weekly on the Internet, soaking up as much knowledge as possible. They may mistake that knowledge for expertise, but the truth is there is a lot of misleading information out there, and much difficulty in discerning what's correct and what is not.

The age-65-and-over prospects are not starved for data on this subject, either. This has been the group of people targeted most for long-term care sales calls and solicitations. They depend more on the mass media than other age groups and there has been no shortage of long-term care information available through a variety of publications. *Consumer Reports'* study of long-term care has been the magazine's most ordered reprint, according to the study's author.[1] You can be sure this activity is not just insurance agents asking for the article.

The educated consumer is the prospect you most likely will be dealing with today. This means that you must be prepared for a working idea and pre-conceived notion of what long-term care is all about. In some ways, it will help significantly if the clients you are speaking with have already thought enough of the potential problem to have read up some on it. Your presentation will either verify what they believe they already know or present the case for long-term care protection in an entirely different light. You will have to be sensitive to the reactions during the talk, stopping often and asking for agreement on the key principles. The main point is that you are likely talking with people who have formed an opinion, good or bad, of long-term care, and you should be prepared to deal with that.

Long-term care represents wealth or income and asset protection just as life insurance and disability income do. The threat of an unforeseen illness or injury can do substantial physical and financial harm. If you currently sell either life or disability income insurance, it is an easy step to add long-term care to your list of needs that a client must address.

In Part One, we noted some of the many different housing considerations for people as they age. Today, there are many types of "retirement" communities all over the country (and not just in the Sun Belt) and these communities present opportunities to work with individuals who are vulnerable to the threat posed by a long-term care need.

The 2000 U.S. Census[2]

- 37,677,952 Prospects age 45 to 54 years old (13.4% of the population)

- 24,274,684 Prospects age 55 to 64 (8.6% of population)

- 34,991,753 Prospects age 65 and older (12.4% of population)

- 96,944,389 Total Prospects

In Central Florida, there is just such a community called "The Villages." Here, the several thousand residents from all walks of life enjoy their own newspaper, *The Villages Daily Sun*. A recent edition displayed the following front page headlines: "Huge Signs Direct Travelers to The Villages," "AP Poll Shows Half Favor Social Security Investment Option," "Participants Consider Villages Games Great Success," and "German Adjusts to New Culture," along with the weather and a warning to set the clocks ahead.[3]

This newspaper, published daily, has three sections and places to advertise your financial advisory services. In addition, there is a list of meetings, seminars and activities available to the residents for the week. Offering a session on long-term care planning as part of an overall financial plan or as a way of allowing one to remain independent will likely draw an audience here. If so, you will have a new set of prospects that have expressed an interest in this type of wealth protection.

This particular community has a reputation for some highly educated residents. Retired CEOs live here. So do retired civil bureaucrats and gas station owners. It is a broad mix of people, all within a few blocks of each other, with the same potential need for financial assistance should long-term care happen. They have their own shopping center and movie theaters, an insulated utopia whose occupants are active, enjoying their retirement and, more important, their independence and freedom – ideals that can be lost once a chronic health problem has set in and taken control. Here, "Paradise Lost" can be a frightening reality for these carefree retirees.

There are an almost overwhelming number of prospects to speak to about the long-term care issues that will affect many people's lives in the years ahead. Women remain the most at risk due to their longevity. Older, single people also represent an important group of individuals to focus on as they have less apparent social support behind them and lack the cloak of Medicaid's spousal protection provisions. Here, you have people that have never married, or are divorced, or widowed. Coincidentally, this group of singles is overwhelmingly female. Due to a number of social and demographic factors, 85% of women will find themselves single during their mature years.[6]

> **Women are at much higher risk for needing long-term care.[4] They are:**
>
> • much less likely to receive spousal support when they have a chronic condition
>
> • twice as likely to remain unmarried after 65, and
>
> • three times more likely to be alone after age 75.

Thus, some of your prospecting might include identifying whether the individual is single, female, and perhaps if she has any caregiving experience. These are the most receptive and the most vulnerable of your potential audience, young (age 40+) and old. As noted in Part One, if you can discover, early on, who the extended family members of your prospect are, you can involve them in this process. Getting agreement

> **The 2000 U.S. Census Bureau:[5]**
>
> • 12,900,103 Female householders, no husband present (12.2% of all households)
>
> • 27,230,075 Householders living alone (25.8% of all households)

from more than just the prospect that this type of wealth protection is a critical part of any financial plan will help cement the program in your prospect's mind.

A number of financial advisors conduct seminars that provide knowledge of this subject area in an effort to find a few in the audience that might wish to pursue this information on a more specific level. Here, with your insider's knowledge of the types of insurance protection that are available, you might team up with a CPA or elder law attorney and conduct a joint session that covers a couple of subjects. For example, a joint presentation where an attorney talks about the importance of durable powers of attorney can also have you discuss wealth protection in general. A discussion of how an insurance product can be a valid funding source for long-term care can be teamed with a CPA pointing out the tax ramifications of the product. This team-work approach can be highly effective in generating prospects.

Top 5 Questions Consumers Ask at LTC Seminars[7]

1. *What's the best age to buy LTC insurance?*
2. *Is this insurance portable to another state?*
3. *How much would LTC insurance cost me?*
4. *What happens to all the money I paid if I never need LTC?*
5. *What if the company I'm insured with goes out of business?*

Source: LTC Learning Institute

THE PRESENTATIONS

"Whoever controls the media – the images – controls the culture."
　　　　　　　　　　　　　　　　– Allen Ginsberg

There are three clear prospect bases to work in the effort to provide as many individuals and families with wealth protection as possible. Each group has a different motivation in securing this form of assistance and, though you will emphasize some similar points to each, there is a difference in the approach.

The target audience was long thought to be the age-65-and-over individual/couple since they were believed to be the closest to needing the care. But this ignores under-age-65 individuals who may find it easier to finance this need as part of their overall pre-retirement planning. Moreover, there are many stories about people under age 65 needing assistance with a chronic condition. Both of these prospects will approach long-term care differently, especially since they are likely in different financial conditions. In any event, you will need to stress certain points and ask some different questions for each of these markets. Finally, the Health Insurance Portability and Accountability Act also sanctioned an entirely new group of prospects – employers. With long-awaited clarification on the taxation of long-term care policies and the corporate deductibility of premium, there is finally a framework in which to operate and add long-term care coverage to an employee benefit portfolio.

> • More than 67% of adult children who think about their parents getting older also think about how this will affect them personally
> • 50% of older parents who think about their own aging, wonder about how it will affect their children.
> But the two generations differ on what this means.
> • 54% of adult children predict their parents will need to rely on them in the future
> • only 27% of older parents believe that they will need their children's help.[8]

The Age-65-and-Over Prospect

There are certain questions that will help you establish the reasons why long-term care funding through insurance might be important to the older prospect. What are the priorities of these older prospects?

- Do they wish to stretch their retirement dollar as far as it can go?

- Do they want to live independently for as long as they possibly can?

- Are they interested in leaving an inheritance to their children and/or grandchildren?

- Do they desire to have the freedom to do as they choose?

Independence. Freedom. Choice. An income they won't outlive. An inheritance they can leave as their last legacy.

These are one or more of the driving factors behind the purchase of long-term care insurance at the older ages. Today's older Americans are the healthiest and wealthiest they have ever been and they want to stay that way for as long as possible. Protection of this living standard and the ability to draw on a resource other than their own children will give them plenty of reasons to add long-term care insurance to their financial plans.

For years, seniors have done their best to fill in the gaps left by Medicare. The great majority of age-65-and-over Americans own a Medicare Supplement. They are not averse to addressing a risk if they understand the scope and breadth of the problem. Once seen, they won't forget it. The easiest way to identify this potential financial problem is to look at the individual/couple's own economic situation and see if assistance with long-term care expenses will be necessary or not.

This will satisfy those who need to see the numbers, and are more logically motivated to solve the problem. But the real need here is emotional, as many older adults do not want to depend on their children for care at an older age. This role reversal is not a desired situation. The older adult does not want to move back to be with the child (as he or she is probably in a different part of the country) nor is it usually practical for the child (who may be employed and/or caring for children) to pick up and move to where the older adult is living. But to do otherwise

> Only about 5% of the non-independent 65 and older are in nursing homes. The remaining elderly, who are past being independent, are being cared for by children in their own or their child's home, or by a caregiver employed by the family.[9]
>
> Source: Eldercare Advocates, Inc.

and have other choices that don't involve a dependency of some sort, there must be advanced planning and that is ultimately what your presentation emphasizes. The whole purpose of the talk you are having with these prospects is to empower them through choice – to let them have the ability to have options other than depending on a child when the long-term care need arises.

> **Older people living alone are:**[10]
>
> • more prone to inadequate diets and poor nutritional status
>
> • less likely to have family caregiver supports and more likely to rely on formal paid services for assistance
>
> • more socially isolated and at a greater risk of depression, and
>
> • often functionally disabled

> The College for Financial Planning says the average net worth of the top 60% of retirees, minus their home, is around $120,000. An extended nursing home stay of five years would wipe out the savings of all but the wealthiest 5%.[11]

Long-term care insurance represents a retirement fund defense to the many older Americans who will be affected by the need to obtain medical assistance or help with the "basics" like dressing and bathing or, on a more simplistic level, doing the household chores or shopping. Older Americans worry a lot about their financial condition They are concerned with outliving the money they have and being forced to depend financially on their children. That a long-term care situation could make them both physically and financially dependent is something most wish to avoid at all costs. This is a good point to focus on when explaining the need to fund this potential future cost.

The Under-Age-65 Prospect
How old do you have to be to need long-term care assistance:

The under-age-65 prospect today faces an incredible number of financial challenges. The age-65-and-over prospect may have gone through the Great Depression, but the under-age-65 prospect may be looking at an unprecedented triple hit at age 65:

1. *Child's educational costs.* Because many adults have waited until late to have children, it is not out of the realm of possibility that the upcoming age 65-year-old will still be putting a child or two through college.

2. *Older parents' long-term care.* At age 65, their parents may well be into their 80s and early 90s, may still be alive and struggling financially and medically with no one but their children to turn to for help.

3. *One's own retirement.* Age 65 has long been the benchmark for retirement due to Medicare availability, and that will gradually increase now to age 67 (and maybe higher in the future). The ability to live off the assets built up will depend in large part on circumstances noted in #1 and #2 above.

> A 49-year-old Nashville, Tennessee woman still raising her 11-year-old son, is bed-ridden in her 11th year of Lou Gehrig's disease, her muscles and body virtually petrified. She taps out Morse code through sensors attached by Velcro to her fingertips that signal a laptop computer to write and speak her thoughts through a synthesized voice.
>
> A 29-year-old had a massive stroke a month before her wedding day. Her fiancé continues to care for her several years later. Her mind is fine, but she communicates with her eyes and is confined to a wheelchair. They live with her parents.[12]

If ever a group were in solid need of financial planning, it's the people under age 65 who are planning for their futures. So much emphasis is put on accumulating wealth, yet wealth protection for these prospects and their elderly parents and relatives can accomplish just as much in preserving the income needed for education, emergencies, and retirement. In working with the younger prospect, there is the potential for working with a number of relatives providing your prospect understands both the financial and emotional need for this protection.

Therefore, two key questions that are more relevant here than with the age-65-and-over prospect are:

Percentage of Americans who indicated that the most important benefit of a long-term care insurance policy is "avoiding using my income":[13]
Under age 65:   40%
Age 65-74:   29%
Age 75+:   25%

1. Do you have children still living at home?

2. How old are your parents and what is their medical and financial situation?

These answers will indicate what kind of financial crunch awaits the prospect ahead.

Most financial surveys and studies indicate that the under-age-65 American is not financially prepared for retirement. If that's the case, education and parents' long-term care costs are not necessarily going to come from these prospects' funds. But they will still have to live off their assets at some point and they will have their own potential long-term care costs that will have to be funded. This is all the more reason the younger buyer is worth some time and effort. Not only do they need the help, but so do others around them, especially if the prospect is not going to be a good source of assistance to them in the future. In about a decade's time, older Americans will spend some $52 billion out of their own retirement savings to pay for nursing-home care, with the cost of long-term care projected to grow by 5% a year for the next decade.[14]

"It's not a surprise that a recent government survey shows that roughly two out of three people providing informal care to a loved one believe that the availability of private long-term care insurance has reduced their level of stress."

— Winthrop Cashdollar,
   Director, Center for Disability
   and Long-Term Care
   Insurance

Indeed, it's the ever-increasing burden of medical inflation that represents a continued serious financial threat to many individuals in the future. The overconfidence in the ability to accrue significant amounts of money in a short period of time, born in the furious bull market of the 1990s, is now yielding to concerns that this is not a never-ending fairytale of ever-accumulating assets and that financial discipline and thoughtful planning is as important as ever. Many of your under-age-65 prospects have seen their retirement account values in free-fall since mid-2000, when the dot was pulled from under the dot.com start-ups. Today, it is a more shaken, concerned prospect who is examining the realities of tomorrow's wealth, with a more down-to-earth focus.

Many under-age-65 prospects have seen a loved one beset with the type of chronic illness that necessitates long-term care treatment. They know the difficulties of caregiving and they have seen the finances of a parent or relative erode quickly in the face of this need. This does not mean they are ready and waiting for you to get in touch with them. There will

The Future Cost of One Year of Nursing Facility Care[15]	
Year	Cost
2005	.$65,466
2010	.$83,555
2015	.$106,640
2020	.$136,100

be the need, as always, to present the reasons, financial and emotional, for this form of wealth protection.

The Employer

The Employer prospect once faced a major employee crisis – childcare – and responded with flexible working hours, Section 125 dependent care spending accounts, and on-site day care. Many of the children have grown up and out, but their parents (and, by extension, their employers) are staring down the barrel of a new problem: that older Americans are aging and moving in.

Once again, employers find their employees preoccupied, this time with the needs of parents or other aging relatives. As so few have prepared in advance for the long-term care situation, these younger ones have seemingly little choice but to respond when their parent calls for help. As a result, employers lose their employees physically (if they need time away from work) and/or mentally (if their minds are half-thinking about their caregiving responsibilities while on the job). This is, needless to say, not helping with the company bottom line.

Questions to pose to an employer prospect:

- Is the aging of America's workforce having an impact on your business?

- Are child care needs being replaced with elder care demands?

- If your employees leave work regularly to take care of family members, will it affect your business at all?

Of caregivers who work full-time:[16]

- 70% give up personal time for caregiving
- 60% from their spouse
- 42% from their children
- 40% had to take time off from work for caregiving, 26% of those for no pay
- 31% have changed, sacrificed or put off career goals because of caregiving responsibilities
- 17% say their work has directly suffered as a result of their caregiving duties.

Under the Health Insurance Portability and Accountability Act of 1996, Congress made it enticing for businesses (especially C corporations) to purchase long-term care insurance with corporate funds. Smaller firms (S corporations, partnerships, and sole proprietorships) also have an incentive – full deductibility of their employees' coverage and, in 2001, a 60% deduction for their own, with the balance possibly deductible on a personal basis. Talking to an employer about paying for something out of the business checkbook is always a more favorable position.

Long-term care insurance is the up-and-coming employee benefit. And, as employers begin retaining older employees, this coverage becomes even more vital. For nearly a century, Americans were able to retire at ever-younger ages and in greater prosperity. But in later years they have begun staying on the job later into life. Many of the pension conversions of the past decade have eliminated incentives for early retirement, as companies have seen a need to retain the 50-something workers they might have removed from the payrolls a decade ago.[18] The older employee is going to have an interest in long-term care. If the employer wishes to keep this kind of experienced worker around, this benefit will become a key part of the employee benefit package.

Employers who are also looking to retain key employees may see long-term care insurance as a competitive advantage for them in the overall employee benefit package. Employees are certain to respond favorably to inclusion of this product in the stable of benefits from which they can choose. There are positives for both employer and employee going forward.

> The analysis of working caregiver data from three national surveys shows that those caring for disabled elders who have long-term care insurance are nearly two times as likely to be able to continue working than those caring for non-insured relatives. In addition, working caregivers of those with long-term care insurance were reported less likely to experience some type of stress related to their caregiving duties.[17]

Advantages for the employer include:

- tax deductibility, in whole or in part

- retention of key employees

- enticement for older workers to stay, and

- curtailing of lost productivity

Advantages for the employee include:

- ease of worksite purchase

- solution to caregiving demands

- avoidance of lost wages and Social Security benefits, and

- better health, less stress

It's families, not facilities, that are the backbone of the long-term care provided in this country today. But it will ultimately take its toll unless employers are encouraged to act. The extent of family caregiving in this country is immense. A recent survey from the National Family Caregivers Association revealed that more than 54 million people were involved in caregiving during the prior 12-month period. Forty-three percent of caregivers had an annual household income of less than $30,000.[19] This is certain to have an economic impact on both employee and employer. The good news is that it may be avoidable with an alternative source of funding that can help hire caregivers to furnish the type of care necessary and enable the working adult to stay in his or her job.

> Today, one in four employees provide assistance to elderly relatives. By 2006, that figure is projected to be one in two. Caregiving affects employees' attendance and attention, resulting in a substantial loss in productivity. It's estimated that the cost to the average company today is over $3,000 per employee per year.[20]

Employers also have the chance, as they do with disability income insurance, to pick and choose the key employees they would like to cover through the use of non-threatening criteria such as years of service, job title, and earnings, or any combination of the three. Thus, a key employee long-term care insurance program may be available, for example, to all employees with at least 10 years of service. The awareness level of others in the company may increase and you should encourage the employer to let you talk to the other employees in the firm about the risk, even if they have to pay for it themselves. They may well be interested.

If corporate America is going to survive in the 21st Century, it will have to include long-term care among its chief employee concerns and address the problem accordingly. For many, using long-term care insurance as a funding vehicle will be the most feasible way of handling the issue. With employer tax incentives likely to improve even more, this is a very favorable employee benefit to concentrate on for the foreseeable future.

**Examples of employer-sponsored
long-term care programs:**[21]

IBM: Employees get a discount on a program that gives their elderly relatives access to emergency care assistance, along with a referral system that helps with a variety of concerns from help in drafting a living will and power of attorney to counseling for workers who have an aging relative who is dying.

AT&T: Employees have access to a referral service for elder care providers and other services. They can also take up to 12 months of unpaid time off in any 24-month period to care for aging relatives.

Bristol-Myers Squibb: Provides employees with emergency back-up elder care nationwide, paying 80% of the cost each time back-up is needed up to $300 per employee each year. Employees may take up to 16 weeks of unpaid leave each year to care for an older parent or relative.

Former CNN news writer Clint Deloatch had a promising career in the news business. Fifteen years in all, first at CNN and then at Headline News as a writer. But the 41-year-old metro Atlantan's career was sidetracked after his diabetic 70-year-old mother had a leg amputated. He and his eight siblings had put together what they thought was a workable schedule, with weekly rotations for caregiving. His parents live in North Carolina, a six-hour drive for Deloatch. Sometimes, he would return from visiting his parents, grab a few hours' sleep and then rush to work. "When you're at work," he said, "you really want to concentrate on your job, but when it's your mother, you are not thinking a whole lot about work." He didn't realize his work was suffering until called into his supervisor's office. Headline News had already announced a job cutback. Deloatch advised about the caregiving duties and the company let him go with a severance package. He now manages a natural products store.[22]

Medicare and Medicaid

Medicare

"Democracy is the art and science of running the circus from the monkey cage."

           – Henry Louis Mencken

The Balanced Budget Act of 1997 has cut spending for home care, mainly by targeting the long-term home care patient, according to the National Association for Home Care. About 2,500 of the home health care agencies that left the market due to the cuts are unlikely to re-enter the market if cuts were restored. In addition, nursing homes received $2.6 billion less from Medicare in the first six months of 1999 versus 1998.[23]

The new Medicare reimbursement system for skilled nursing facilities is encouraging the use of older, cheaper medicines, rather than newer and more appropriate medications, threatening the health and quality of frail elderly residents who are particularly vulnerable to medication related problems. The American Society of Consultant Pharmacists called for Congress to restore the $7.1 billion in cuts that was removed from the Medicare skilled nursing facility program.[24]

The song remains the same. The chorus might be slightly different, but let's face it, Medicare has never been a viable funding alternative for long-term care and Medicaid is the program turned to when you run out of money.

Medicare has its place, no question. Thanks to this 1965 legislative creation, only 1.1% of those age 65 and over lacked basic health insurance coverage in the year 1998.[25] The word to concentrate on is *basic*, since that's the primary objective of Medicare – acute, basic care provided in a hospital or doctor's office setting (see Figure 2.1). Short-term recoveries are great, long-term chronic problems are not.

"Democracy encourages the majority to decide things about which the majority is ignorant."
— John Simon

Perhaps the key component of Medicare's rules is the requirement that the condition must be improving. This has jettisoned some of the true long-term care cases, since maintaining is often considered a positive result. Despite these strict requirements, Medicare spending simply has run into the dual dilemma of more older Americans living longer and healthier. The needs of these people are less acute and more chronic in nature and this has created significantly higher than expected expenditures for this type of treatment. During the past 30 years, there has been a shift in the distribution of spending among different types of Medicare services. Spending for hospital inpatient services as a percentage of the total for persons age 65 and older declined from 70% in 1967 to 49% in 1998. Spending for inpatient services for persons age 85 and older showed a similar but more marked decline. The percentages spent for home health and skilled nursing facility services increased greatly, especially for the oldest old. The drop in the percentage of total spending for skilled nursing facility care from 1967 to 1977 was the result of strict enforcement of the rule that Medicare does not cover custodial care.[27]

"I think it's an open secret that Medicare and Medicaid reimbursements are not truly adequate for any of our providers... [W]e all need to figure out ways to reimburse our facilities and health care professionals.
-Senator Charles Grassley (R-IA)[26]

As you can see from Figure 2.2, the Balanced Budget Act of 1997 (BBA '97) had some immediate effect on home health care payments. To see the steady growth over the period 1987-1997 come down significantly in 1998, it's obvious Congress achieved its goal of slowing

Figure 2.1

QUICK GUIDE TO MEDICARE

The federal Medicare program was not designed, in general, to provide financial assistance for medical expenses for chronically ill individuals due to the long-term nature of such expenses. There is some coverage provided for skilled nursing care received in a skilled nursing facility and some home health care coverage.

Nursing home coverage:

To qualify for long-term care coverage in a nursing facility, the individual must meet all of the following requirements:

1. The stay in the skilled nursing facility must be preceded by 3 days in the hospital not counting the day of discharge, and the patient must go to the skilled nursing facility for the same medical reason the patient was in the hospital within 30 days of leaving the hospital.

2. The care must be certified by the patient's physician as necessary.

3. The patient must require skilled care.

4. The skilled facility must be a Medicare-approved facility.

5. The medical condition must be improving.

If all of these requirements are met, the 2001 Medicare skilled nursing coverage is:

Days	2001 amount
1 – 20	Up to 100% of the Medicare-approved amount
21 – 100	All but $99/day
101+	Nothing

Home health care coverage:

To qualify for home health care reimbursement under Medicare, the patient must meet all of these requirements:

1. The patient must require part-time or intermittent home health care only. Medicare does not pay for 24-hour full-time care.

2. The patient must be homebound, meaning to have a medical condition that restricts one's ability to leave the house except with assistance.

3. The patient must be under a physician's care and that doctor must certify the need for home health care.

4. Medicare must certify the home health care agency providing the services.

5. The medical condition for which the care is sought must be improving.

Covered services include part-time or intermittent skilled nursing care, physical therapy, speech therapy, occupational therapy, medical social services that are under the direction of a physician, medical supplies, and 80 percent of the cost of durable medical equipment (DME). DME devices would include canes, walkers, wheelchairs and hospital beds.

Medicare will not pay for full-time nursing care, meals delivered to the home, prescription drugs, 20% of the cost of DME, transportation, and homemaker services primarily needed to assist in meeting personal care or housekeeping needs.

the Medicare spending in this, the fastest-growing area of expenditure in the program.

The BBA '97 made several changes to control spending, provide incentives for agencies to deliver care more efficiently, and rein in the use of the home health benefit to deliver long-term personal care. The most important change was to legislate the development of a prospective payment system (PPS) for home health reimbursement, calling for an interim payment system as a temporary measure in the meantime.[28]

Unquestionably, Medicare spending on long-term care types of treatment had increased dramatically over the past few years. This was more than just a function of a greater number of beneficiaries, especially those over age 85. Medicare developed a practice of reimbursing home health agencies their actual costs up to an annual limit, based on a national per visit amount for each type of visit multiplied by the agency's number of visits of each type. An agency then could increase its Medicare net income simply by providing more visits while keeping its average costs per visit below the national limits. The result was Medicare spending on home health increasing an average of 31% per year, annual visits per user jumping by 343% and yearly payments per user rising 374%, an inflation-adjusted average yearly increase of 14.4%.[30]

As part of the Balanced Budget Act of 1997, Congress placed an arbitrary cap on the amount of services Medicare patients could receive for therapy services in skilled nursing facilities. They set two caps: $1,500 for physical therapy and speech therapy combined, and $1,500 for occupational therapy. As a result, beneficiaries' care is being affected, according to the American Health Care Association.[29]

Congress obtained what it sought – a cutback in Medicare spending for what it perceived as a non-covered benefit: long-term

Figure 2.2

Percentage Distribution of Medicare Per Capita Payments for Skilled Nursing (SNF) and Home Health Care (HHA), 1967 – 1998

Age 65+	SNF	HHA
1967	.6%	.1%
1977	.2%	.2%
1987	.1%	.2%
1997	.7%	10%
1998	.7%	.6%

Age 85+	SNF	HHA
1967	14%	.2%
1977	.3%	.3%
1987	.2%	.4%
1997	14%	16%
1998	15%	10%

Source: Health Affairs, March/April 2001

Sun Healthcare, the 3rd largest nursing home company, is reeling from losses it has blamed on changes in the Medicare payment system for long-term care. The company lost $761.1 million in the fourth quarter of 1998. It also reported a first quarter 1999 loss of $113.1 million.[31]

care. Providers protested mightily as did some of the Medicare beneficiaries left out in the cold as a result, deserted by their home health care agency that no longer viewed their care as a profitable undertaking. The Health Care Financing Administration put into place an adjusted Prospective Payment System in October 2000, providing yet another set of financial incentives for agencies. The new PPS now provides reimbursement on a case-mix adjusted capitated payment for a 60-day episode of care. It allows an unlimited number of episodes as long as these are authorized by a supervising physician. Agencies will again have incentives to treat longer-term patients (60 days), but it will likely not be

Use of Medicare Home Health Services, Fiscal Years 1997-1999

(in 1000s)	1997	1998	1999	% change
Number of users	3,296	2,953	2,518	-24%
Number of visits	259,816	183,510	116,276	-55%
Payments per beneficiary	$499.90	$373.21	$247.66	-50%

Source: Health Care Financing Administration data

financially feasible for them to deal with high-cost, shorter stay patients receiving care for less than 60 days.

Congress has been more than willing to review their work over the last 15 years. Remember the Medicare Catastrophic Coverage Act of 1988? Portions of that were repealed within a year. Technical corrections acts pop up from time to time, trying to get it right in hindsight. The BBA '97 brought out a huge number of lobbyists and the resulting give-and-take resulted in a late year, post-election passage of the Medicare, Medicaid and SCHIP Benefits Improvement Act of 2000, essentially a health care provider relief bill. Only Congress could use the word improvement to fix something it broke. At any rate, among the changes this Act made were:

- Skilled Nursing Facilities (approximate cost: $350 million)

    - It increased SNF payments, on average, by 3.2% in fiscal year (FY) 2001.

    - In FY 2002 and 2003, the increase will be 0.5 percentage points less than the increase in the market basket index.

    - The nursing component of the rate (about 1/3 of total payment) is increased by 16.66% for services furnished from April 1, 2001 to October 1, 2002. A study will be done to see if SNFs spend increased payments on staffing and recommend whether added payments should continue.

- The moratorium on the $1,500 per year therapy caps would continue through 2002.

- Home Health Care (approximate cost: $675 million)

    - It delays for one year, from October 1, 2001 to October 1, 2002, the 15% reduction in the interim payment system (IPS).

    - It increases home health payments, on average, by the full increase in the market basket index in FY2001, rather than the BBA's market basket less 1.1 percentage points.

    - Payment rates will be increased by 10%, or about $210 per episode on average, for home health services furnished to beneficiaries in rural areas, effective April 1, 2001 through March 31, 2003.

    - It liberalizes requirements for "homebound" status to receive home health care.

You can be sure there will be some monitoring of the effects of the payment restorations under the Benefits Improvement Act of 2000. This political jockeying only underscores that Medicare will constantly be subjected to funding ebbs and flows. That it was not primarily established to provide long-term care benefits means this area of coverage will continue to receive the most scrutiny in the future. As a funding vehicle to assist with an individual's long-term care expenses, it is both inadequate and unreliable to count on in any meaningful way.

Medicare Supplements

Where do these policies, owned by a substantial majority of the age-65-and-over population, fit in? Are they a viable source of long-term care funding?

Alas, these policies (there are ten standard models, although that is under analysis by a NAIC working group now) fill in some of the marginal gaps left by Medicare, but do little to ensure any *long-term* help. Detailed below are the two areas that some of the Medicare Supplements (check Policies A through J for specifics) address:

- Skilled Nursing Care (Plans C through J)

    - covers the co-payment that the insured is responsible for from day 21-100 in a SNF ($99 per day in 2001); and

    - after 100 days, the supplement pays $0.

- Home Health Care (Plans D, G, I, and J)

    - provides a $40 per visit at-home recovery benefit (not to exceed $1,600) following an illness or injury, but only if the physician orders the follow-up care.

There are many age-65-and-over prospects who, though knowing that Medicare will not likely help much, believe that their supplements represent a major source of funding for long-term care expenses. Unfortunately, this is not the case. Insurers have always had the ability to expand the benefits of the basic plans, but simply have chosen not to do so. Supplements, at best, round out the *short-term* funding nature of Medicare itself. As we know, long-term care's economic and emotional threat is not from a short-term problem. It's the lengthy chronic condition that must be supported, and this is the type of care Medicare and Medicare supplements are definitely not designed to handle.

*"It is even harder for the average ape to believe that
he has descended from man."*

– George S. Patton

Medicaid

The Medicaid program was established as a joint federal/state plan to provide the *indigent* among us with access to medical health services. (See Figure 2.3.) It was created as part of President Lyndon B. Johnson's war on poverty. That we are discussing it as part of a review of long-term care is due to its coverage of long-term care services for the needy, and its historic relevance as a primary source of this type of benefit for the elderly.

The 10 Fastest Growing States in Medicaid Expenditures

| | Millions of $ | | |
State	1995	2030	% Change
Nevada	$52	$768	1389%
Utah	75	761	909%
Idaho	63	618	881%
Alaska	26	238	823%
Colorado	224	1,978	781%
New Mexico	80	695	764%
Wyoming	33	281	740%
Georgia	361	2,733	657%
Oregon	157	1,184	655%
Montana	80	597	650%

Source: American Council of Life Insurance

The increases in Medicaid spending have been expanding state budgets to the breaking point for several years, and the load appears not to be letting up. Medicaid does so much in terms of long-term care reimbursement that it is a major provider of funds for this treatment and second only to out-of-pocket individual expenditures in terms of a resource for these health care services.

Individuals qualify for Medicaid coverage for long-term care services in one of three ways: as recipients of SSI (Supplemental

Figure 2.3

QUICK GUIDE TO MEDICAID

This federal welfare assistance program is to help low income individuals with their medical expenses. It has rapidly become one of the primary sources of funding for long-term care expenses. Medicaid assists more than 35 million people, five million of which are over the age of 65. Two-thirds of all nursing home residents rely on this government program.

Medicaid is jointly funded by both the federal and state governments. Each state is eligible for a federal Medicaid subsidy ranging from 50% to 76.82% in Mississippi in 2001. The responsibility for administering Medicaid resides with each individual state. The states are allowed to set their own individual limits with records of asset and income eligibility.

Individuals: Persons who are single will most likely be required to spend down their assets to the federal poverty level ($2,000-$5,000). They will also only be allowed a token income allowance (usually less than $100) on a monthly basis. Each state has its own rules as to these levels and you should check with the state department that administers the Medicaid program.

Couples: To protect the spouse who is not in need of long-term care services, each state sets asset and income allowances that are not countable by Medicaid. The asset figure, adjusted annually, is typically called a Community Spouse Resource Allowance (CSRA). In 2001, in many states, this figure can be as high as $87,000. The income figure is called the Community Spouse Income Allowance (CSIA). In 2001, in many states, this amount can total as high as $2,175 ($1,407 spouse allowance, plus $423 excess shelter costs, plus $194 utility allowance).

Non-countable assets: In spending down assets to attain the required level for Medicaid qualification, there are some assets that may be retained and not counted (in addition to the community spouse allowance noted above). These assets are: the home (in some states, the home is always protected even if the patient is single), one automobile, household and personal belongings, wedding and engagement rings, life insurance cash value up to $1,500, burial plots and funds up to $1,500, and property used in a trade or business.

Asset transfers: Congress has, over the years, removed many of the legal incentives for people to transfer assets for purposes of Medicaid qualification. The Omnibus Budget Reconciliation Act of 1993 (OBRA) required that transfers of assets must occur 36 months prior to applying for Medicaid and transfers out of a trust must occur 60 months prior to applying for Medicaid. Applications made to Medicaid that show transfers made within these time frames will result in the imposition of a penalty period before Medicaid eligibility. In addition, OBRA directed states to create their own legislation, called Estate Recovery Acts, to recover Medicaid costs following the death of the Medicaid beneficiary and any spouse.

Security Income), as "medically needy," or as individuals with incomes below a state-designated cap. In medically needy states, individuals can qualify for medical care (including long-term care) if their assets are below a specified amount (usually $1,000 - 2,000) and they agree to pay monthly income in excess of a specified amount to the custodial provider. In income states (there are around 20), if individuals' monthly income exceeds a cap ($1,500 or so, on average), eligibility for Medicaid benefits is denied regardless of health or need.

The states listed below are the ones whose budgets will be stretched in the future. Combine these with those listed in the fastest-growing chart presented on page 98 (ten different states), and you have at least 20 states whose budgets will be straining the local coffers, and for whom some changes will have to happen.

The Ten Largest States for Total Medicaid Expenditures

	Millions of $		
State	1995	2030	% Change
New York	$3,907	$17,707	353%
Pennsylvania	2,072	8,650	317%
California	1,811	7,916	337%
Ohio	1,580	7,533	377%
Texas	1,040	7,184	591%
Florida	1,058	6,491	514%
Massachusetts	1,263	5,873	365%
Minnesota	806	4,394	445%
North Carolina	598	4,107	587%
New Jersey	882	3,858	338%

Source: American Council on Life Insurance

Since long-term care represents one of Medicaid's fastest growing expenses, not to recede anytime soon in light of current and future demographics, states (and the federal government) are already working on ways to limit their fiscal responsibility.

The federal government reimburses states for their Medicaid expenditures on a weighted scale. Not all states receive the same assistance, although the minimum amount of help is 50%. Listed in Figure 2.4 are the states and their Federal Medicaid Assistance Percentages (FMAPs) for 2001 and projected for 2002.

Medicaid has long concentrated its efforts on the long-term care front on skilled nursing facility arrangements. However, it is just now beginning to yield to the more preferred alternative to institutionalization – reimbursing costs for home and community-based care. In October 2000, the U.S. Department of Health and Human Services announced its proposal of new rules allowing obtainment of Medicaid coverage while living at home instead of having to transfer to nursing care facilities. Essentially, the proposed rules give more flexibility to the states to level the playing field on requirements for eligibility for either nursing facility or home-based long-term care treatments.[32]

This concession may save the program some money as home care often is less costly than the same services delivered in an SNF. If the past is any indication of the future, however, this loosening of past Medicaid rules could encourage more people to artificially qualify for the program, now that they see home care is now an option. The Medicaid program rules have not proven too difficult to get around.

Ten years ago, Pennsylvania found a loophole whereby it could claim more federal funding than it actually deserved to have based on its actual expenditures. The idea caught on, other states found similar ways to accomplish the same thing, and soon some 26 states were grabbing some extra funds from the government. They might still be flying along except that a few states couldn't contain their enthusiasm and word leaked back to the federal government about the accounting loophole that had been discovered. As if the program didn't already

Many state governments are using accounting gimmicks to drain more than $3.5 billion annually from the Medicaid program in what a top investigator likened to "legal money laundering." Officials say states have used different methods to increase their federal reimbursement, but they boil down to this: The states claim to spend more on the program than they actually do, so they can obtain more federal money. Pennsylvania started the idea in 1991 and has received an extra $1.9 billion in the past three years as a result.[33]

Figure 2.4

State	2001 FMAP	2002 FMAP
Alabama	69.99%	70.45%
Alaska	56.04%	53.01%
Arizona	65.77%	64.98%
Arkansas	73.02%	72.64%
California	51.25%	51.40%
Colorado	50.00%	50.00%
Connecticut	50.00%	50.00%
Delaware	50.00%	50.00%
District of Columbia	70.00%	70.00%
Florida	56.62%	56.43%
Georgia	59.67%	59.00%
Hawaii	53.85%	56.34%
Idaho	70.76%	71.02%
Illinois	50.00%	50.00%
Indiana	62.04%	62.04%
Iowa	62.67%	62.86%
Kansas	59.85%	60.20%
Kentucky	70.39%	69.94%
Louisiana	70.53%	70.30%
Maine	66.12%	66.58%
Maryland	50.00%	50.00%
Massachusetts	50.00%	50.00%
Michigan	56.18%	56.36%
Minnesota	51.11%	50.00%
Mississippi	76.82%	76.09%
Missouri	61.03%	61.06%
Montana	73.04%	72.83%
Nebraska	60.38%	59.55%
Nevada	50.36%	50.00%
New Hampshire	50.00%	50.00%
New Jersey	50.00%	50.00%
New Mexico	73.80%	73.04%
New York	50.00%	50.00%
North Carolina	62.47%	61.46%
North Dakota	69.99%	69.87%
Ohio	59.03%	58.78%
Oklahoma	71.24%	70.43%
Oregon	60.00%	59.20%
Pennsylvania	53.62%	54.65%
Rhode Island	53.79%	52.45%
South Carolina	70.44%	69.34%
South Dakota	68.31%	65.93%
Tennessee	63.79%	63.64%
Texas	60.57%	60.17%
Utah	71.44%	70.00%
Vermont	62.40%	63.06%
Virginia	51.85%	51.45%
Washington	50.70%	50.37%
West Virginia	75.34%	75.27%
Wisconsin	59.29%	58.57%
Wyoming	64.60%	61.97%

Source: Health Care Financing Administration

have enough pressure, these extra dollars allowed states to draw down billions of dollars in hospital and nursing home reimbursements, with no guarantee that the payments were being used for that intended purpose. The Department of Health and Human Services estimates that approximately $6 billion extra went out in the past year as a result.[34]

In July 2000, HCFA sent a letter to state Medicaid directors expressing concern about the states' use of the loophole – the Medicaid upper payment limit (UPL) – as a means of maximizing federal matching funds. The result was a new rule developed in March 2001 that modifies the UPL for several providers, including nursing facilities.[35] It's no wonder that for years Medicaid estate planners were able to work the system to qualify ordinarily wealthy, ineligible people for Medicaid reimbursement when long-term care needs surfaced, without actually having to spend down the money.

ASSET TRANSFERS

It took Congress some time, but they finally wised up to the Medicaid transfer game as it was played in attorney conference rooms from Boston to New York to Philadelphia to Washington, D.C. and points south and west. These lawyers described it as simple to their wealthy clients: Transfer your assets within the guidelines set up by Medicaid (36 months before Medicaid application for a simple transfer, 60 months for transfers involving a trust), and you can let the government pick up the tab for your long-term care needs without having to part with a cent of your assets.

There were certainly people that this appealed to, and attorneys specializing in Medicaid transfers were the popular planners of the 1990s. Legislation, in several parts, has now taken the wind from beneath the sails of these individuals, and given some teeth to the state to deal with transfers after the fact. But even before that, there were some problems both before and after the need for care surfaced – little details that perhaps the attorney hadn't explain very well:

1. When assets and income are transferred to get below Medicaid qualifying levels, these funds are completely out

of the transferor's hands. Now, if money is needed for anything – for example, the country club membership or an Alaskan cruise – a call must be placed to the recipient of the assets to obtain a loan. This proved dicey for some of the people not used to having to ask anyone for money, let alone for their own money.

2. When long-term care was needed, Medicaid generally only reimbursed costs for this treatment if delivered in a skilled nursing facility. Ordinarily, this wouldn't have been a problem, but the patient and family didn't realize the list of facilities was Medicaid's choice, not theirs, based on which SNFs accepted Medicaid reimbursement, typically the lowest payor of any third party taking care of long-term care costs.

3. Finally, once the patient was packed off to the not-so-desirable facility, one more important point was discovered – the person would have 2-3 roommates for the rest of his or her life. Forced to triple up in many cases, these facilities could only accept Medicaid when combining the expenses of three or four patients in one room.

Needless to say, the bubble burst for many who adopted this approach to funding their long-term care costs. But the government wasn't through. The Omnibus Budget Reconciliation Act of 1993 contained a mandatory edict in it that required states to develop legal, enforceable language to allow them to recover assets that were transferred (even within the stated 36/60 rules) for the purposes of avoiding Medicaid spend-down. These laws, enacted by all states by late 1995, were called Estate Recovery Acts. (See Figure 2.5.)

> *"The great tragedy of Science: the slaying of a beautiful hypothesis by an ugly fact."*
> — Thomas Henry Huxley

Figure 2.5

MEDICAID: ESTATE RECOVERY QUICK GUIDE

The purpose of estate recovery is, in the words of legislators, to assure that all of the resources available to an institutionalized individual not needed for the support of a spouse or dependent children will be used to defray the costs needed to support the individual in the institution. OBRA legislation passed in 1993 required states to aggressively pursue recovering costs of Medicaid care; to recoup some of the costs of long-term care by collecting from former patients' estates. In effect, this nearly changes Medicaid from welfare assistance to a loan program.

Any state that doesn't comply with its own estate recovery legislation runs the risk of losing that minimum 50% federal subsidy. Some states pursue this recovery more vigorously than others, and some have outsourced the collection to private companies.

The message is clear. Congress did not want to ruin families financially who were unprepared for long-term care expenses. The asset and income exemptions for the community spouse reflect this desire. Conversely, Congress did not want Medicaid to become another entitlement program, where wealthier individuals circumvented spend down through creative asset transfers and accessed public funds for their long-term care needs.

Federal law requires that states recover assets from a Medicaid recipient's probate estate – the property owned by the individual in his or her own name. States can go further and to make claims against other property in which the Medicaid beneficiary had an interest, including property held jointly with right of survivorship, joint bank accounts and pay-on-death accounts. A clarification last year from the Health Care Financing Administration stated that annuity proceeds may be included in the definition of estate for the purposes of Medicaid estate recovery.

Transferring assets and relying on Medicaid can have other drawbacks in addition to heirs facing estate recovery bills from the state. Relying on Medicaid means forfeiting choice. You must use an institution that accepts Medicaid reimbursement – and Medicaid pays the lowest of any of the third party payment sources for the institution. In addition, you will likely have one, two, and perhaps three roommates since the institution must double or triple up or more to properly cover its expenditures based on Medicaid's low reimbursements.

Estate recoveries are catching many by surprise, mostly because states do not adequately publicize their plan to bill heirs (and transfer recipients) after the patient (and spouse) pass away. But the laws have been on the books for several years now and, in 1999, California's program collected about $40 million from more than 2,400 estates, according to the Health Care Financing Administration.

The idea is that states have a budget battle each fiscal year and ways to curb expenditures are always being explored. Estate Recovery Acts are one way states are recovering money they feel should have been spent by the individual needing care *before* applying for Medicaid. Since that didn't happen, they are coming back after the fact to obtain their money. Pay me now or pay me later. The bureaucrats behind this feel that there are fair and adequate spousal asset and income protection provisions to avoid devastating a family financially. In order to prevent the program from becoming an entitlement, these bureaucrats instituted laws to collect on the money that was "advanced" to the family for the patient's long-term care.

What's interesting about the states that have been the most vigorous in their pursuit of these recoveries is that most of them are at the low end of the federal reimbursement level (see previous FMAP charts). For some states, this aggressive posture pre-dates the OBRA '93 federal law that mandated the recoveries. It was actually the Tax

Equity and Fiscal Responsibility Act of 1982 (TEFRA) that explicitly authorized Medicaid estate recoveries as a state option and states like Oregon have been a leader in charting the recovery course since that time. The 1993 federal law finally made it a mandatory practice as a condition of receiving the federal matching funds.[37]

There is still a planning option or two left. Miller Trusts may enable individuals, who would otherwise have too much income, to meet the income test for Medicaid coverage for nursing home care or, now, nursing home level care delivered at home. Arising out of a federal district court opinion, *Miller v. Ibarra*, this case authorized the creation of trusts to evade Colorado's income limit qualifications on nursing home care. Money goes into the irrevocable trust and the trust must provide that any amounts remaining in the trust will be paid to the state upon death as reimbursement for cost of care.

This trust is a device that lets some money operate to pay for normal expenses of the patient without impeding qualification for Medicaid. It may be that some later recovery will occur, but it may be another legal way to qualify for Medicaid reimbursement. It should be noted that there have been court opinions that have criticized the holding in *Miller v. Ibarra*. It is probably safe to say most people would rather think about planning ahead in other,

Annuity proceeds may be included in the definition of "estate" for the purposes of Medicaid estate recovery according to a January 24, 2000 letter written by the Region IX HCFA Office to the California Department of Health Services.

In Michigan, a workgroup sponsored by the state's Department of Community Health recommended closing all loopholes for asset transfer by middle and upper income individuals, and gradually raise the 5-year look-back period to 10 years.[38]

Figure 2.6

The "Dear Heir" Letters[39]

Illinois: Please accept our condolences regarding the death of
_____.We regret the necessity to discuss business during
your time of bereavement, however, we must advise you that the
Illinois Department of Public Aid has a claim against any assets
owned by _____ at the time of ____ death. It is necessary to
provide you with information immediately so that you will have
the opportunity to make the necessary arrangements for proper
distribution.

California: Please send your payment in the amount of $106,424.92 (or the
value of the estate, whichever is less), within 30 days. A self-
addressed envelope is enclosed for your convenience.

Delaware: Since deceased patient received $3,517.38 in Medicaid benefits, the
Department of Health and Social Services hereby gives you notice
of its claim for that amount against any real property and/or assets
in her estate.

Nebraska: The Department cannot file a claim if _____ was survived by
a spouse, a child under the age of 21, or a child who is blind or
totally and permanently disabled. Our information shows that this
situation does not apply.

---

simpler and safer ways, especially higher income people for whom the
cost of a long-term care insurance premium (if they qualify) would be
far less burdensome than borrowing their own money from their children or entering a nursing facility they would never think of going to
otherwise. Long-term care insurance as a funding vehicle is about
choice – the Medicaid program, for obvious reasons, is not.

THE FINE ART OF BENEFIT DESIGN

"We think in generalities, but we live in details."

– Alfred North Whitehead

If one sees the typical funding alternatives – Medicare, Medicare
supplements, Medicaid, and savings – are not going to be adequate
and there is a definite need for some financial assistance, then the

long-term care insurance policy should take center stage. In its simplest terms, it is the payment of a relatively small, budgetable amount of money to a third party (an insurance company) in exchange for that carrier accepting the future unknown liability of long-term care costs.

That being said, there are a lot of choices to be made in purchasing the right long-term care policy and it is here where mistakes can be made and coverage can be inadequate. If one goes to the trouble of understanding the need and then trying to do something about it, why not get it as right as you can?

> The main regret of long-term care policyholders at claim time: they wish they had bought more coverage.

There are several key factors to consider first and some other components that may be more or less critical to the individual depending on personal preferences and circumstances. The initial choices to make are the type of policy, the kind of reimbursement, the daily benefit amount, the elimination period, and the length and type of benefit period. None of these vital parts of the coverage should be taken lightly, but in many cases, informed decisions can be made relatively quickly.

> A LifePlans, Inc. study for the Health and Human Services Department and the Robert Wood Johnson Foundation found that the average nursing home claimant had $1,144 in monthly **non-covered** expenses, around $14,000 per year. The study also found that policies covered only about the first 36 of the average 59 hours of home care the typical policyholder received each week.[40]

Choice #1: What type of reimbursement is desired?

This is an option between policies that pay the daily benefit amount without regard to the actual long-term care expense incurred (called an indemnity plan) or those that pay either a daily benefit or the cost of the actual expense, if lower (called an expense-incurred plan).

Indemnity	*Expense-Incurred*
Advantage:	Advantage:
• a better opportunity to cover the extras over and above the actual charges	• likely less expensive than the indemnity plan since it may not pay policy benefits as fast
Disadvantage:	Disadvantage:
• may run into taxation of benefits if daily benefit exceeds a certain level ($200 per day in 2001; adjusted annually)	• may not be adequate to cover the unanticipated expense; the add-ons in a facility; instrumental activities of daily living

Choice #2: What type of policy is desired?

This means choosing between a tax-qualified and non-qualified plan. Briefly, the Health Insurance Portability and Accountability Act of 1996 (HIPAA) sanctioned tax-qualified plans as receiving the utmost tax favorability. Benefits under tax-qualified plans will never be taxed and businesses receive a tax deduction, while there may also be a chance for policyholders to deduct all or a portion of their premium, too. The trade-off was the elimination of one important benefit qualification and a limitation placed on another. For a more complete discussion of these two product types, see Part Three of this book.

Tax-Qualified	*Non-Qualified*
Advantage:	Advantage:
• known positive tax consequences	• more opportunities to qualify for benefits
Disadvantage:	Disadvantage:
• some claims may not be paid as a result of modified, standardized policy language	• possible taxation of benefits; insurers now complete Form 1099-LTC to report benefit payments under non-qualified plans

Choice #3: What daily benefit amount should be selected?

This selection depends on the area of the country where the individual would most likely seek long-term care benefits. Remember that daily benefits will vary not only by geographical location, but also by the type of care needed and the setting in which it will be delivered. Traditionally, planners have used the area's average nursing home cost to determine an adequate benefit level (see Part One for more discussion). Around-the-clock home health care can be far more expensive than daily room and board and services in a skilled nursing facility, however, so one must be careful of any benchmark used. The inflation option can help the initial amount selected keep up with the ever-increasing expenses of this treatment. This choice may also be based on what one can afford in the way of premium payments, too. One level to keep in mind: the per diem limitation for tax purposes. As noted above, it is $200 per day in the year 2001. Coverage at or just below this amount will be quite sufficient in most areas of the country. If the daily benefit amount selected is too low, the individual will have to fund the difference at claim time out of his or her own pocket – something that insurance was meant to avoid if it all possible.

Choice #4: What elimination period should be chosen?

The elimination period is the number of days at the beginning of a long-term care claim during which the individual will self-insure. An individual can elect first-day benefits, or self-insure for 15, 20, 30, 45, 60, 90, 100 days, or longer. This is not an easy decision. Witness the following 12 questions that should be asked before a decision is made:[41]

1.   Are the elimination period days cumulative?

2.   Do the days need to be consecutive?

3.   Are the days a singular occurrence?

4. Does the period of accumulation have time limitations?

5. Does the elimination period need to be satisfied within a benefit period?

6. Is the elimination period a singular occurrence for both facility care and home care?

7. If the elimination periods are separate for facility and home care, do they offset one another?

8. Is the elimination period for home health care treated differently than the elimination period for facility care?

9. If so, how is it different (waived, accelerated, or credited for care management, etc.)?

10. Is the elimination period for home health care based on days of services?

11. Do the Medicare days of service count towards satisfying elimination periods?

12. Are the home health care elimination periods credited based on days of services or from point of claim?

That's a lot of analysis for only one of several choices that have to be made. But all of these questions are valid. If an individual selects first day coverage (0 days), most of these questions go away as long as there is not a separate election for facility and home care. This is also the most expensive option and electing to take a longer elimination period can save some premium.

There are elimination periods that need be met only once over the lifetime of the policy. Some of these are cumulative where once a day is satisfied, it need never be counted again even if the particular long-term care situation isn't long enough for benefits to be paid.

There are elimination periods where one day of home care can equal seven elimination period days if the care is only needed once a week. The more liberal the interpretation, the higher the premium in all likelihood, but it might be worth it for ease in claims handling and in understanding how the policy actually works.

Choice #5: What type and how long a benefit period is needed?

Benefit periods come in all shapes and sizes just as elimination periods do. There is an unlimited benefit period (that is, lifetime) where the claim will go on for as long as the patient does. Any other choice means a finite period of time, such as two, three, four, five and six years most often. I've always recommended a minimum of four years to cover some of the statistical probabilities in lengths of stay at a facility. There was a time when planners recommended a three-year benefit period based on the ability to immediately transfer assets upon need for care and then applying to Medicaid once the benefit period had expired. Estate Recovery Acts (discussed earlier) have discouraged this practice upon which to base the choice of a benefit period.

There are two types of benefit periods – straight time calculation or a pool of money concept. Straight time is easy – four years is four years, for example. Once benefits have been paid that long, the claim is over. The pool of money benefit period is a different idea.

Rather than use a straight time measurement, a pool of money plan takes the days in the benefit period selected (1,460 days in a four-year benefit period) and multiplies it by the daily benefit amount elected ($150/day, for example) to determine a lump-sum amount (1,460 x $150 = $219,000). This $219,000 then becomes the total claim account. Benefit period time is now forgotten. An individual can draw down the money from the account based on the expenses incurred up to the daily benefit amount (unless the plan is an indemnity plan where the daily benefit amount is always paid and the money will last, in this example, exactly four years). If less is taken from the policy than the daily benefit amount because the expenses were lower, no money is lost – it's still parked there in the pool of money account. Reimbursement at a slower rate than the daily benefit amount means the money may last well past the four-year point in this example. The key is the individual is now working with dollars rather than number of days.

> *"If all else fails, immortality can always be assured by spectacular error."*
> – John Kenneth Gailbraith

These initial choices – type of policy, type of reimbursement, daily benefit amount, elimination and benefit period – are made when designing the plan the individual will need to carry into the future to help pay for long-term care costs. Inflation options will be reviewed later in this section. These elections must be made carefully with thought given to each. It is important to know why a non-qualified plan is selected over a tax-qualified plan or an indemnity contract instead of an expense-incurred one. One must understand how the daily benefit amount was determined and why the elimination and benefit periods were chosen. An understanding of plan design reinforces the reason to have this product as a wealth protection vehicle in one's financial plan. Mistakes can be made and, in some cases, these errors may cost money. But the decision to purchase long-term care insurance as a funding vehicle for possible future medical expenses is the first and most important step – and one that is already taken if one is now reviewing plan design details.

Attention: Disability Income Producers!

It's time to examine the most common policy definitions. Long-term care is a disability-based contract. One must have a disability event – illness or injury – to begin the qualification process for benefits under the product. For those who have marketed and/or purchased disability income coverage, this should be a heartening thought. There will be a parallel between some of the definitions in both contracts.

The key definitions to review are:

*   policy renewability, and

*   definitions of disability.

The purpose of the long-term care contract is to furnish dollars for the purposes of paying for medical expenses that will likely go un-reimbursed otherwise. It is meant to preserve assets and income that would be spent for this need if no other financing alternative is in place. A disability income contract's primary objective is also to pre-serve assets and income that would go towards paying for normal monthly expenses without any economic assistance from the disabil-ity policy. For many people, there will simply be no other reasonable options with which to finance the fragile risk of their health. Understanding the key provisions of this vital and necessary coverage is a pre-requisite for selling or purchasing.

Policy renewal provision choices

Disability income: Long-term care:

*   Non-cancelable   *   Guaranteed renewable
*   Guaranteed renewable
*   Conditionally renewable

Both disability and long-term care products can be guaranteed renewable. This is the minimum and (to this point) only renewal pro-vision in effect for long-term care policies. It means that the insurer can never cancel the policy – it is obligated to guarantee its renewal as long as the policyholder continues to make timely premium pay-ments as required.

The inability of an insurer to cancel was of overriding concern to the National Association of Insurance Commissioners (NAIC), who made this minimum provision standard in their long-term care model policy. This renewal language does allow the carrier to raise the premium rates, as long as it does it for a class of business and can justify it with the insurance departments. Insurance companies are not permitted to single out any one insured for a rate increase. Increasing premiums to a specific policy form – and, therefore, to all purchasers of this policy form – is the type of "class" that can see a rate hike.

Disability policies have a better and a worse provision. A policy that is conditionally renewable means that there are a number of circumstances that have to be met for the policy to be renewed. Long-term care policies, as defined by law, do not carry this sort of restrictive provision. Nor are they non-cancelable (non-can) as are some disability insurance contracts. This is a misleading term since we know that guaranteed renewable contracts cannot be canceled either. What "non-can" adds is a premium guarantee, usually until age 65. While this is a welcome concept in this type of coverage, no long-term care insurer feels comfortable with this pricing structure yet. Let's face it – it has to get the premium right the first time. Long-term care experience is still relatively new and the confidence level in adding a non-can renewal (which costs about 10-15% more for this provision in a disability income contract) is just not there.

Some insurers are willing to make a 10-year rate guarantee on their long-term care product and this has been a popular choice so far among long-term care purchasers. Others are offering a paid-up at age 65 policy that is more about accelerating the premium payments than any type of guarantee.

The disability insurance industry was hit fairly hard with poor claims experience on its non-can block of business, but that was likely due as much to the liberal disability definitions and improper pricing than the inability to raise premiums. Certainly, insurers couldn't overcome the poor experience with rate increases, but this was not the underlying factor.

We are likely to have "guaranteed renewable" as a standard renewal provision in long-term care for some time to come. Whether insurers expand their rate guarantees will probably depend on the ever-increasing knowledge base of claims experience developed with the long-term care product line.

Definitions of Disability

Disability income:	Long-term care:
• Own occupation	• Loss of ADLs
• Residual disability	• Standby assistance
• Presumptive total disability	• Cognitive impairment
• Under a doctor's care	• Medical necessity

In a disability-based insurance contract, it follows that the definition of disability is the key provision to understand. It is in this language that insurance company claims examiners will determine the eligibility on the part of the insured for benefit payments under this policy. Naturally, it is in this language that one finds the closest parallels between the two types of insurance plans.

Own occupation:	Loss of ADLs:
"Inability to perform the duties of one's own occupation"	"Inability to perform two of six activities of daily living"

Easy comparison – the inability to perform duties as a result of some disability event; an injury or illness that affects one's performance. In the case of long-term care policies, it is an inability to perform basic and necessary tasks – that is, activities of daily living (ADLs). The six ADLs are listed below:

1. bathing,

2. dressing,

3. eating,

4.   toileting,

5.   mobility, and

6.   continence.

There are variations on both the "own occupation" definition and the "loss of ADLs" definition, but these are the primary standards. The two of six ADL loss requirement is the standard language in a tax-qualified plan. There are some disability insurers that are contemplating using the ADL language for their plans, and paying benefits for both types of expenses covered in the two contracts – basic monthly bills and long-term care treatment.

Residual disability:	Standby assistance:
"Inability to perform one or more of the duties of your occupation, or the inability to perform these duties for as much time as was done prior to disability"	"The presence of another person within arm's reach of the individual that is necessary to prevent, by physical intervention, injury to the individual while the person is performing an ADL"

In both cases, the insured is performing a normal task, but in each situation, is limited in his or her ability to carry out the duty. In the case of long-term care, there is an overriding concern that the individual may need some help. If help is not needed, fine, but simply the need to have someone there constitutes the loss of an ADL for policy purposes. This language was introduced with the tax-qualified plan and represents an interim step in the disability process. It is a recognition that there is a partial loss of ability and, hence, the need for someone to supervise the carrying out of an activity of daily living.

With disability income, this partial loss triggers a payment of a portion or all of the benefit. In long-term care, standby assistance means the loss of the ADL and the payment of the appropriate daily benefit amount. An expense will be incurred because someone has to be within a physical distance from the individual. That charge is what is reimbursed under an expense-incurred policy up to the daily benefit amount and the full daily benefit would be payable under the indemnity version of the policy.

Presumptive total disability:	Cognitive impairment:
"Loss of sight, speech, hearing or use of two limbs"	"deterioration in or loss of the insured's intellectual capacity"
Examples	*Examples*
Blindness	Alzheimer's disease
Deafness	Senile dementia

The idea behind this qualifier for policy benefits is a type of catastrophic disability from which recovery is virtually impossible. Policyholders having an infirmity that meets the language in these policy provisions are automatically eligible for claim payments. There is no need to meet any other policy provision. This disability is significant on its own.

Under a doctor's care:	Medical necessity:
"Insured must be under the care of a physician to receive benefits. This provision may be waived if continued treatment would be of no benefit to the insured"	"Insured is considered benefit-eligible if a physician directs that long-term care services are needed to assist the patient"

In both cases, the insured's doctor is the one that has the individual's best interests at heart and is acting accordingly. For long-term care policies, "medical necessity" became a fallback provision when the insured needed the care but did not qualify under either the ADL or cognitive impairment definition. This often fit the frail elderly, who simply needed daily help as the process of performing ADLs consistently over the course of the day would take its physical toll.

This definition was developed with assistance from the medical professionals actually furnishing long-term care. It is available in non-qualified long-term care insurance policies, but not in tax-qualified plans.

IADLs

Prior to the inability to perform an ADL will likely come the inability to perform one or more instrumental activities of daily living (IADLs). While not normally covered in a long-term care policy, the inability to perform these important, but not vital, life duties will be a precursor to the loss of ADLs. These chore-oriented tasks can be performed by a home care aide to make life a little easier for the individual who may be on a physical decline but is not ill enough to warrant assistance with the customary activities of daily living. Insurers were experimenting with the coverage of IADL loss prior to the passage of HIPAA. There is still room to develop coverage for this loss, perhaps as an extra option on a policy, paying at a low benefit level, but helping defray the costs in some way. Disability insurers used to offer a small emergency room accident expense benefit in much the same way.

Instrumental Activities of Daily Living:[42]

- *Shopping*
- *Housekeeping*
- *Money Management*
- *Food preparation*
- *Transportation*

For individuals with adults who need help with one or more of these IADLs, they should take note that there may be worse ahead. Loss of IADLs can provide the opportunity to start thinking about long-term care costs and services. Unfortunately, if the adult hasn't purchased a long-term care insurance policy yet, it is likely too late to exercise that funding arrangement option.

> *"It has yet to be proven that intelligence has any survival value."*
>
> – Arthur C. Clarke

Both disability and long-term care contracts are packed densely with language only an attorney could love. The discussions of policy provisions above were an overview at best, intended to help you generally distinguish between the key eligibility triggers in these types of contracts. But make no mistake about it. It will be critical to obtain a specimen policy of the coverage one is contemplating marketing or buying prior to making any final sale or purchase. The omission of a word or inclusion of another can make a world of difference in benefit eligibility.

If this sounds suspiciously like President Clinton's "[i]t depends on what the definition of 'is' is," it is.. Or, as has been pointed out by many analysts, it may be more a case of the words "and" and "or."

ADL: Transferring/Mobility	ADL: Transferring/Mobility
Transferring means moving into **or** out of a bed, chair **or** wheelchair.	*Transferring* means your ability to change positions, including moving from bed to standing, chair to standing, bed to chair, **and** the reverse of these activities.

The definition on the left is NAIC suggested language: short, succinct and to the point. However, to be considered unable to perform this ADL, one would have to lose the ability to perform all of these transfers: in and out of bed, in and out of a wheelchair, or in and out of a chair. An ability to do any one of these would technically disqualify the individual from receiving benefits.[43]

On the right, this definition means you must be able to perform all of these tasks – from bed to a standing position and back, from a chair to standing and back, from a bed to a chair and back – or you will be deemed unable to perform this ADL. The inability to perform any one would qualify as an ADL loss in this definition whereas the *ability* to perform any one of the mobility functions on the left would not qualify as an ADL loss.[44]

It is important to read "and/or" language closely. In general, when "or" is used as part of the definition, then the language can be interpreted more restrictively to mean that the insured must lose *every single one* of the functions listed in the definition to constitute the loss of that activity of daily living. The use of the word "and" will give a more liberal interpretation, meaning that the individual must be unable to do *only one* of the listed functions to be certified as not being able to perform that ADL. That's a huge swing, and the policy developers and claims examiners know it. Careful study of each of the ADL definitions would be the proper due diligence strategy.

Other Key Provisions
Home Care

Arguably, this might be the most useful of all the policy provisions in the long-term care insurance contract. It goes right to the heart of what this coverage is about: maintaining independence, control, and freedom of choice. Being able to receive needed care in familiar surroundings can be an emotional boost – to all concerned.

Simply, home care benefits provide for expense reimbursement for care furnished in this setting. Coverage for home care is triggered by the same benefit eligibility definitions noted earlier in this section. Once qualified, home care is an option, and one that many tend to choose rather than institutional care. It might be the patient's own home, or the home of a child or other relative, friend or neighbor. There may be a separate elimination period from facility care and this should be checked and understood at the time of purchase. Many comprehensive long-term care policies use the same elimination period for both, while others may offer first-day home care coverage even if the basic policy has a specified elimination period for other basic benefits.

In light of the reduced expenditures by Medicare on home health care, the long-term care policy becomes more vital for those that consider this the optimum way to receive care. It is definitely one of the features to highlight in any presentation of long-term care insurance since it diffuses the belief that this coverage is only about nursing home or institutional care.

Home care benefits are usually paid at the daily benefit amount rate. There may be policies that offer you the option of reducing your premium payment by electing home care benefits at a percentage of the daily benefit (for example, 50% or 80%). This means, in the case of a 50% option, a policy with a $130/day daily benefit amount will pay up to $65/day for home care benefits.

When choosing homes today, Boomers typically favor floor plans with less defined space that allows them to tailor rooms to meet their specific needs. Many people have hobby rooms, place a lot of emphasis on the kitchen and set up home offices with high-speed Internet access.[45] This flexible room development may make it easier to transform a room for the purposes of providing long-term care services.

Since home care costs are many and varied, electing a lower home care percentage may not be the best choice in benefit design. In general, home care costs are lower, but it all depends on what is needed. As noted several times in this text, around-the-clock home care can be more expensive than facility care, but more desirable emotionally for the patient and family. It's probably wiser to elect daily benefit amounts that pay the same for care delivered in most every setting.

The other element to look for today in a home care benefit is how benefits are paid. This has become very important in part because of the way home health care agencies schedule their appointments, preferring often to put two to three visits in the same day for various needs. Patients (and any family members living with them) may find this method of delivering long-term care services more convenient. Insurers are experimenting with different ways to calculate the benefit.

Using a daily benefit amount purchased at $150/day, let's look at how a claim would be paid if the insurer paid the expense-incurred benefit up to either the daily, weekly or monthly amount. Let's look at a four-week claim with the following home care expenses incurred:

Daily Benefit	Weekly Benefit	Monthly Benefit
$150	$1,050	$4,500

	Day 1	Day 2	Day 3	Day 4	Day 5	Day 6	Day 7
Week One	$130	$210	-0-	-0-	$500	$130	-0-
Week Two	130	210	-0-	-0-	500	130	-0-
Week Three	130	130	-0-	-0-	500	130	-0-
Week Four	130	130	-0-	-0-	210	130	-0-

The first two weeks were consistent in the visits and services delivered. In weeks three and four, the need for some care diminished and the visits (and expense) dropped off somewhat. It is important to remember that home care visits and needs can and often do change during the course of long-term care treatment.

There are currently three ways home health care benefit payments can be calculated. The first is the standard way – paying up to the daily limit. Some carriers have added a second way – a weekly pool of benefits. Here, the daily benefit is multiplied by seven, giving the claimant a weekly total to draw benefits from even if the daily benefit amount is exceeded on any one day. Finally, other insurers are working with a monthly pool, multiplying the daily benefit by 30 and paying benefits each month from that total. In Figure 2.7, these three methods are applied to the above outlined home care claim.

Figure 2.8 shows the totals for each of the three payment methods.

As you can see, the daily benefit limit policy can leave the insured with out-of-pocket expenses. Home care expenses will vary

Figure 2.7

WEEK ONE AND TWO
CLAIM PAYMENTS

Policy Type	Day 1	Day 2	Day 3	Day 4	Day 5	Day 6	Day 7
Daily ($150/day)	$130	$150	0	0	$150	130	0
Weekly ($1,050/week)	130	210	0	0	500	130	0
Monthly ($4,500/month)	130	210	0	0	500	130	0

WEEK THREE PAYMENTS

	Day 1	Day 2	Day 3	Day 4	Day 5	Day 6	Day 7
Daily	130	130	0	0	150	130	0
Weekly	130	130	0	0	500	130	0
Monthly	130	130	0	0	500	130	0

WEEK FOUR PAYMENTS

	Day 1	Day 2	Day 3	Day 4	Day 5	Day 6	Day 7
Daily	130	130	0	0	150	130	0
Weekly	130	130	0	0	210	130	0
Monthly	130	130	0	0	210	130	0

Figure 2.8

TOTAL EXPENSES	BENEFIT PAYMENTS		
	Daily	Weekly	Monthly
Week 1 - $970	$560 ....$970 ....$970		
Week 2 - $970	560 ....970 970		
Week 3 - $890	540 ....890 890		
Week 4 - $600	540 ....600 600		
Total - $3,430	$2,200 ....$3,430 ....$3,430		
Not covered	$1,230 ....-0- ....-0-		

and the greater the policy flexibility with regard to payment, the less likely one will have substantial out-of-pocket costs. The daily limit policy covered less than two-thirds of the claim, while the weekly and monthly benefit calculations covered the entire amount of expenses incurred.

The weekly benefit would cover any home care expenses up to, in this example, $1,050. The total expenses incurred were $970 at the highest; thus, there were no out-of-pocket expenses. Should the weekly expenses have exceeded $1,050, there would have been out-of-pocket costs to the insured.

The monthly benefit would be paying benefits until the total reached $4,500, in this example, in a month's time. This gives the insured even more flexibility and should hold out-of-pocket expenses down.

Check the policy form for the type of benefit calculation accorded the home care and home health care benefits. The more flexible, the higher the premium in all likelihood, but it could mean a tremendous savings later on during a time when it is most needed. The better this calculation, the easier it is for the home visits to be scheduled, since the impact on out-of-pocket costs is minimal.

ASSISTED LIVING FACILITY CARE

Many adult children promise their parents they won't put them in a nursing home. This was easier said than done at times as, aside from care being delivered in one's own home, there were few reliable alternative institutions in which an individual could receive long-term care treatment. The recent negativity surrounding nursing homes has only added to elders' anxieties regarding this particular type of facility. It is also true that many people that were placed in a skilled nursing facility did not need highly skilled levels of care, but needed more basic assistance with activities of daily living. Certainly a different type of facility could handle this type of patient. And so up grew an opportunity for a mid-range level of long-term care housing.

Hands-on assistance with activities such as bathing, dressing, and taking medicine has become a staple of these new assisted living facilities. This type of help rarely requires skilled nursing care, so the cost of living in these residences is far more reasonable than a nursing home. When you add in the psychological factor of not remotely resembling what people think of as a nursing home, the steadily increasing popularity of these places is no surprise. Designed to first help people with their instrumental activities of daily living and then regular ADLs as their health situation worsens, these facilities are more laid-back, and filled with people who are more livelier than the average nursing home resident.

A National Academy of Sciences study recently found that 2.3% of older Americans now live in assisted living facilities, with more than half the residents reporting no disabilities of any type. Such facilities provide some help, such as meals and home maintenance, while giving independence to the residents.[46]

Assisted living facility care, as a result, is a less expensive alternative for people who need assistance but are not sick enough to need a skilled nursing facility. Benefit dollars under a long-term care policy can last longer. Naturally, because individuals placed in assisted living

A recent study published in the *Journal of the American Geriatrics Society* found that nearly a third of 3,262 seriously ill patients interviewed said they'd rather die than live in a nursing home.[47]

facilities are not as ill, they may be receiving long-term care for a longer time than those in a nursing home.

The typical ALF resident is about 82 years of age, female, mobile, but with a need for help with two to four basic activities of daily living.[48] It is important to keep in mind that the ALF may not be the last stop on the long-term care ladder of care, as few are staffed and able to handle the needy patient.

> "Linda Cope thought an assisted living facility would be ideal for her brother, Bill. But after he broke a hip at a Virginia ALF … and began using a wheelchair to get around, the story changed. "They kept saying they weren't equipped to handle him," Cope says. This, despite the administrator's earlier assurance, she says, that her brother "would move right through the system as his abilities decreased." The company's promotional brochure, it turns out, even includes a picture of a wheelchair-bound resident. For confidentiality reasons, the administrator would not comment on Cope's case, but says the facility is obligated to discharge residents whose needs it cannot meet. For Cope, however, the reality was simple: She had just weeks to clean out her brother's belongings."[49]

Assisted living facility coverage is a standard in most comprehensive long-term care policies. For one insurer, eight out of ten "nursing home type" claims are currently for assisted living facilities.[50] This is more than enough to warrant discussion and for potential LTC insurance buyers to understand what type of coverage is available for stays in this emerging type of residence.

INFLATION COVERAGE

Medical costs are constantly going up. This has been true for years, and this economic reality should be addressed by reviewing the inflation protection options available to for long-term care policies. The Federal Reserve Board worries about inflation and so should purchasers of long-term care policies. Otherwise, an individual will be working with the same policy benefits year after year to handle the ever-increasing costs of the long-term care treatments being received.

It will add extra premium to the cost of the policy, but the most expensive option is better off purchased at a younger age when the premium is still relatively manageable.

The American Council of Life Insurers (ACLI) recently published a study, projecting the following increases in long-term care costs by the year 2030:[51]

- Nursing home care will cost about $190,600 per year.

- Assisted living facility costs will be at $109,300 per year.

- Home care visits will cost $260 per visit (averaging $68,000 annually).

- Adult day care will increase to $220/day ($56,100 on average per year).

If you purchase a $150/day policy ($54,750) without any inflation protection, in year 2030 the annual policy benefits will still be $54,750, eclipsed by all of the projected services costs, some substantially more than others.

Here are the choices:

1. Do not purchase inflation protection.

2. Purchase simple inflation coverage.

3. Purchase compound inflation coverage.

4. Purchase a higher daily benefit amount than currently needed.

Let's consider each of these circumstances.

1.   DO NOTHING.

Benefits would stay level from year to year. An individual could apply for more coverage at periodic intervals, but unless there was some benefit purchase guarantee, the individual would have to qualify medically each time he or she asked for a benefit increase and pay the rates in effect for his or her age at the time the new coverage is added.

2.   SIMPLE INFLATION.

Most insurers offer this type of inflation coverage, usually at a 5% flat increase each policy anniversary. This is the option that many purchase because it is the more affordable choice. It is best selected when a buyer is in one's 60s and that much closer to potentially needing long-term care. The difference between simple and compounded inflation in the early years of a policy is not that significant.

3.   COMPOUNDED INFLATION.

The best, and most expensive, form of inflation protection also usually provides a 5% annual increase but one that inflates benefits faster than the simple approach. The younger buyer (under age 60) should seriously consider this choice since it may be some time between the purchase of the policy and the claiming of any benefits. In that time, long-term care costs could soar dramatically. Without inflation coverage, there would likely be a lot of out-of-pocket costs to the younger buyer.

4.   PURCHASING A HIGHER BENEFIT AMOUNT.

Instead of purchasing an inflation option, the older buyer (over 70) can consider taking a higher-than-needed daily benefit instead. With needs at $150/day, this individual may take $200/day instead and combat inflation that way. Doing the math is important here. As one analyst notes, you should compare the daily benefit purchased without inflation to the daily benefit that can be purchased for the same premium with inflation. For example, at age 80 one could purchase a $140/day benefit without inflation for the same price as a $100/day benefit with inflation. After just seven years, the $100/day plan with inflation would have increased to more than $140/day. Further, if this presumably healthy 80-year-old outlives life expectancy and goes into an institution at 95, the benefit and, presumably the cost of care, will be well over $200/day.[52]

If one buys inflation protection, the cost of the option is included in the regular premium. The policy benefit increases annually without a further increase in premium as a result. Variations of this are being introduced in the market on a regular basis. One such type has a nominal price when purchased, but a 5% increase in premium each time the benefits are increased by 5%. Be sure you know how the inflation option you selected charges the premium for this privilege.

Figure 2.9 shows the difference in the four approaches over a few years. The policy purchased is $100/day, except for option 4 – buying a higher daily benefit – where $150/day was taken instead.

In the first few years, the advantage belongs to the higher daily benefit amount purchase. This is why this is sometimes recommended for the over-age-70 client. There is very little difference early between the simple and compounded approaches – about $3,700 in annual payout by year 10. However, as time moves forward, the difference in the compounded rider becomes obvious. By the 25th year after purchase, the policy with the compounded rider could pay out over $37,000 annually more than the coverage with the simple inflation option, and substantially more dollars than the higher daily benefit amount or the do-nothing strategy.

Figure 2.9

Year	Annual Payout no inflation	Annual Payout 5% simple	Annual Payout 5% compound	Buying a higher benefit
1	$36,500	$36,500	$36,500	$54,750
2	36,500	38,325	38,325	54,750
3	36,500	40,150	40,241	54,750
4	36,500	41,975	42,253	54,750
5	36,500	43,800	44,366	54,750
10	36,500	52,925	56,623	54,750
15	36,500	62,050	72,267	54,750
20	36,500	71,175	92,233	54,750
25	36,500	80,300	117,715	54,750

Knowing the differences in the payouts can help illustrate the bottom-line effects of each of these ways to address the problem of rising long-term care costs.

Premiums

*"Money frees you from doing things you dislike. Since
I dislike doing nearly everything, money is handy."*

– Groucho Marx

As is true in most aspects of life, decisions often come down to money. The initial information gathering that helps to pinpoint whether or not long-term care funding is a need for a client will also help you find how much is likely available to be spent on long-term care insurance. This is done by a careful analysis of liquid assets and cash flow.

But there are many considerations where premium dollars are concerned and there are numerous ways to pay the cost of a long-term care insurance policy.

Annual premium and more frequent payments. The most common method is to buy a policy and pay for it on an annual, semi-annual, quarterly or monthly basis. The premium is regular. The notices of payment due are sent or, in the case of a monthly premium, the premium can be deducted automatically from one's bank account.

Accelerated payment methods. Becoming increasingly popular with the younger buyer is the ability to pay up the premiums on a long-term care insurance policy early. A number of companies have filed "10-pay" and "paid up at age 65" variations of premium payments. In these cases, one pays a higher premium than would be paid under the first option stated above, because payments are accelerated.. For the younger buyer, this may make sense as even a higher premium to achieve this can be affordable in one's 40s and 50s. The idea of buying long-term care coverage, thinking of it as a retirement need and then paying it off at age 65 means you eliminate that cost from your retirement budget. Premium payments are over at age 65 on the "paid up at 65" option and there is no need to worry about rate increases in the future.

Single premium. Both stand-alone and life insurance and annuity-based long-term care policies offer the chance to pay for this coverage in one lump sum. For those individuals that have a liquid asset that isn't that productive, this might be a way to obtain the coverage and not worry about future payments or rate increases. Again, the identification of such a liquid asset would be uncovered during your information gathering efforts.

All of these are ways to pay the premium for a long-term care insurance policy. Each individual's financial circumstances and needs will be different. If the need exists, how best to solve it will be determined by the economic realities of the individual's current situation. This is another reason why it is important to gather all the numbers up front as part of the overall analysis.

Today, premium variations can have incredible ranges for what would appear to be similar coverage. An American Council of Life

Insurers study put together a composite of five, large long-term care insurers for a $100/day plan with a 5% compounded inflation option. The study showed the following average annual premium results:

Average Annual Premiums

Ages	2-year Benefit period	5-year Benefit period
35-39	$394	$558
40-44	.443	.666
45-49	.550	.807
50-54	.645	.905
55-59	.892	1,204
60-64	1,265	1,709
65-69	1,849	2,432
70-74	2,638	3,610
75+	3,851	5,274

While these are average costs, it is very important to understand that studying the premium rates alone can be very misleading. While there may be a general variation between insurers, substantial differences usually mean the coverages being compared are not exactly the same. The next chart shows some differences between carriers:

Average Annual Premium By Age

	40	50	60	70	80
Insurer 1	$400.48	$584.72	$1,072.21	$2,191.38	$5,079.77
Insurer 2	215.70	472.00	940.90	1,795.00	5,345.70
Insurer 3	212.00	375.00	850.00	2,226.00	6,832.00
Insurer 4	466.05	496.51	830.70	1,925.35	5,511.63
Insurer 5	286.85	450.84	756.40	1,582.11	3,937.58
Insurer 6	109.00	312.00	604.08	1,462.32	4,161.72

$100/day, 0-90 day EP, 3- or 4-year BP

Source: Weiss Ratings, Inc.

What makes one carrier charge $109.00 for the same program for which another charges $466.05? Can this be an error?

The first thing to do is to check the basic plan differences: daily benefit amount, elimination period, benefit period and inflation option. Given that these are all the same, one must delve further into the policy analysis. Does one plan offer home care and another not? Does one offer assisted living or other type of facility care and another does not? Is one plan non-qualified with an extra benefit eligibility trigger (medical necessity) and the other tax-qualified? Be sure the products being compared are essentially the same before deciding on whether one is more expensive than another.

If benefits are comparable, and the premium difference substantial (as the above $109 vs. $466 for a 40-year-old), one must be cautious again about insurers that are "buying" their way into the market by offering low premiums as an incentive. Because not long after buying one of the low-cost long-term care plans being offered around the country, individuals and couples may find themselves being faced with extremely high rate increases just a short 2-4 years into the policy and suddenly their low-cost bargain has priced them out of the market. If they are forced to drop coverage for affordability reasons, and have had a health problem that prevents them from then qualifying for a new plan, what service has been done for these people? To lose the coverage as they near the point of need after shelling out thousands in premium dollars is a deceitful practice, but one that is carried on by some insurers today.

How can you assess the likelihood of a future rate increase? Past history or lack of it can both be indicators of possible premium hikes ahead. As part of your analysis of an insurer, ask for the length of time the carrier has been marketing long-term care. If it's only a year or two, there's

A retired couple had bought a long-term care insurance policy as an element of their financial plan while they were still working. After they retired, their insurer raised premiums by 18% one year, 21% the next year and a comparable percentage in the year after that. They were on a fixed income and couldn't afford to carry on their policies. They admitted they had initially shopped for the lowest premium.[53]

good reason to be concerned, as the company has assembled no track record in either its pricing accuracy or its claims handling. If the company has priced the product too low, it may be scrambling to make it up quickly. On the other hand, if the company has five to ten years of experience or more, ask for its rate increase history. How many times has it raised premiums? By what percentage? For which policy series? If it's for an older series and the increase was a one-time adjustment of, say 12%, this may not be a problem. But if it's occurred more than once, and the rates adjusted upward early on in the policy series life (within the first 5 years), this is a carrier that is quite likely to raise rates, leaving clients stranded.

In Figure 2.10 is a copy of a flyer distributed in Florida regarding long-tem care insurance. The insurer distributing the information was comparing its product to one of the traditionally lower cost long-term care plans being marketed.

Figure 2.10

WE ARE THE COMPETITION
0 Day EP/$100 per day/Unlimited Benefit

	Low-Cost Insurer 1	Insurer Distributing Flyer
Age 65	$1,890	$1,431
Age 70	2,860	2,068
Age 75	4,480	3,226
Age 80	7,070	5,457

Same Benefits – Dade/Broward County

	Low-Cost Insurer 1	Insurer Distributing Flyer
Age 65	$2,060	$1,431
Age 70	3,100	2,068
Age 75	4,820	3,226
Age 80	7,570	5,457

Call for your starter kit and contract today.

Unquestionably, broker and client will be drawn to the presumably lowest rates in the industry. Is this a reasonable strategy? It all depends on how one estimates the chances of a future rate increase. There is no reason that one policy should be more than $2,000 less annually for the same coverage. The company listed on the left in the flyer is currently having some financial difficulties with this product line. What is the chance that the even lower priced competitor will repeat this experience? What will an advisor's credibility be like if a product recommendation results in a situation where an individual or couple have to drop coverage because of high rate increases?

This type of rate sensitivity is every bit as important to the client's ultimate well being as is knowing the differences between a tax-qualified and non-qualified policy. There is good reason to be concerned about the industry in light of the recent experience in both the health and disability income insurance product lines.

Quite simply, the lowest premium is almost always the wrong route to take in selecting a health insurance type of plan. Rate increases have been notorious in the health insurance field. Indeed, some analysts feel the insurance industry has lost its ability to successfully manage a health insurance product line today. In disability insurance, carriers were locked into long-term rate guarantees on their mispricing of these products and so they took an aggressive posture towards claims that has brought forth a record number of lawsuits contesting these narrow claim decisions. One hopes this is not what lies ahead in the future of the long-term care marketplace.

There are ways to legitimately keep your policy premium down, without attaching your star to an insurer that's priced its plan to take a bite out of market share. The first, as seen in the chart on the next page, is age. Buying the policy early may make more sense in the long run, even though the chances are you may not have the need for benefits so early. The key is a lower price due to age and an easier chance of qualifying medically for the coverage. Some average rates:

Long-Term Care Rates As You Age

Age at Purchase	Average Annual Premium
50	$ 736.00
55	877.00
60	1,169.00
65	1,704.00
70	2,646.00
75	4,466.00
80	7,280.00

Source: Weiss Rating, Inc.

As you can see, new business rates rise very rapidly once the individual reaches age 60. The younger buyer has the advantage of getting into the coverage early, and any future possible rate increases are going to be made against that initial low premium, minimizing the impact of that action. Even though the younger buyer pays premiums for a longer time over the life of the policy, it is still a good buy compared to the cost of waiting and eventually looking at a much higher premium – if the individual can even qualify.

Listed below is an example of a 45-year-old LTC insurance buyer contrasted with someone who waited until age 65 to purchase the coverage figuring he or she wouldn't have a need for long-term care services in those 20 years and could "save" some money.

Coverage: $130/day, 0 day EP, unlimited benefit period, simple inflation

At age 45: Annual premium: $1,182.35

At age 65: Annual premium: $3,463.59

Source: New business rates from a major LTC insurer

Assuming that both individuals require long-term care services beginning at age 85, we can measure the amount of premium paid prior to the need for benefit payments.

Simple calculation of premiums paid
(ignoring the time value of money)

Age 45: 40 years of premium payments = $47,294.00

Age 65: 20 years of premium payments = $69,271.80

On a simple basis, the number of years one is paying premiums is deceiving. Since the 45-year-old's premium payment was that much lower, the total payout isn't close. Even if you applied the time value of money principle, the 45-year-old will likely have made the better investment especially if coverage was needed or a health event occurred that affected insurability in the first 20 years of coverage.

However, this assumes that there would be no premium increases and that seems overly optimistic. Applying rate increases of 15% every 10 years, the 45-year-old still has a lower outlay despite having three rate increases to the 65-year-old's one rate increase:

Applying 15% rate increases every 10 years

Age 45: 40 years of premium payments = $59,040.10

Age 65: 20 years of premium payments = $74,471.00

There can be a cost for waiting – either in dollars or in the ability to purchase coverage or receive benefits, something that should help to motivate the younger buyer.

Inflation protection will also have a dramatic impact on rates, although as pointed out earlier, it's a vital part of the overall strategy to seek an alternative funding vehicle for these medical expenses. Long-term care insurance can become quickly outmoded unless care is taken to monitor the amount of coverage versus current charges for this type of treatment.

Figure 2.11 illustrates the rates of several insurers and the differences between purchasing a policy without inflation coverage versus one that has a 5% compounded inflation option:

Figure 2.11

TOTAL ANNUAL PREMIUM

	With Inflation	Without Inflation
Insurer 1	$1,670.00	$1,010.00
Insurer 2	2,047.00	1,073.00
Insurer 3	1,950.00	1,054.00
Insurer 4	1,251.00	834.00
Insurer 5	1,930.00	1,070.00
Insurer 6	1,798.00	1,097.00
Insurer 7	2,859.00	1,313.00
Insurer 8	2,561.00	1,366.00

Coverage: $100/day, 4-year BP, 30-100 day EP, age 65-year-old

Source: Weiss Ratings, Inc.

These policies all charge up front for the inflation protection option, meaning that there is no additional cost when the benefit is being increased each year. At the end of 10 years, a 5% compounded rider would have raised the $100/day benefit to $155/day after ten years (nine increases). Assuming there were no overall premium rate hikes, the annual premium would have remained the same.

Spousal discounts. There are discounts available that can reduce the premium. The most common of these is a spousal discount applicable when both husband and wife apply for coverage. This can help reduce the premium up to 10% and even higher, saving couples a substantial amount of money. Most carriers still allow the discount if, say, both apply for coverage and one is declined due to health history. The other applicant can still obtain the plan with the spouse discount even though his or her partner was not issued a policy.

There is a legitimate reason for insurers' generosity here. In its National Nursing Home Survey, the Center for Disease Control and the National Center for Health Statistics found a distinct difference in nursing home admissions based on family status.[54]

Average Length of Time Since Nursing Home Admission

Status	Number of years
Female	2.6
Male	2.3
Married	1.6
Single/Never Married	3.8
Widowed	2.3
Divorced/Separated	2.7

Clearly, there is the likelihood of a shorter claim for a married individual versus any other marital status. The obvious explanation is the presence of a caregiver spouse, who probably tended to the individual longer prior to any facility admission. As previously noted, this caregiver is usually female and the ability to tend to the partner's needs so as to keep him home longer contributed to the results noted above. These statistics have been relatively consistent for several years.

One last way to measure the value of the premium paid is through a Premium Recovery Chart. This illustration shows the number of days of facility care that it takes to equal the premiums paid in for the coverage. In the example below, the chart depicts the number of days, based on the daily benefit amount, required to recover the premiums paid. The daily benefit amount is assumed to have an inflation feature added that increases the benefit by 5% compounded each year. The calculation is based on an initial $100/day benefit, no elimination period, a lifetime benefit period and inflation protection.

Age at Issue	Annual Premium	Years That Premiums Are Paid					
		5	10	15	20	25	30
		Days to Recover Premiums Paid					
50	$1,410	58	91	107	112	109	103
55	1,785	73	115	135	141	138	130
60	2,030	84	131	154	161	157	148
65	2,840	116	183	215	225	220	207

Except for the 65-year-old, no other buyer listed above has to receive even six months of facility care to recover the premium paid in. Consider the nursing home statistics that indicate the majority of admissions going on Medicaid within similar time frames and long-term care insurance holds up well as an alternative funding vehicle for this need. This example is yet another in which it might pay to consider adding the coverage as a wealth protection instrument in one's 40s or 50s.

While the example above does not consider the possibility of premium increases in the higher number of premium years, it does indicate the high cost of long-term care versus the low cost of protecting against the possibility with long-term care insurance.

DUE DILIGENCE

"We're all in this alone."

– Lily Tomlin

So you understand the need. You have a good grasp of the basics in plan design and the various items that should or can be included and what effect these benefits have on the overall price. But is this enough? What other questions are important in the overall planning process to complete the long-term care sale and then to retain the individual as a client in the future, monitoring lifestyle changes to be prepared to adapt any LTC insurance coverage accordingly? This product is sensitive to changes – a physical move by the insured to another part of the state or another state entirely, health problems, rate increases and their implications, and tax and legislative changes that may be forthcoming. This is one of the primary reasons for annual reviews – to check for changes and make any appropriate adjustments. This will be even more important as retirement living changes in the future.

Listed below are a number of questions that should be explored both during a sale and after policy delivery as a means of distinguishing important changes that will affect this vital coverage.

1. Where is the individual likely to be when he or she might begin accessing long-term care services?

2. What are the average LTC costs (nursing home, assisted living facility, home health care) for this specific area?

3. What does "tax-qualified" mean?

4. Does the individual understand the difference between non-qualified and tax-qualified plans?

Demographers see the "halfback" moving trend [i.e., retirees who moved to Florida from the north and are now moving half way back to North and South Carolina and Tennessee] as a sign that the nation's retirement patterns are changing. According to recent Census data, fewer than 5% of Americans ages 60 and older move out of state. But as the nation's Boomers near retirement age, experts predict that retirees will become more mobile. Boomers are expected to live longer and retire earlier. A higher proportion of them are likely to be in a high-income bracket when they retire and more of them are expected to move more than once during their retirement.[55]

5. How long has the insurer been marketing long-term care plans and administering long-term care claims?

6. What is the rate renewal history of the insurer in the health insurance business – long-term care, disability income, health insurance?

7. What type of care and living arrangements best suit the individual?

8. What kind of budget does the individual have for wealth protection vehicles like long-term care insurance?

9. How are "activities of daily living" defined in the policy?

10. How are the coverage and facility options defined?

11. Why are two (or more) seemingly similar products priced so differently?

12. Does the product offer a daily, weekly or monthly home care benefit?

13. Is there claims-management language that places a limitation on the individual's care options?

14. Does the individual have a liquid asset that might be made available, in whole or in part, to pay for long-term care on a lump-sum basis?

15. Are there rate acceleration options to pay up the policy early?

16. What financial obligations are looming in the individual's future?

17. Does the individual have any major health conditions?

This due diligence is necessary and critical to make the proper need diagnosis and recommend the proper solution. Failure to understand the policies or the insurers or the clients involved can mean mistakes will be made that can have consequences for these individuals in need of wealth protection.

Figure 2.12

TO OUR VALUED FLORIDA SALES FORCE:

"As part of our overall capital restructuring plan, we have deemed it appropriate to discontinue the issuance of new business in certain of our key states in order to decrease the strain on surplus. Therefore, effective immediately, we will not be accepting any applications for new business in the state of Florida that are completed and dated after _____. We will continue to accept any insurance applications that were completed and dated on or prior to _____. We are taking this action according to Florida statutes sections 624.4095(1) and 624.408.

"We expect that this restriction will last only as long as it takes for us to address our capital needs as approved by the Florida Department of Insurance and are hopeful that we will be writing new business again in Florida in the near future.

"We are grateful for your support and understanding."

What does a financial advisor do when the notice in Figure 2.12 arrives in the mail? Does one tell present policyholders that their insurer is no longer accepting new applications? Do you seek immediately to switch the insured policyholders to another insurer? What if they are unable to change due to the inability now to qualify medically? Does one take a chance that the insured will ultimately have some protection under the state guaranty funds? Should you prepare the client in the event that letter is forthcoming or do you ride it out in the event that financial circumstances change for the better for this insurer?

Difficult questions that may have been avoided if one did due diligence a bit better or prepared clients in advance for this possibility because of the aggressive nature of the carrier. No one in the industry wants to see a long-term care insurer taken into receivership. But there are carriers taking broad risks out there in terms of pricing and underwriting philosophy that may seem terrific from a marketing standpoint today and a disaster for your clients in the future.

This is why the due diligence portion of your homework is just as important as the financial assessment and recommendation you make. You are the one with the background in the insurance industry and the supposed ability to distinguish a solid carrier from a riskier one.

The use of waivers and releases as a form of disclosure with your clients is becoming a common due diligence practice. These forms may have no legal foundation, but they do serve to advise a client of the potential consequences of a decision. In addition, some insurers are requiring a *Personal Worksheet* from the agent or broker submitting a long-term care insurance application that the applicant must sign, indicating an understanding of some of the broader issues involved here.

These types of forms are shown in Figures 2.13, 2.14, and 2.15.

Figure 2.13

NON-QUALIFIED LONG-TERM CARE COVERAGE WAIVER

My agent, _____, has explained to me the differences between tax-qualified long-term care and non-qualified long-term care insurance contracts.

I understand that the purchase of a non-qualified long-term care insurance contract could result in adverse tax consequences for me. Further, my agent has advised that only policies for which specific tax standards have been issued are tax-qualified contracts. I understand that no tax clarification has yet been given to non-qualified plans.

After considering these factors, I have elected to purchase a non-qualified long-term care insurance policy. My agent has explained the possible adverse tax consequences and the final decision to purchase the non-qualified long-term care insurance plan was mine and mine alone.

_____   _____
Signature   Date

_____
Printed name of applicant

_____   _____
Witness #1 signature   Witness #2 signature

Figure 2.14

LONG TERM CARE PERSONAL WORKSHEET [56]

People buy long-term care insurance for a variety of reasons. These reasons include to avoid spending assets for long-term care, to make sure there are choices regarding the type of care received, to protect family members from having to pay for care, or to decrease the chances of going on Medicaid. However, long-term care insurance can be expensive, and is not appropriate for everyone. Please complete this worksheet to help you and the insurance company determine whether you should buy this policy.

Premium: The annual cost of this coverage you are considering will be $ _____.

NOTE: The company has the right to increase premiums in the future.
Have you considered whether you could afford to keep this policy if the premiums
were raised, for example, by 20%? _____ yes

Income: Where will the money come from to pay each premium payment?

____ Income   ____ Savings   ____ Family members

What is your annual income? ___ under $10,000   ____ $10-20,000

____ $20-30,000   ____ $30-50,000   ____ Over $50,000

How do you expect your income to change over the next 10 years?

____ No change   ____ Increase   _____ Decrease

Note: If you will be paying premiums with money received only from your own income, a rule of thumb is that you may not be able to afford this policy if the premiums will be more than 7% of your income.

Savings and Investments: Not counting your home, what is the approximate value of all your assets (savings and investments)?

___ under $20,000   ___ $20,000-30,000   ____ 30,000-50,000   ____ Over $50,000

How do you expect your assets to change over the next 10 years?

___ Stay the same   ____ Increase   ____ Decrease

NOTE: If you are buying this policy to protect your assets and these assets are less than $30,000, you may wish to consider other financing options for your long-term care needs.

_____ The information provided above accurately describes my financial situation.

_____ I choose not to complete this form, but do wish to purchase this coverage.

Signed: _____   _____
                    Applicant   Date

____ I explained the importance of completing this information.

Signed: _____   _____
                    Agent   Date

STATEMENT: My agent has advised me that this policy does not appear to be suitable for me. However, I still want the company to consider my application for long-term care insurance.

SIGNED: _____   _____
                    Applicant   Date

Figure 2.15
LIABILITY RELEASE FORM

Note: Please review this form and sign your name. As a professional and ethical insurance agent, I have covered the reasons why I feel it is important that you protect yourself with this coverage. However, at this time you are choosing not to protect yourself with long-term care insurance. This form requires your signature in the event that, at some point in the future, the need for long-term care services arises and this interview is not remembered. It will serve as a reminder that we did discuss the alternative of financing your wealth protection needs with long-term care insurance.

DATE: _____

CLIENT: _____

ADDRESS _____

PHONE: _____

AGENT: _____

Long-Term Care Insurance Plan Presented _____

I acknowledge that on the above date I was presented information about long-term care insurance, including both facility and home care. Also explained to me were: (1) how long term care benefits work; (2) the cost for the long-term care insurance coverage; (3) why this coverage is important as a wealth protection vehicle; and (4) the potential costs I may face in the future for long-term care.

Even though I may want coverage at a later date, I acknowledge that on the above date I am choosing NOT to protect myself with long-term care insurance. (If a couple is applying, use one form for each person.)

PRINT NAME: _____

SIGNATURE: _____

AGENT NAME: _____

SIGNATURE: _____

_____ Client will not sign form.

AGENT SIGNATURE: _____

These forms are generally self-explanatory and will prove useful to you in your efforts to provide wealth protection to those who need it. You will not close every sale and you will have individuals who want the coverage despite a lack of need as well as those who want to buy non-qualified coverage. The documents here cover all of these possibilities and are part of your own due diligence efforts.

> "What most people do not realize is that America's long-term care service delivery and financing system is a disastrous mess. Seven major nursing facility chains have declared Chapter 11 bankruptcy. Between 10 and 20% of all nursing home beds in the country are in bankrupt facilities today. Hundreds of home health agencies have gone under financially. Many new assisted living facilities are filling far more slowly than anticipated. Long-term care stock prices are down precipitously. New capitalization by debt or equity is almost non-existent for publicly held long-term care companies. Caregivers are in desperately short supply, whether they are low-wage nurses' aides in long-term care facilities or unpaid friends and family in private homes. Formal long-term care services are too expensive for most Americans to afford, but Medicare and Medicaid pay too little to assure quality home care or nursing home care. Litigation against nursing homes and assisted living facilities for providing allegedly poor care is on the rise and is driving liability premiums through the roof. Only 7% of seniors and virtually none of the baby boomers own private insurance that could help them pay the catastrophic cost of long-term care. America's gigantic and rapidly aging baby-boom generation guarantees that the challenge of long-term care will become greater and far more expensive with time. As of now, long-term care is well on its way to trumping Social Security and Medicare as our country's most challenging social problem."[57]

The challenge has been issued. There is much to do to prepare people for the financial burdens of long-term care expenses. For many, long-term care insurance is a way out of the emotional and monetary landmines that this largely unfunded medical service represents. How well we succeed as an industry may very well dictate the type of 21st Century we will all have.

Long-Term Care Underwriting

Ultimately, underwriting is the key to success for any insurance product line. Sure, it helps to have solid pricing strategies and a well-trained sales force, but often the bottom line results rest with the faceless individuals who turn thumbs up or down on the applicant whose paperwork you've sent in for long-term care insurance coverage.

Long-term care products as they currently exist are less than two decades old. This is not much time to accumulate much reliable experience on this risk, and this puts underwriters on unfamiliar ground. Insurers are feeling their way through this, trying to develop guidelines for preferred risks on down to high substandard applicants.

Underwriting begins with the typical informational tools at hand. These are the application itself, medical records, cognitive testing, telephone assessments and personal history interviews. From time to time, a paramedical exam or other diagnostic test may prove helpful in quantifying this risk.

"The probability of needing some type of paid care increases rapidly with age. For example, the probability of a male having a qualifying nursing home admission is only about 1 in 1,000 at age 45, but shoots to about 60 in 1,000 at age 85. In addition, a person's perception of his or her potential need for LTC also increases dramatically with age. The end result is that, in the individual market, most LTC sales are to the elderly (average issue age in the 60s). This self-selection makes the underwriting process that much more critical, since it is estimated that as many as 15 to 25% of the over-age-65 group are uninsurable for long-term care.[58]

The applications are very specific to the risk being assessed. This is where the agent can help out all concerned by having this completed properly and in detail. The medical history is pointedly directed at the likelihood of a future long-term care need and is important to fill out in full since it generally foregoes the need for a paramedical exam. Medical records can reveal as much as one wants to know about the risk, especially if there is a history of a degenerative disorder that promises to worsen in the future. Both the telephone and personal interviews are tools that can identify some cognitive difficulties by asking specific questions designed to unearth this risk. Generally, a geriatric nurse is very capable of recognizing a potential problem when seeing or hearing it. All of this information is assembled and then evaluated with an eye towards assigning it to an underwriting class or declining the case.

Underwriters will also tap into the Medical Information Bureau (MIB) for assistance in determining the risk involved. Of the more than 80 conditions that were identified as posing potentially significant situations in the underwriting of long-term care insurance, the MIB has codes on 70 of them. This enables underwriters to see codes on a particular applicant that may indicate some health history of concern. They would then check their paperwork to see if that information has been disclosed and, if not, initiate a search to obtain the medical records on the condition. This MIB check has a "protective value" to the underwriter. Protective value is the ratio of dollars spent finding information to the net present value of claims saving as a result of this checking. A 50:1 protective value means that for every $1.00 spent in this form of underwriting work, a $50 savings can potentially result for uncovering a physical or emotional condition that may have presented itself as a future claim.[59]

Cognitive testing can be especially significant in setting the proper risk quotient for a long-term care applicant. The elderly are at a significant risk for depression and a proper set of questions asked by phone or in person can actually pinpoint whether this disorder is present in the applicant. It is an under-recognized emotional problem that can affect the mental and physical health of an individual.

*Underwriting
Cognitive Screens*

- *Short Portable Mental Status Questionnaire – a series of 10 questions designed to test a person's orientation as to time and place.*
- *the Mini-Mental State Exam – the most widely used test*
- *the TICS – Telephone Interview Cognitive Status exam*
- *the Cognistat – a longer exam with independently scored subtests*
- *the Delayed Word Recall Test*
- *the 7-Minute Screen*
- *the Minnesota Cognitive Acuity Screen – a recently developed tool that incorporates the Delayed Word Recall test and appears to have high reliability.[60]*

Depression is recognized to be the most common psychiatric condition seen in individuals over age 65. The incidence of depression in individuals over the age of 65 who live independently and require no assistance in any activities of daily living is estimated to be at 10 to 15%. This percentage rises sharply among the institutionalized elderly, reaching as high as 25 to 30%. There are any number of signs that can point to this risk, including poor self-care, social withdrawal, weight loss or gain and insomnia.[61] As the individual in contact with the person and doing the proper field underwriting, you are in a position to help to assess this situation and assist the underwriter in identifying this possible risk.

Underwriters have to take this information and determine what kind of risk the applicant represents and act on it, assigning the individual to a risk classification where premium and benefits may be affected. It helps the underwriter when a variety of product types are available. The insured may not qualify for a comprehensive long-term care plan, for example, but perhaps can be issued a facility-only plan, or a tax-qualified plan instead of a non-qualified one.

Part of the accumulation of experience is to be able to compartmentalize various medical conditions as being from not that much of a risk all the way to high risk or uninsurable situations. As claims experience develops, underwriting will become somewhat easier and should result in a less conservative approach. Already, the pricing of long-term care products figures underwriting to be less than normally effective due to the unknown risk some conditions represent. Perhaps as information becomes clearer about the pricing versus claims experience, the premium determinations will be more confidently calculated. Already, the Society of Actuaries have noted a substantially high persistency on this product, much better than the pricing of the policy reflects. But the February 2001 findings show that lapses can reach an ultimate level around 2% very quickly. This should start to show up in pricing in the near future.[62]

Claims

It's a heady time in the long-term care business. Long-term care sales are beginning to increase and in-force cases are still relatively new and claims experience is great. But it should be, being that many of the policies are in an early duration stage. Since long-term care policies are disability-triggered for claims, it makes sense that if there was any decent underwriting involved at all, claims would be low in the early years. Traditionally, for disability policies, it takes about 7-10 years for the true experience on a block of business to emerge. So, today's optimism can easily yield to industry problems in the future once the experience shakes out for the insurers writing the largest amounts of premium. Agents can call for more liberal underwriting and lower rates today because there is no experience yet to contradict them. But it's coming, and let's hope that these important products have been priced with reasonable accuracy.

Improved underwriting experience has helped keep claims in check to date, but as in health and disability insurance, future claimants will learn better how to utilize their policies and claims will exponentially increase. How well insurers have anticipated this will soon be seen as claims reach a peak for the 1993-96 business shortly. It is hoped that past experience in the health markets will not be indicative of the future claims results. Both the industry and the consumer public need this financing alternative to work properly for the good of all.

"We got out of this market because we didn't believe that there was a way of underwriting long-term care," says a spokesperson for a former LTC insurer. "In our view, long-term care lends itself to social underwriting. There are different forms of social underwriting and unfortunately this lends itself to false claims."

This type of social underwriting, typically with permissive standards for large groups, will happen with long-term care because the triggers for benefits – the inability to perform specified activities of daily living – are set low and can be arbitrary.[63]

For the moment the industry number-crunchers can step forward and take a bow. The claims experience is running remarkably close to predicted results despite a dearth of information about claims types and durations. As noted, many of the poorer risks were caught in the underwriting process. This has helped produce the numbers, shown in Figure 2.16 from years 1992 to 1998, as provided by Milliman & Robertson, Inc. from NAIC compiled data.[64]

Figure 2.16

NAIC LTC EXPERIENCE EXHIBITS: CUMULATIVE EXPERIENCE

Cumulative Through Calendar Yr.	Premiums Earned (Millions)	Claims Incurred (Millions)	Loss Ratio	Actual to Expected Ratio
1992	$ 3,180	$ 958	30.1%	99.7%
1993	5,290	1,685	31.8%	104.5%
1994	7,211	2,351	32.6%	103.8%
1995	9,509	3,113	32.7%	102.8%
1996	12,727	4,094	32.2%	97.0%
1997	16,079	5,198	32.3%	94.4%
1998	21,112	7,012	33.2%	94.6%

NAIC LTC EXPERIENCE EXHIBITS: RESULTS BY DURATION

Calendar Duration	Premiums Earned Incurred (Millions)	Claims Incurred (Millions)	Loss Ratio	Actual to Expected Ratio	Ratio
0	$3,792	$ 540	14.3%	89.6%	
1	4,856	1,033	21.3%	100.0%	
2	3,628	1,083	29.9%	104.4%	
3	2,654	1,004	37.8%	104.3%	
4	1,985	873	44.0%	100.4%	
5-9	3,960	2,273	57.4%	90.1%	
10+	237	205	86.6%	79.6%	
TOTALS	$21,112	$7,012	33.2%	94.6%	

There's many a collective breath being held about the next 5-7 years of claims results. If the industry can weather the storm in this period, there will be a huge confidence surge in the long-term future of the long-term care business.

Footnotes

1. Jesse R. Slome, "More LTC Sales: As Easy as 1,2,3," *Life Insurance Selling* (April, 2000), p. 136.

2. "Profile of General Demographic Characteristics:2000," U.S. Census Bureau, Census 2000.

3. Headlines from *The Villages Daily Sun*, March 31, 2001, p. 1.

4. Carroll Busher, "Agents: Sell LTC Policies to Women," *National Underwriter*, Life & Health/Financial Services Edition, April 30, 2001, p. 11.

5. "Profile of General Demographic Characteristics:2000," U.S. Census Bureau, Census 2000.

6. Mark Francis, "Market Segmentation Key to LTC Sales," *National Underwriter*, Life & Health/Financial Services Edition, May 10, 1999, p. 22.

7. "What the Public Wants to Know," *National Underwriter*, Life & Health/Financial Services Edition, January 22, 2001, p. 34.

8. "Talking About Growing Older: The Last Taboo?" *PR Newswire*, May 1, 2001.

9. Rosemary Carlson, "Caring for Elderly Loved Ones without Going Broke," *Bankrate.com*, March 29, 2001.

10. "Older People Living Alone," from a U.S. Administration on Aging report called *The Many Faces of Aging*, www.aoa.gov, March 29, 2001.

11. "The Pitfalls of Medicaid Planning," *Associated Press*, December 15, 1999.

12. Phyllis Shelton, "Framing the Conversation," *Financial Planning* (September, 2000), pp. 170, 172.

13. Linda Koco, "Reaching for Younger LTC Buyers is Starting to Pay Off," *National Underwriter*, Life & Health/Financial Services Edition, February 12, 2001, p. 31.

14. "The Cost of Long-Term Care," *SmartMoney.com*, March 29, 2001.

15. "Long Term Care Insurance," from California Office of Statewide Health Planning and Development (March, 2001).

16. "Caregiving Sacrifices Personal Lives and Careers," *PR Newswire*, May 15, 2001.

17. "Caregiving Employees Stay in Workforce Twice as Long When Long-Term Care Insurance is in Place for Care Recipient," *Business Wire*, April 20, 2001.

18. Mary Williams Walsh, "Leaving Jobs not an Option for Many," *Fort Lauderdale Sun Sentinel*, March 11, 2001, pp. 1G, 3G.

19. "54 Million Americans Involved in Family Caregiving Last Year, Double the Previously Reported Figure," *National Family Caregivers Association News Release*, March 29, 2001.

20. "Rules Give Corporations Attractive Tax Advantages to Buy Long-Term Care Insurance," *Business Wire*, February 27, 2001.

21.   Stephanie Armour, "Employers Stepping Up in Elder Care: More Workers Taking Care of Aging Relatives," USAToday.com, August 3, 2000.

22.   Shelia M. Poole, "Elder Care Reshaping Workplace," *Daytona Beach Sunday News-Journal*, 2000.

23.   "Medicare is Paying Less and Less," from American Independent Marketing monthly newsletter *Road Runner.*

24.   "Medicare Skilled Nursing Facility Prospective Payment System Threatens Seniors' Access to Needed and Appropriate Medications," *PR Newswire*, April 28, 1999.

25.   Horace B. Deets, "Health Insurance is the Key to Successful Aging," from an *AARP Bulletin*, 2000.

26.   Harley Gordon, "LTC Financing and Your Business," *Advisor Today* (February, 2000), p. 110.

27.   James Lubitz, "Three Decades of Health Care Use by the Elderly, 1965-1998," *Health Affairs* (March/April, 2001), p. 19.

28.   Nelda McCall, et al., "Medicare Home Health Before and After the BBA," *Health Affairs* (May/June, 2001), p. 189.

29.   "American Health Care Association Applauds Introduction of Medicare Rehabilitation Act," *PR Newswire*, May 28, 1999.

30.   Nelda McCall, et al., "Medicare Home Health Before and After the BBA," *Health Affairs* (May/June, 2001), p. 189.

31.   "Banks Block Sun Healthcare Payments," *Associated Press*, June 2, 1999.

32.   "HHS Proposes Changes Allowing States to Expand Medicaid Coverage," *HHS News*, U.S. Department of Health and Human Services Web site (www.hhs.gov/news), October 27, 2000.

33.   Edward T. Pound, "Loophole Draining Medicaid," *USA Today*, August 21, 2000, pp. 1A, 7A.

34.   Laura Meckler, "Administration to Confront Medicaid Loophole," *Associated Press*, March 26, 2001.

35.   "Medicaid Upper Payment Limits," *NCSL State Health Policy Brief* (March, 2001), p. 2.

36.   "LTC Bullet: Medicaid Estate Recovery," *LTC Bullets*, provided by the Center for Long-Term Care Financing, November 8, 2000.

37.   "LTC Bullet: Medicaid Estate Recoveries Clarified by HCFA," *LTC Bullets*, provided by the Center for Long-Term Care Financing, March 7, 2001.

38.   "HCFA OKs Estate Recovery of Annuity Proceeds," from American Independent Marketing's newsletter *Road Runner* (Summer, 2000), p. 1.

39.   Melynda Dovel Wilcox, "Will Nursing Home Bills Haunt Your Estate?" *Kiplinger's Personal Finance Magazine* (April, 1998), pp. 115, 116-118.

40.   Kimberly Lankford, "Do You Have Enough Long-Term Care Coverage," *Kiplinger.com* (March, 2001).

41.   Kim Purnell, "Specialization Key to Addressing LTC Complexity," *National Underwriter*, Life & Health/Financial Services Edition, June 14, 1999, pp. 29-30.

42.   "ADLs/IADLs Assessment Measures," from *arcmesa.com* Web site.

43.   Claude Thau, "Two Little Words Can Spell All the Difference in LTC Contracts," *National Underwriter*, Life & Health/Financial Services Edition, May 7, 2001, pp. 26, 29.

44.   *Ibid.*

45. Cecily Fraser, "Extending the Limits of 55-plus," *CBS MarketWatch.com*, May 18, 2001.

46. Paul Recer, "Elderly Americans Seem to Thrive," *Associated Press*, May 7, 2001.

47. "The Gray Charade," from *SmartMoney.com*, April 5, 2001.

48. Howard Carver and Michael Berne, "Assisted Living Market Could Mean Strong ROI for Insurers," *National Underwriter*, Life & Health/Financial Services Edition, May 10, 1999, pp. 33, 34.

49. "The Gray Charade," from *SmartMoney.com*, April 5, 2001.

50. Glen A. Levit, "Long Term Care Insurance and Assisted Living Facilities," *Health Insurance Underwriter* (July/August, 2000), p. 33.

51. "Study Finds Rising Long-Term Care Costs, Demographics Will Make 'Aging in Place' Harder Than Boomers Think," *PR Newswire*, April 26, 2000.

52. James M. Glickman, "A Long-Term Commitment," *Best's Review* (October, 2000), pp. 137, 138.

53. Ron Panko, "Good for the Long Term?," *Best's Review* (March, 2000), p. 97.

54. "Nursing Homes," *AARP Research Center* (March, 2001).

55. Haya El Nasser, "Meeting Retirement Halfway," *USA Today*, August 31, 2000, p. 3A.

56. *Long Term Care Insurance Personal Worksheet*, from Bankers United Life Insurance Company.

57. Stephen A. Moses, "Long-Term Care Due Diligence for Professional Advisors," The Center for Long-Term Care Financing, (March, 2001).

58. Dawn E. Helwig, "Underwriting Individual Long-Term Care Insurance," *Disability Newsletter*, published by Milliman & Robertson, Inc. (September, 1999), p. 1.

59. Robert S. Littell, "New Advances in LTCI Underwriting," *Health Insurance Underwriter* (April, 2000), pp. 41, 42.

60. Dawn E. Helwig, "Underwriting Individual Long-Term Care Insurance," *Disability Newsletter*, published by Milliman & Robertson, Inc. (September, 1999), pp. 4-5.

61. Lisa Duckett, "Depression in the Elderly Raises Life Underwriting Issues," *National Underwriter*, Life & Health/Financial Services Edition, November 1, 1999, p. 7.

62. Gary L. Corliss, "The State of Long-Term Care Insurance," *Florida Agent* (April, 2001), p. 16.

63. Ron Panko, "Long-Term Scare," *Best's Review* (March, 2001), p. 82.

64. Dawn E. Helwig and Michael S. Abroe, "LTC Industry Experience: Is It on Track?" *Disability Newsletter*, published by Milliman & Robertson, Inc. (October, 2000), p. 7.

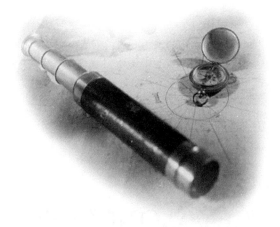

PART THREE:
WHICH PRODUCT

"An expert is a person who has made all the mistakes that can be made in a very narrow field."

– Niels Bohr

Key Concepts

Understanding

- the essential differences between TQ and NQ plans,

- the other key provisions of long-term care policies,

- the various alternative ways of covering long-term care through the use of life insurance and annuity coverage, and

- group long-term care trends.

A WORLD OF OPPORTUNITY

"'If we do not change how we deal with long-term care, we are going to have a crisis,' says Florida's secretary of elder affairs. 'We will have more elders, no infrastructure for alternative care, and nursing homes will continue to absorb the biggest part of our budget.' Originally designed as a short-term solution for the endgame of life, nursing homes have become long-term residences for a population extending the limits of old age. At the same time, community and home-based programs that would allow more old people to maintain their independence and dignity have been shortchanged by lawmakers, the secretary said. To avoid an oncoming catastrophe in long-term care in the 21st Century, the Florida Legislature is contemplating some fundamental changes in the way Florida cares for its oldest population. If the increasing usage of long-term care services continues as it has for the last 15 years, Florida will spend an additional $3 billion in tax money for long-term care in the next 10 years."[1]

Florida is not alone. Most states are coping with the financial consequences of older Americans unprepared for their long-term care needs. Florida simply has an older population base than most states and is on the leading edge of the problem; an impending crisis that could be eased by the availability of long-term care insurance as a legitimate financial funding tool to help with the burden of these oppressive expenses.

Long-term care products have been around in some form for over 35 years. Today's current design has been around for more than a decade (excluding the definitional changes made by the Health Insurance Portability and Accountability Act of 1996 – HIPAA), yet very few people will be able to rely on insurance for funding all or a portion of their long-term care need.

Arguably the best long-term care sales year was 1996, aided in large part by the fire sale that went on before HIPAA regulations took effect in 1997. Sales were up 17% in 1996 over the previous year. In 1997, sales went up only 11% and in 1998 the sales increase was around 7%. Many reasons were given for these lackluster results, including the public's lack of knowledge about the product, complex government regulations that make the coverage difficult and time-consuming for agents to explain to prospects, and a shortage of agents willing to devote the time necessary to sell these complicated policies.[2]

Perhaps it's the latter excuse that is the more telling. A great number of agents have, and likely always will, shy away from a health insurance type product. It's too complex, many say, and its these intricacies that can get agents or advisors in trouble if they don't explain the products properly. I've heard the same comments for over 25 years from planners who prefer to stay in a comfort zone with what they know, rather than trying to fill out the rest of the needs their clients have. Most of the excuses are in their own self-interest. Rarely do you hear any real concern about their clients' potential future problems with regard to their health. Even if these agents or advisors would simply find a referral for their clients' long-term care needs, it would greatly help their clients and save the agents or advisors from dealing with the issue themselves.

Long-term care insurance has to be sold. Rarely do people seek you out on this coverage, even if they know the risks involved. Talking about being sick or hurt in the future is the least favorite topic to discuss especially if you're a healthy person. Yet this is what agents must do – motivate people to consider the future. The need is not that difficult to pin down; it's getting the client to take the next step and apply for a policy. It hasn't helped that the health insurance industry has a deserved reputation for volatility. Experienced agents have seen health companies come and go and many believe this could be the fate of a number of long-term care insurers, too. Some of the early industry consolidation that has been happening, along with increasingly negative publicity about insurers raising rates on in-force business, has only served to confirm those underlying fears.

The year 1999 was a reasonably better one from the standpoint of long-term care insurance sales. Premium revenue from new sales to individuals and associations rose 13% to $900 million.[5] The top five public carriers all reported double-digit gains. It has never been all that easy to track long-term care sales as insurers have opted for different ways to help consumers deal with their long-term care needs. Long-term care products are not only sold on a stand-alone basis, but as part of a life insurance and annuity policy as well. This diversified approach addresses clients of all financial shapes and sizes. It has also helped bring more agents into the mix, as those comfortable with the life or annuity sale are able to add long-term care to it without having to travel too far afield from their base of knowledge. Expanded distribution was felt to be responsible for the recent up-tick in long-term care sales, a trend one hopes will continue.

Richard Lehman, 47, remembers the day his friend Jim, also 47, had a massive stroke and ran through his family's finances. Lehman said the experience was a wake-up call. "I decided I needed to get my life in order. I run a successful business, but you can have all the money in the world and an illness can wipe it out." So he bought long-term care insurance for his wife and himself. He's glad he can afford to pay for the policies to protect the rest of his assets.[3]

G.E. Financial Assurance Holdings, Inc. has announced an agreement to acquire 90% of Citigroup Inc.'s long-term care insurance business. The agreement would also give GE the ability to sell long-term care insurance through Travelers, Citibank, Primerica and other Citigroup units. GE and Citigroup announced their deal just three months after John Hancock Financial Services, Inc, Boston, agreed to acquire Fortis, Inc.'s LTC unit.[4]

Long-term care represents a healthy growth market for insurance companies that can help them strengthen their ratings while gaining an edge against competitors in financial services, according to Standard & Poor's. In selling traditional products like annuities and term insurance, carriers and their agents compete with rival financial services. LTC allows them to take advantage of their established position as protection providers. "LTC stands out as a product that insurers can provide better than competing industry sectors because it requires not just asset management expertise but also the ability to underwrite, sell and manage a long-term care protection-based product," said Standard & Poor's.[6]

Many analysts saw 1999 as more of a transformational year than the years preceding it. Some large insurers bowed out while others joined the marketing fray. There was consolidation as acquisitions were a faster way for some insurers to grow their market share, even if not ultimately as profitable. Competition had increased substantially, not only between stand-alone long-term care products but with a growing number of alternative product combination types using life insurance and annuities. State regulators continued to maintain a close watch on the activities in this market and concerns about rate stability had begun to yield to specific statutory action. Experienced insurers monitored their underwriting and claims experience amidst cautions not to get carried away with competitive concerns.[7] The disability insurance industry had already been down this well-traveled path and had not fared well.

Product development has begun to focus on features that would appeal to an entire family, realizing that it's not just the afflicted insured that has needs during a long-term care event, but those immediate family members in attendance. As previously noted, long-term care has a far-reaching impact on more people than the person in need of assistance. Encouraging people to look to their own homes for care and providing training and dollars to family members for caregiving has been a way of addressing this multi-person need, while focusing on the potentially more economically efficient community-type care rather than an emphasis on resident facilities.

The insurance industry has some public relations problems. Market conduct is a serious issue. Educational gaps are a major problem. Commodity-type products that place more emphasis on commissions than on policyholder value do a disservice to the consuming public. The industry may well have forever fouled up the financing of health care through an insurance product. It is badly in need of a product that can truly be viewed as doing some good. Long-term care insurance, in its many forms, is just such a product.

- It may well serve a senior population previously victimized by Medicare Supplement abuses.

- It may create a safety net for assets that people will definitely need as they live longer and longer.

- It has the potential to relieve the financial pressures being placed on the shoulders of the Medicare and Medicaid programs.

In other words, this is the product that presents the industry with an image-changing opportunity. The market for this coverage will only increase in huge numbers over the next three decades. Long-term care insurance can be the standard bearer for an industry in search of a more presentable identity. The key is to convince individuals of the need, if any, and then select the best products to suit individual needs. The ultimate difference it will make will not be felt for some time. But, in the final analysis, this product could mean more to people and affect many more lives positively than anything else the industry markets in the 21st Century.

The long-term care insurance product – which one should you choose? Obviously, the one that best fits your client's situation. This section points out all of the possibilities you have of selecting the proper funding vehicle for an individual. The key is to create enough opportunities for yourself to make this selection a reality.

Tax-Qualified vs.
Non-Qualified Plans

"You can observe a lot just by watching."
                                        – Yogi Berra

For a number of years, consumers, financial advisors, agents and insurers repeatedly called for a clarification of the tax benefits of long-term care insurance policies. Year after year, many Congressional representatives introduced legislation that would generally place long-term care under "accident and sickness" policies for tax purposes. This would create a greater market for employer-based long-term care that had never really lifted off the ground due to the questionability of tax deductibility.

In 1996, this persistence was rewarded with LTC tax clarification that was part of a broader Act dealing with a number of health insurance related issues. This was the Health Insurance Portability and Accountability Act (HIPAA) that began a seemingly never-ending dialogue among these same consumers, financial advisors, agents and insurers over the effects of this federal legislation. For, by formally defining long-term care insurance, the government has created more confusion about this product than it may have intended, and opened up a gap between the new tax-qualified plans and the pre-HIPAA policies, now labeled as non-qualified plans.

What's happened since the HIPAA legislation passed in 1996?

First, there was a fire sale on the now non-qualified "triple trigger" policies that, at least on the surface, offer more ways to qualify for benefits. In the last quarter of 1996, the industry enjoyed its finest sales quarter ever as agents and financial advisors rushed consumers into a decision to purchase what they viewed as a better policy while it was still able to be grandfathered as a "tax-qualified" plan.

Second, people in the industry began to line up on either side of the policy fence. One side argued that tax-qualified plans were better

Figure 3.1

A QUICK OVERVIEW

Tax-Qualified Plans

The 1996 Health Insurance and Portability Act (HIPAA) created a new tax code for long-term care and new language for a tax-qualified long-term care insurance policy. This law established what long-term care policies would be treated on a tax-favored basis, from tax-free payment of proceeds to deductibility of premiums. These are the key features of tax-qualified plans.

Chronically ill: To be a tax-qualified plan under this legislation, benefits must be paid only to chronically ill individuals. There are currently two ways to qualify as chronically ill:

1. inability to perform, without substantial assistance (including standby assistance) from another individual, at least 2 out of 6 activities of daily living (ADLs) due to a loss of functional activity that will last at least 90 days in length, OR

2. require substantial supervision to protect the individual from threats to health and safety due to a severe cognitive impairment.

The six ADLS are: eating, bathing, dressing, toileting, transferring and continence.

Benefit Proceeds: Benefit payments under a tax-qualified plan are distributed income tax-free.

Individual Premium Deductibility: Premiums paid for this coverage may be tax-deductible if the insured itemizes medical expenses (exceed 7.5% of adjusted gross income). If so, there are also maximum deduction limits, changing each year. For 2001:

> Age 40 or younger . . . .$ 230
>
> Age 41 – 50 430
>
> Age 51 - 60 860
>
> Age 61 – 70 2,290
>
> Age 71 or older 2,860

Per diem: For tax-qualified long-term care policies that pay benefits on a per diem basis (without regard to the expense incurred), the maximum tax-free benefit payment in 2001 is $200 per day.

Figure 3.1 (continued)

<u>Business Premium Deductibility</u>: C-corporations can deduct the entire premium cost of a tax-qualified plan paid on behalf of an employee as a reasonable and necessary business expense under Section 162 of the Internal Revenue Code. The amount of the deduction is also not considered income to the employee. Sole proprietors, partners or more-than-2% S-Corporation Shareholders can deduct in full the premium paid on behalf of their employees. For themselves, they can take 60% of the cost as a business deduction in 2001. The balance of the cost can be deducted individually up to the maximum deduction limits above, as long as the taxpayer is able to itemize medical expenses.

Non-Qualified Plans

The taxation of long-term care insurance plans that are not tax-qualified is still unknown. The Treasury Department (and Congress) continues to remain silent on the consequences. The Internal Revenue Service has created Form 1099LTC that must be completed by any third party dispensing long-term care benefit payments. This form asks specifically if the distribution was made from a tax-qualified plan or not.

Most non-qualified plans offer a more liberal method of qualifying for benefits. These plans give insureds a "triple trigger" method of qualifying for benefits:

1. inability to perform 2 of 5 ADLs, or

2. suffers a medically diagnosed cognitive impairment, or

3. physician certifies the need for long-term care services (often referred to as medical necessity).

Note: There is no 90-day requirement for the first trigger.

State Income Tax Deductibility

There are many states that offer either a deduction or credit against their state income tax. These states are: Alabama, California, Colorado, Hawaii, Illinois, Indiana, Iowa, Kentucky, Maine (both credit and deduction), Maryland, Missouri, Montana, Minnesota, New Mexico, New York, North Carolina, North Dakota, Ohio, Oregon, Utah, Virginia, West Virginia and Wisconsin.

Check with your financial and tax advisor for more details about this potential tax savings. These laws are being enacted every year, so those residents in states not listed should check to see if their state legislature is considering such an action to benefit its taxpayers.

for all concerned because of the known tax favorability and the more sensible approach to covering people who were chronically ill, reining in "non-essential" claims and preserving the product line from higher than expected loss ratios and resulting premium rate increases. The other side felt that tax-qualified plans would not cover all of the potential long-term care claims people faced, especially through the elimination of the medical necessity trigger, a feature that was primarily added through the efforts of experienced LTC providers who felt the ADL and cognitive impairment triggers alone would leave a number of claims uncovered. As time progresses, both sides have solidified their arguments and are quick to interpret studies and data as clearly favorable to their points of view.

"Sales of long-term care insurance have been reported to be flat for well over a year, even though the market for these products is expanding daily. This begs an obvious question. Is it possible that the federal government's effort to encourage consumers to purchase LTC through the [HIPAA] legislation permitting tax-qualified LTC policies is beginning to backfire?... It certainly wouldn't be the first time a well-intentioned government program has fallen flat.... Given the positive marketing spin the industry has bestowed upon HIPAA over the last two years, one might wonder how anyone could take the view that HIPAA may be a villain rather than a savior. However, the doubt that remains about taxation of benefits received from non-qualified LTC contracts has had negative effect on the entire issue of LTC funding mechanisms."[8]

There is no question of the passion of the discussion, and that both sides truly believe they are right. And both may be, in their own way. I'm sure there are some claims that will be covered under non-qualified plans that tax-qualified policies will not be required to cover. There is also the very real possibility that non-qualified plans present the industry with a challenge neither its health or disability insurance counterparts have been able to deal with well – that the competitive pressures to market the most liberal policy with the best rates and the highest commissions have resulted in claims disasters that make the long-term future of both health and disability product lines very questionable indeed.

There are three major issues in the TQ-NTQ debate. These are:

1.   the 90-day ADL loss requirement;

2.   the medical necessity trigger; and

3.   taxation.

90-Day Loss Requirement

As part of the "chronically ill" definition mandated by the federal government for long-term care plans, some type of health practitioner ranging from physician to social worker must certify that the expected loss of two ADLs will last at least 90 days. If it doesn't, the certification should still stand. In other words, insureds will not be asked to return claim dollars because their long-term care treatment lasted only 75 days instead of the expected 90 days.

There are many that feel this stipulation will mean TQ policies will avoid paying in most post-acute care situations, where the individual is discharged from the hospital (or moved to a skilled nursing wing) but is not yet well enough to function entirely on his or her own. This was likely the intention. Medicare patients (with Medicare Supplements) are probably safe in having this short-term care paid for (as long as skilled nursing is required) through these third party outlets. Under-age-65 patients will receive financial assistance through a major medical policy, the majority of which reimburse this type of short-term care. Those uninsured by Medicare or private health insurance are in the same position they would be in for any type of necessary medical care. It seems highly improbable that those people who do not purchase regular health insurance are likely to opt for long-term care insurance.

Will there be situations where a NQ policy pays (and a TQ does not) because of the 90-day requirement? Probably, although for the above noted reasons, it may not be as often as many claim. The real problem that the 90-day language is starting to present is that some TQ insurers are using the 90-days to avoid paying claims right away when a shorter elimination period is in effect.

For example, a TQ policyholder has a 20-day elimination period on the policy. A long-term care event occurs, a claim form is filed, along with certification from a health practitioner that the loss of at least 2 ADLs is expected to last at least 90 days. This should trigger benefit reimbursements 20 days from the start of the claim. But an insurer may challenge the certification on the basis of the medical information received, saying that it doesn't believe the ADL loss will extend 90 days. This means that the insured will not see long-term care bills paid early in the claim and may be receiving due notices from health care providers while the insurer is still making up its mind as to the legitimacy of the claim.

While no one is denying the right of the insurer to adjudicate a claim, there is great potential for abuse here. How long does the insurer wait until it believes the 90 days will be reached? How much extra financial pressure does this put on the claimant who bought long-term care insurance for just this purpose only to see the claim held up – perhaps unjustly? We have all seen health insurers go into this "Four Corners Stall" before with health and disability claims and it creates a mountain of public relations work for the agent to explain to the client. If this becomes a common practice, the 90-day requirement will have created difficulties unforeseen by those that passed the HIPAA language.

One thing is certain, NQ advocates will tell you. There is no 90-day requirement on a NQ long-term care policy.

Medical Necessity Trigger

HIPAA deleted this trigger entirely from its "chronically ill" definition. This effectively removed the "triple trigger" qualifying that became the buzz-word in the early 1990s for the best in long-term care coverage. NQ supporters point out that this policy type has three ways in which one can qualify for benefits, while TQ policies have only two. The medical necessity trigger was added to the long-term care policy definitions in the late 1980s, largely on the suggestion of long-term care providers themselves. These providers pointed out many situations where an individual (usually a frail elder) will not consistently qualify under an ADL loss or cognitive trigger, but still will require a need for assistance. Medical necessity placed the responsibility on the shoulders of the individual's physician, who could certify the need for care under this trigger if it was felt to be necessary.

The question ultimately becomes – what is an insurable event? Does the person truly need help or is this trigger a convenient way to make life a little easier for someone who is undoubtedly in some physical discomfort? Should insurance cover *all* of the possible long-term care events or only those that are more catastrophic in nature? More important, can insurance afford to reimburse for virtually every situation?

Some of the medical necessity claims are going to pay very little – primarily for help with instrumental activities of daily living, such as a housekeeper, someone to drive, someone to shop for the individual. The TQ policy may not cover such claims, but the majority of people may be able to self-insure them.

Other medical necessity claims may require the person to live in a supervised facility. Here, the expenses increase substantially once one is paying a room and board daily cost (and perhaps some extras). While NQ policies will undoubtedly pay here, there may be situations where TQ policies also reimburse the costs. Frail elders, where the majority of these questions will arise, may well be able to perform an ADL, but due to their frailty, may require the *supervision* of that ADL. TQ policies contain language that stipulates that stand-by assistance constitutes the loss of an ADL. These individuals may well need some supervisory assistance with the two most fragile ADLs – bathing and dressing – even though the individuals are still generally performing these routine activities. This is often why the doctor has recommended a facility residence, so that the *supervisory* assistance is there.

Those passionate TQ supporters have also expressed a legitimate concern as to whether the medical necessity trigger represents a bigger claim bite than most insurers can chew. When HIPAA was introduced, the evidence was not yet all in regarding this contention. With the majority of policies now being sold as TQ, the potential claims volatility of medical necessity may not be accurately measured for some time. It is known that at least a couple of insurers with "soft" (easy to qualify) benefit triggers have been hit hard with claims losses over the last decade. With the history of claims problems in the health and disability insurance markets, the concern about "medical necessity" may be a legitimate one, but there is still no way to tell at this point. It is interesting that there is very little premium differ-

"These claims would not have been paid under tax-qualified long-term care policies:

"Client A: This 89-year-old woman resides in an assisted living facility. Her conditions are diabetes, abdominal aortic aneurysm, peripheral vascular disease and osteoarthritis. She receives assistance with one ADL only; however, she is a frail elder and the company is paying benefits under the medically necessary trigger.

"Client B: This 77-year-old woman had a laminectomy. She can perform her ADLs, but needs assistance with other instrumental activities. The NQ insurer has approved a plan of care offering her three hours of help, two days per week for four weeks at a cost of $13 per hour."[9]

ence, on average, between TQ and NQ policies being sold by the same insurer. The difference might average 5-10%. That suggests carriers don't expect NQ policies to cover all that much more in claims than TQ plans. Only time will tell.

Taxation

TQ policies have a clear tax treatment. Benefits under these policies are never taxable (unless a per diem TQ policy pays more than $200/day in 2001) and the premium may be deductible by individuals and is certainly deductible in whole or in part by all types of businesses. NQ policies have nothing spelled out about their taxation. NQ advocates say that the IRS has repeatedly said that they consider NQ policies as "accident and sickness" plans and this means they would not receive unfavorable tax treatment. I can say that IRS regional offices are not as unified in this belief as NQ supporters would have you think. There are some IRS officials who refused to tuck NQ plans under the "accident and sickness" wing and others who said they can only speak for TQ plans in terms of known tax consequences. While it seems absurd that they would tax these benefits paid for by individuals with their own non-deductible dollars, it is impossible to say for sure what the IRS will ultimately do.

The IRS has issued Form 1099-LTC and insurers are required to report all long-term care policy disbursements, from both tax-qualified and non-qualified plans. When a 1099 is issued, the individual must account for it somehow on his or her tax return. With TQ plans, there is Form 8853 that can accompany an individual return that avoids the 1099 amounts being included as income.

But what do NQ policyholders do? Should they report the income on their 1040 as "other income"? What are people doing with these 1099s? Are there enough NQ plans that have been issued since the beginning of 1997 for which a claim has already been presented where this would be necessary? How is the IRS handling the non-inclusion of these 1099 amounts on individual returns? The client should be aware of the potentially negative tax consequences because you had him or her sign a waiver form (see Part Two).

*"I am not promoting non-tax-qualified plans over
tax-qualified. I am simply saying that choices are
available and the public needs to know what those
choices are. As agents, we do a disservice to our
clients when we do not present to them all of their
options. Who are we to determine in advance of
ever meeting with prospects what is best for them
and their family? Would a doctor decide what
medicine a patient should take prior to the office
visit? What about our responsibility to perform due
diligence? Of course it is easy to say, 'Well, I don't
want my client to have a tax bill so I will only
explain tax-qualified LTC.' However, consider this:
Is it better to have the client receive a net 70 cents
on the dollar (after-tax result in the worst scenario)
or receive no benefit at all? I always present both
TQ and non-TQ plans to my clients so that they
can make an informed decision."*[10]

While confusion reigns in the individual market, businesses
have focused solely on tax-qualified plans. For them, the only known
for premium deductibility and subsequent favorable tax treatment of
benefits is in a TQ plan. My guess is that virtually no NQ plans are
being marketed to businesses. Advisors have learned their lesson after
the Section 125 fiasco where, prior to the passage of HIPAA, many
were telling employers that long-term care was bound to be included
in these employee benefit plans because they were "accident and sickness" type plans similar to those the IRS was allowing to be placed in
a Section 125 plan. Many employers took this advice. When HIPAA
was ultimately passed, the language in the law specifically excluded

LTC from Section 125 plans, and left employers scrambling to cover up this error in their employee benefit plans. There is still hope that TQ plans will be made a part of Section 125 plans and there is federal legislation introduced every year seeking to make this happen. For now, employers can only feel completely comfortable with the known tax consequences of TQ plans.

The majority of insurers maintain both a tax-qualified and non-qualified LTC portfolio. Many currently offer *only* the TQ plans (except in California where they are mandated by the state to offer both). Many of these same insurers offer a conversion privilege for policyholders to exchange their TQ plans for the "triple trigger" NQ plans should the taxation of NQ plans ever be cleared up favorably.

For now, the arguments both for and against TQ and NQ plans will rage on. This internal squabbling has not changed the need for this type of protection among many of the consuming public. As long as these discussions do not preclude advisors from talking about long-term care and presenting clients with their options in this regard, we as an industry will be doing our job.

STAND-ALONE LTC POLICIES

In Parts One and Two, various key policy provisions were reviewed. Renewability, elimination periods, benefit periods (or pool of money contracts), nursing home, assisted living facility care, home health care, hospice care and inflation protection were all examined. These provisions either will be or should be considered as part of every LTC contract. The differences between tax-qualified and non-qualified plans have also been noted, especially since the distinction changes the eligibility triggers for benefits.

There are several types of product choices that can be made when attempting to fill a long-term care need with a funding solution. The most common way is with a stand-alone long-term care insurance plan.

Aside from the policy provisions noted above, there are a number of other features of these plans that should be noted as you review the coverage that best fits the needs of an individual client.

Community-Based Care

Home care, the most prevalent of the community-based options, has already been discussed. However, there are other parts of this overall long-term care component that are worth mentioning.

Adult-day care. Just as one drops a dependent child off at a day care program on the way to work, the same option is available in communities to do likewise with a dependent adult. For single parent households where there is one employed individual, there is a need for someone to supervise the dependent adult during the day. This is not about a need for skilled nursing assistance, but more for intermediate or custodial type care. If this type of service is utilized and the insured meets one of the policy benefit triggers, the cost of this care can be reimbursed under the policy.

Respite care. This provision is intended to relieve the primary caregiver. It pays for temporary help – a few hours or a few days – to care for the dependent adult while the caregiver takes a break or attends to other affairs. There is generally a policy limit in terms of either (or both) dollars and days, but it is meant to provide the caregiver (more than the insured) a chance to be freed up for a short time.

Caregiver training benefit. This feature is intended to encourage and help individuals who would prefer to be the primary caregiver for the insured. This most likely will be a family member or friend, caring for someone in his or her (or the insured's) own home. This provision would pay for the actual training of the individual to be a qualified caregiver and then ultimately pay the same individual (on a home health or home care charge basis) for ongoing caregiver duties. This allows a family member or friend to be the caregiver instead of an employee of a local home care agency.

Care coordinator/personal care advisor. Many policies today offer to pay for the services of a care advocate who can help a family and the disabled insured through the maze of local long-term care services. These consultants often develop a plan of care involving the proper use of various health care workers depending on the patient's condition. The coordinator can arrange for the appointments that are necessary and will work in conjunction with the insured's physician to ensure that all is being done to follow the doctor's wishes in regards to the individual. While this may not be a costly expense to the insurer, it is often both a good will gesture to help a family suddenly caught up in the need for long-term care and a way to use advisors that will work to deliver necessary care on a cost-effective basis.

Durable equipment/home modification. Some policies pay for home-based devices like a medical help or alert system or similar equipment if it ensures that the insured can remain in his or her home for care as a result. In pursuit of this goal (as home care can be less costly than facility care and more desired by the insured and family), insurers may help pay for any home modifications within reason to allow the person to remain at home. From building a wheelchair access ramp to adding rails to the bathtub, there are many possibilities here that can help an individual stay at home longer and (from the insurer's point of view) potentially keep the claims costs lower as a result.

Miscellaneous. The community-based care provision of a long-term care policy is the place where insurers can exercise some flexibility with regard to covering items that are not specifically listed as being reimbursable under the policy. This is a claims judgment call, but some services are better off being reimbursed here than the alternative – facility-based care. An example of this might be to pay for home-delivered hot meals that assist someone who is not well enough to prepare meals, but otherwise does not need to be in a facility where meals are served. This expenditure can keep a person home longer and also can help to ensure a balanced diet that can help keep the homebound individual healthier longer.

Some of the more innovative policy features can be found under the "community-based care" provision, so it is important to read this section of the policy "Outline of Coverage" fully in this regard.

Other Provisions or Features

Alternate plan of care. Most policies also provide for the development of an alternate plan of care for an individual in need of long-term care services for items that are not specifically noted in the policy provisions. Generally, if the insurer, physician, insured and, if applicable, the care coordinator all agree on the validity of certain non-named services, this provision allows them to be reimbursed. The idea of basing reimbursement on qualifying through the benefit triggers rather than "locking" insured in to only the services and facilities spelled out in the policy can lead to easier claims handling, potentially lower overall costs to the insurer, and more preferred methods of treatment for the insured.

Restoration of benefit. This provision would apply when the insured has elected a benefit period less than "unlimited" or "lifetime." In this case, an insured may qualify for and have need of policy benefits for some time. Then, a recovery takes place where no benefits are payable under the policy. If this recovery time lasts long enough (usually 180 days), the original Maximum Policy Benefit can be restored to its initial amount. This puts the insured in a position to draw down the full policy benefit even though some benefits had already been accessed in the earlier claim from which recovery was made.

Waiver of premium. The concept behind this policy provision is to relieve the insured (and family) of having to continue paying LTC policy premiums in order to keep the policy in force and collect benefits. However, this provision can be quite complex and careful attention should be paid to the policy language. First, some policies only waive premium if the insured is confined to a facility, excluding community-based care. Second, some policies begin waiving the premium after either the expiration of the elimination period (first day if a zero-day EP exists) or a specified period of time – 30, 60, or 90 days without regard to elimination period length. Third, there are policies that have different waiver stipulations for facility care and home care. Fourth, some policies have a designated time frame where, if the insured has had the premium waived for a certain length of time, no premiums will ever be due again even if the insured recovers from the present medical condition. Because of these variations and conditions, it is recommended that one look carefully at the entire policy outline of coverage to be sure one has found all of the contract language referring specifically to premium waiver.

Non-forfeiture benefits. This extra feature is often offered to the insured as an optional benefit for an additional extra premium. The idea behind non-forfeiture benefits is to allow the insured to have some type of consideration due to the amount of premium paid into the policy should the individual wish to no longer pay premium costs. Rather than having the policy simply lapse with no further protection available, this feature gives the insured an option or two when this happens. The more common choice is to have the daily benefit payable for a shortened benefit period based on the amount of premium paid into the policy at the time of lapse. This has the effect of continuing coverage even though the insured is now paying nothing for the policy. In life insurance, there are non-forfeiture benefits in this event, where the dollars paid in are not necessarily "wasted." This is the same idea – extended coverage until the "value" of the premium paid in has been exhausted.

Return of premium. Along this same line of thought is an option called Return of Premium. Here, if the insured dies and the policy is still in force, some insurers will take the last premium payment and return all or a portion of it to the insured. For an extra premium, carriers will go a step farther by returning premium paid less any claims. In general, one has to die or surrender the policy to activate this option, rendering it potentially impractical. A more living-type benefit can reimburse a percentage of premium paid if the insured is claim free for a specified period of time. This type of approach has a fairly high cost to it, and no guarantee that it will ever be used if the insured has a substantial claim since most of these options subtract claims paid from the premiums paid in as part of the calculation.

Coordination of benefits. Tax-qualified plans coordinate with Medicare so as not to duplicate coverage. Generally speaking, if Medicare pays a benefit for long-term care, the policy will not. TQ plans must be expense-incurred plans for this provision to be in effect. Indemnity, or per diem, contracts do not coordinate with Medicare even if they are tax-qualified. Non-qualified plans are not required to coordinate benefits with Medicare.

Married couple benefits. It has already been noted in this text that insurers have good reasons to provide incentives for married couples to acquire long-term care insurance together – lower incidence of claims among married couples than those who are single, widowed, or divorced. In addition to the premium discounts offered married couples, there are some other features for them as well.

- Survivor premium waiver: If both husband and wife are insured under an insurer's long-term care plan, in the same or two different policies, this provision allows that if one of the two passes away, the survivor of the two can continue his or her own policy and the premium will be waived forever if the policy has been in force long enough (usually ten years). This encourages the surviving individual to keep his or her policy and recognizes that there may be some financial ramifications upon death of one of the spouses.

- Shared benefits: This option creates a separate pool of money that either or both spouses can draw upon should they exhaust the benefits in their policy. For those electing less than a lifetime (or unlimited) benefit period, this can be a way of saving money by taking a shorter benefit period (3, 4, or 5 years) and ultimately creating a longer one through the use of the extra benefits. One spouse may use the entire extra amount or either one may use a portion of these benefits until they are depleted in full.

Bed reservation. Most long-term care insurance policies will provide a benefit where if a stay in a facility is interrupted by a hospitalization, the insurer will keep paying the daily room rate to ensure that the insured's accommodations are kept intact until his or her return. There is usually a maximum number of days that this benefit will be paid – generally 30 days per calendar year. A long-term care stay can be interrupted several times by the need for more acute care and in long-term care facilities where beds are scarce, this provision can prevent further disruption caused by the lack of available space.

Cognitive reinstatement. Insurance policies traditionally, by law, have a 31-day grace period. In the case of long-term care policies, the grace period is generally extended farther out than that. Some insurers allow copies of the premium due notices to be sent to a designated third party to further prevent any lapses in coverage. In this provision, the insurer will take it a step farther if the insured has a cognitive impairment or functional incapacity and allow reinstatement of the policy up to six months from the date of lapse, recognizing that the individual's impairment likely resulted in the failure to pay premium. It seems unfair to punish the claimant about the lapse so payment of back premiums can put the policy back in force along with the doctor's certification of the medical condition.

Cash benefit. There are some insurers who will allow the policyholder to elect to have a long-term care policy pay on an indemnity basis. As noted previously, indemnity or "per diem" plans, even issued as a tax-qualified plan, have tax issues above a certain daily benefit amount ($200/day in 2001). There are advantages to having an indemnity plan such as the lack of necessity to submit a bill for reimbursement. If you meet the definitions under one of the eligibility triggers, you qualify for the full daily benefit. Some high-income individuals, who have maximized the amount of disability income insurance that can be purchased, have looked to this type of policy to provide more dollars in the event of a disability. For this rider, they would have to meet different criteria for benefits to commence as opposed to their disability policy definitions. But for those individuals more concerned about the more catastrophic type of disability that would limit their ability to perform 2 or more ADLs, they can supplement their disability policy with benefits payable under this option. If a $200/day option is elected and a lifetime benefit period, that's $6,000/month to be directed towards whatever the insured decided needed to be paid. Some insurers allow up to $300-350/day of benefits; thus, an individual could supplement DI coverage with, potentially, around $10,000/month of benefits, with some taxation of those dollars above $6,000/month. For those who have been stymied in the individual disability insurance marketplace, this may be an opportunity in which your clients may have an interest.

Pre-existing conditions. Policies are generally issued without any pre-existing condition limitation at all. The underwriting of the policy has typically satisfied the insurer as to the person's present state of health and, if issued, there is not the added complication of determining whether a condition was in existence prior to the issue date of the policy.

Limitations and exclusions. This is a specified list of conditions or situations for which no benefits are payable under the policy. It could, but not necessarily, include:

1. condition due to a war, or act of war, declared or not;

2. self-inflicted injury or suicide attempt;

3. charges for a condition due to participation in a felony, riot or insurrection;

4. charges in connection with chronic alcoholism or chemical dependency;

5. charges covered by state or federal workers' compensation laws;

6. care provided outside the United States, its territories or Canada.; and

7.   services or supplies that would normally be furnished free in the absence of insurance.

These limits will vary from insurer to insurer and it will be necessary to fully review each policy's specific listings to see what exclusions apply. A list of these limitations is generally required to be in the company's sales literature that addresses policy benefits, so the information should not be hard to find. At any rate, the policy outline of coverage will contain the specifics for your review.

Non-insurance benefits. In the always vigilant practice to include value-added benefits to a policy to make it more attractive, long-term care plans have been promoting different types of benefits in the past couple of years not related to a disabling event. The most common of these is a toll-free help line where insureds (and family members) can contact an independent third party to ask for resource information, inquire about facilities in a given area, or clarify some points about Medicare and Medicaid. For families not in the know about long-term care (and most are not), this can be a helpful extra that also takes some pressure off the insurer's own phone lines. The other perk is access to a discounted provider service. If the claimant has a long-term care need, that individual can go to a provider (skilled nursing, home care, assisted living facility) where a lower rate is charged because the patient is a policyholder of the specific company offering this benefit. In a way, it's like an in-network/out-of-network type of program where benefit dollars go farther if a recommended group of providers is sought out, but nothing prevents one from getting treatment wherever one wishes. If a facility would normally charge $150/day, but as part of a preferred group, the same accommodations are available for $125/day, that's $25/day ($750/month, $9,000/year) that can be saved from any pool-of-money totals, helping the insured to extend coverage out that much further.

Stand-Alone Product Variations
Most of the stand-alone products sold today are comprehensive in nature. In many states, to qualify as long-term care insurance, products must include both facility and community-based care. But

there is the availability of other products focusing on a specific type of long-term care. Insurers continue to market "home care only" plans and "facility care only" policies. These products are designed for lower pricing and to appeal to consumers looking at the likelihood of a need for just one or the other type of care. Some people cannot envision ever going to a facility and believe they would be able to get all their care at home. Others are not concerned about the home care end of things, believing they would have some adequate caregivers at home. However, they are concerned about becoming so ill that they could no longer be taken care of by a loved one and they do not believe they could afford the cost of a facility, so the insurance would come in handy should the situation arise. These more care-specific plans can be either tax-qualified or non-qualified, and provide added flexibility in trying to meet a client's needs and/or budget.

There will likely be more variations and innovations emerging over the next few months and years. This is still a new product line really, and insurers are becoming more comfortable with creating new ways to approach and insure the market. In an effort to streamline the underwriting and issue process, one carrier has begun an "express" program, where the applicant has a choice of a few customized plans and the agent need only complete an "order form" signed by the applicant, requesting coverage. There is no need to ask health questions or virtually any other question so common in the application process. Simply send in the signed ticket and the insurer takes care of the rest. Someone contacts the applicant and asks the questions directly. It cuts down on an agent's (and applicant's) time and avoids the often-annoying repeat of questions that both slows down the process and disturbs the applicant. On paper, it seems like it should be a successful program. If so, there will be other insurers following with this concept close on its heels.

COMBINATION POLICIES

A number of market factors have contributed to a growth in the presence of combination insurance products in the last few years that link long-term care with other types of insurance, packaging them under one wrapper for maximum effectiveness. First, there is the relative ineffectiveness of the stand-alone LTC policies to date. No one said long-term care was going to be an easy product to sell. Despite the need, the market penetration numbers are weak. Second, many financial planners often pass on the health insurance needs of their clients. They may refer the business elsewhere, but essentially they do not want to be bothered with either its complexity or volatility. This is not an accusation or a judgment, simply the way it is. Third, there is a growing consumer demand for value in any type of insurance product if it is not utilized or needed for a claim. In other words, if money is placed into an insurance product for a number of years and benefits are not accessed or are used only sparingly, there is an expectation that there will be some sort of refund for non-use. Fourth, insurers are trying to appeal more to the under-age-65 buyer for long-term care purchases, as the sales of long-term care plans to date have been dominated by the age 65-and-over market. All of these trends have worked to produce a new way to provide long-term care protection – in conjunction with another type of coverage.

Life Insurance-Based Long-Term Care

> *"Anyone can get old. All you have to do is live long enough."*
>
> – Groucho Marx

Life insurance is almost the perfect vehicle for this type of hybrid product. When joined with long-term care, the insured has the necessary long-term care protection, and also has a death benefit or cash value in the event the policy benefits are not used to any great degree for a long-term care event. This yields the safety net many are looking for in case they do not ever need the LTC coverage. Both males and females are good prospects for this type of product. Males may well pass away before using much or any of their long-term care benefits, while females are usually underinsured when it comes to life insurance and this is an opportunity to both rectify that and provide the equally important feature of long-term care coverage.

Jane Bryant Quinn column, April 22, 2001:

Long-term care is growing ever more complex. As the population ages, many people are purchasing coverage. Meanwhile, the industry hopes to reach younger, more affluent buyers by combining long-term care with life insurance....[With this type of product] you put up a single cash premium that will buy you a lump-sum benefit that can be used for either life insurance or long-term care protection. Women currently account for 70% of the business of [one insurer for this plan].... A 65-year-old woman investing $50,000 in the policy would get $92,150 in death benefits and pay about $252 a year for the long-term care protection.[11]

Those financial planners who position long-term care as an estate-planning tool can cover a couple of bases with this type of product. The information gathering process where one calculates the net worth and cash flow of a prospect can often reveal the way to fund this type of plan. An asset that is being underserved, earning little or no interest, can be repositioned to provide a death benefit, cash value (maybe earning a higher interest rate) and long-term care coverage. Taking $75,000 out of a Certificate of Deposit and getting a tax-deferred interest rate and, more importantly, long-term care funding and an expansion of one's life insurance can accomplish much from a planning standpoint.

Consumer shopping today has fashioned into more convenient options. You can pick up a lot more than prescription drugs at your chain pharmacy today, just as you can do your grocery shopping at

Massachusetts has enacted a law that could help insurers develop new approaches to helping consumers prepare for long-term care expenses. The state's governor recently signed a bill, S.B. 1996, that permits Massachusetts insurers to combine any form of accident or sickness insurance with an annuity, an endowment policy or a life insurance policy. Lawmakers are expecting insurers to start by using the statute to develop products that combine traditional annuity features and life insurance coverage with "living benefits," "accelerated benefits," and other mechanisms designed to cover some or all of the cost of long-term care.[12]

Wal-Mart if you choose to do so. An individual who understands the need for both life insurance and long-term care might appreciate accomplishing these goals with one policy.

Most of the policies work best with a single premium payment, although many insurers offer a more traditional annual (or more frequent) payment approach. You deposit the money into the product – universal life, whole life, variable life – and this obtains both life insurance and LTC protection for you. Sometimes the coverage is completely separate where one accesses the long-term care portion for LTC needs and a death benefit if the life insurance proceeds become necessary. Other plans use a single benefit amount where either long-term care claims can be subtracted or a death benefit paid, or both. In this plan, a $50,000 death benefit where an insured uses $27,000 for long-term care needs and then passes away, will leave the remaining $23,000 as a death benefit to a designated beneficiary. The single premium deposit can include the total cost for both the life and LTC coverage or there may be a separate charge for the LTC protection taken each month or less often from the cash value in the policy.

If the policy is set up so that the LTC benefits are separate from the death benefit, then the drawing of LTC claims dollars has no effect on the amount of the death benefit or the cash value. This means that planners can count on each benefit standing on its own to solve specific needs. Plans that combine the benefit into one lump sum may not accomplish the same thing, but these product types are sold more for LTC protection with a life insurance safety net than for filling a particular life insurance need.

The long-term care portion of these unique products can be written to conform with HIPAA language as a tax-qualified plan. This type of TQ plan was included in the tax favorable language of the HIPAA legislation. So, by changing the status of an asset – a savings account, money market fund, CD – to an asset protection device, one can answer a long-term care funding need and obtain a safety net to return money in the event benefits are used little or not at all, giving this product hybrid a distinct advantage over a stand-alone LTC plan.

VARIABLE LIFE VERSION

Variable life and its spin-off, the popular variable universal life (VUL) product, have been the lead "bulls" in market-oriented life insurance products. It was only natural for the trend of adding LTC coverage to life insurance policies to catch on with the variable life insurers. People have purchased a VL or VUL policy most likely for tax-deferred cash accumulation, not long-term care, but variable insurers expect that to change by combining the excitement of the variable product with the often unrecognized need for LTC. One carrier revamped its VUL policy that was sold with a minimum face amount of $100,000 to issue ages 20 to 75 to include a tax-qualified LTC acceleration rider. The flexible premium VUL had 22 funds, a fixed account, 15 money managers, dollar cost averaging and automatic asset rebalancing. By adding an LTC rider to access death benefits, this product was aimed at a different market than the traditional LTC plan. Younger people, this insurer felt, were more interested in death benefit protection and all the great features of VUL like accumulation, investment opportunity, and supplemental income. Some of these buyers may also see they may one day need LTC coverage.[13] The VUL policy appeal combined with the LTC coverage is targeted at the early-30s-to-middle-50s market. Still others position the VL product as a sort of super-annuity – a Modified Endowment Contract with tax and life insurance benefits over a single-premium annuity.[15]

A notable feature of VUL products is their ability to reflect market performance directly in policy values. The question is, can this performance be reflected in the amount or duration of LTC payments? The link between LTC cost inflation and such performance is at best tenuous. However, we know exceptional growth in values leads to higher death benefits via the operation of corridor factors of Internal Revenue Code section 7702. Some insurers are unwilling to increase the LTC risk, so their rider designs will limit LTC payments to the initial specified amount. Others will find the growth in equities and hence the death benefit to be attractive policy features, so the full death benefit is available for the support of chronically ill insureds.[14]

There has been much discussion over the practice of issuing 1099s for the premium charges each year on the LTC portion of the coverage. The essential cost is moved from the equity account(s) to the insurance company to pay for the pure insurance costs of the long-term care insurance protection. This premium charge transaction is then considered a distribution from a Modified Endowment Contract and, as such, is considered income to the individual insured.

The popularity of variable insurance seems to rise and fall with the tide of the market. Throughout the 1990s, this was the product to buy. Funds have been largely going sideways over the last two years, taking some of the spark out of the fire these policies have lit in the consumer marketplace. Many policyholders have stayed the course in this latest "Bear" lull, meaning using LTC in these plans might make more sense than in the days where these policyholders dropped their policies after their cash values sunk nearly out of sight.

ACCELERATED BENEFITS

The predecessors to the life insurance-linked long-term care insurance products were the Accelerated Benefit options introduced in the mid-1980s. This life insurance policy feature recognized that life insurance can and should function as an accessible living benefit, not only activated upon the death of the insured. Advances in medical technology were helping people sidestep death for a time, but this led to an increase in the number of years with some form of disability. Medical expenses eroded assets and frustration grew among families who needed money but their insured loved one was still alive and draining dollars from the family nest egg.

Accelerated benefits moved up the timetable on the payment of the death benefit. Families could access all or a portion of the death benefit to offset medical costs and normal living expenses. This is what the money would likely have been used for anyway. The majority of insurers charged a cost up front initially for this privilege, but over the last decade, this charge has yielded to a transaction fee upon processing the request for early death benefit money. Insurers also limited the types of situations where this money could be withdrawn, but those events have been expanded and re-defined over the years.

Most of these options now include the need for extended long-term care in an institution or at home, or permanent confinement in a nursing home.[16] This type of medical need certainly can drain assets, as previously shown, and the opportunity to tap into a source of dollars like a policy death benefit was at least an alternative to spending down and eventually qualifying for Medicaid. If the death benefit was originally intended for some other purpose, this will disrupt some planning strategies. Better to have this as a fallback or extra option if there is a specific reason for the death benefit, such as providing an income stream to the family.

For those that have not planned otherwise, the Accelerated Death Benefit provision can be an important funding source to help pay for long-term care costs. Accelerated benefits are another insurance option that was blessed with tax favorability by HIPAA. Certain distributions of life insurance proceeds under the Accelerated Death Benefit option are not considered a taxable event.

When doing your information gathering, check to see if the life insurance policies owned by your prospect/client contain this feature. Review the language to see what type of long-term care for which it will specifically allow this disbursement. This can assist in the overall planning process.

Annuity-Based Long-Term Care

"People who say you're only as old as you feel are all wrong, fortunately."

– Russell Baker

There are a number of insurance agents and financial planners who work each year with individuals to help them acquire annuities as part of their planning strategies. Many of these annuity buyers are also in need of long-term care insurance protection but this has generally not been handled by their financial advisors. Annuity sales have grown dramatically over the years, but long-term care sales have not experienced these same increases.

Why not? One of the primary reasons is likely to be that annuities are a quick issue – a turnaround in days (even hours), as opposed to long-term care underwriting that can be expressed in terms of weeks. If you are used to a 72-hour return on an annuity policy, there will be more frustration with the long-term care application's lengthy review by the underwriting department. This does not mean the need is any less for these annuity buyers, only that the level of patience of their advisors is less.

"Annuity and long-term care combination contracts are a product innovation you need to follow. These are annuity contracts that have LTC benefits embedded inside of them. Not many exist today, but more will debut in the face of rapidly rising demand. A definite market basis for the product already exists, given the huge buildup that has occurred in annuity ownership. As owners of these contracts approach retirement age and beyond, they will become less concerned with asset accumulation and increasingly concerned with asset preservation and independence."[17]

Annuity insurers are beginning to see the appropriateness of combining both of these needs into a single policy. There are several ways that carriers are approaching the annuity/LTC combo market and one should be careful to distinguish between the various products.

A true annuity/LTC combination has a separate benefit for both needs. This is a product where a lump-sum deposit is made and this not only establishes an annuity account, but then also creates an extra long-term care benefit. There is at least one insurer that is marketing this product today. The individual funds a tax-deferred fixed annuity with $100,000, for example. This buys an additional $200,000 of long-term care protection. The initial $100,000 grows at a fixed interest rate, tax-deferred. All the annuity options are in play here. However, if the individual suddenly has a need for long-term care, the entire annuity/long-term care fund is activated.

The annuitant begins drawing down the annuity money first. When that is exhausted, the money created for long-term care when the initial deposit was made is now tapped. The annuity owner, in essence, tripled his or her protection for long-term care simply by buying this annuity. Because the policyholder is withdrawing his or her own money first, there is a substantial length of time before the insurer has to dip into its own pocket. As a result, underwriting has been streamlined to bring the policy issuance down to near annuity turnaround levels.

When attached to annuities, LTC riders can have their premiums paid outside of the annuity or deducted from the annuity values. Currently, it appears that any deductions from annuity values for paying premiums on long-term care riders will be treated as taxable withdrawals for purposes of tax law.[18]

There are many other ways that annuities can interact with long-term care needs:

1.   Using annuity proceeds to help pay for long-term care insurance premiums is a method of paying for this coverage that has been used for a number of years. At least one insurer has a formalized program for taking the income out of the company's immediate fixed annuity and transferring it to the carrier's long-term care insurance product. This was done to make life easier for policyholders, and helped to prevent lapses in coverage because of a missed due premium. Annuity holders simply elect either a life with cash refund option for lifetime premiums or a period certain option if the individual is trying to accelerate the payments of the LTC policy to pay it up in a certain time frame (10 or 20 years, or at age 65).[19]

2.   A nursing home waiver is a policy provision of an annuity that permits withdrawal of annuity money to help pay for nursing home costs without applying any applicable surrender charges. The potential to fund nursing home care is

one of the reasons more than 40% of fixed annuity owners buy a contract. Thus, it follows that nursing home waivers are the most common of all waivers in annuity policies. These waivers may take some time to go into effect after the annuity purchase and also may require an elimination period before the waiver is effective.[20]

3.   Access to non-insurance features like a long-term care provider network and a hot line also can be found as a feature of an annuity. The provider networks furnish a discount on all types of long-term care services and facility charges while the toll-free hot line can help the policyholder and family to access information about long-term care related issues, such as Medicare and Medicaid qualification, costs, and other resources.

4.   Fixed annuities can offer an interest rate specifically for long-term care. This type of policy accepts a lump-sum deposit and keeps two account records. The account that can be used to withdraw funds for long-term care needs grows at a higher interest rate than the regular fixed annuity fund. Withdrawals from either fund reduce the value of both, but a policyholder can utilize either or both, recognizing that the policy is not creating a new benefit for LTC, only a higher interest rate and a faster-growing account of money should funds be accessed for this medical purpose. This can help those individuals who do not medically qualify for long-term care insurance, or who cannot afford the cost of the stand-alone product.

5.   A variable annuity can also contain some type of consideration for long-term care. Again, realizing this is not a specific long-term care insurance product, it can help to supplement present funding vehicles established for this purpose. These annuities provide features from waiver of surrender charges for an LTC need withdrawal to payment of a small monthly crediting (up to a maximum amount)

to the VA account value due to satisfaction of the usual LTC triggers (loss of 2 ADLs or cognitive impairment). Individuals can then access the higher account values for their LTC needs.

6.   Impaired risk single premium immediate annuities are designed for people who may already need long-term care and have done nothing to prepare themselves financially for it. For example, a family who needs to assure care for a person diagnosed with progressive diseases such as Alzheimer's can move some assets to an immediate annuity that can generate cash to help fund care and protect other assets for the ultimate surviving beneficiaries. The advantage here is actually in the *underwriting* of the application. The insurer evaluates both the medical history and the type of long-term care arrangements that have been made on behalf of the potential annuitant. This helps the insurer to estimate life expectancy from the current point forward. This enables it to require *less* money to be deposited to generate the monthly amount needed since this is a different scenario than a healthy applicant with great potential longevity placing funds in the same product. In this case, being in poor health is an advantage. After all, immediate annuities are a financial bet on how long one will live. In one such product for example, the insurer required $111,000 in a deposit to provide a $3,000 monthly income stream for an 85-year-old with moderate Alzheimer's disease. Here, the underwriting helped! If it were a normal, non-underwritten immediate annuity, it would have taken $214,500 to generate the same amount of income. This will help families utilize their assets in a more productive way than a straight spend down to qualify for Medicaid.[21]

Long-Term Care and Health Insurance

Long-term care is a disability-related need. There are many who are covered by health insurance and a smaller number of people who own disability coverage that pays a benefit to insureds to help pay for living expenses during a protracted illness or injury. Many younger people own both types of coverage. If the long-term care industry is going to bring this protection to the younger market, it may well have to do so in combination with these other health-related products.

It is the same issue. Only the lack of long-term care insurance is leaving one part of the recovery or maintenance equation out – reimbursing costs for physical therapists, home care, or facility care and other LTC expenses. Health insurance has limited help for long-term care costs – mostly short-term in nature. Disability insurance pays a benefit to the individual but will there be enough left over to pay for occupational therapy or speech therapy? Very rarely.

Lex Frieden, senior vice president at the Institute for Rehabilitation and Research in Houston, was in an automobile accident at the age of 18. Since 1967, he has earned a master's degree, founded an independent living research program and joined the faculty of Baylor College of Medicine. But he continues to depend on family members for home care. He sees the effects of the LTC coverage gap when talking to young patients who are coping with the effects of strokes, automobile accidents, and other catastrophic illnesses and injuries. He can't remember hearing about a patient under age 45 who came in owning long-term care insurance.[22]

One answer to reaching more people is to utilize the member channels already created by the HMO/PPO distribution network. Various managed care organizations have a substantial number of subscribers. These MCOs are already marketing other products to their members like vision, dental and disability insurance. What about long-term care?[23]

There are some disability carriers that have both disability and long-term care benefits under the same policy umbrella, recognizing that these are distinct needs. At least one insurer is also taking that approach with group disability insurance coverage. If disabled individuals also lose the ability to perform two or more ADLs, their monthly benefit will increase by a certain percentage to provide extra dollars to deal with the long-term care expenses. These funds can be used at the claimant's discretion, an important cash infusion at what is sure to be a difficult time.[24]

Group LTC

Group long-term care has been years in the making. This is one of those rare times in the insurance industry where individual policies have preceded group plans by a significant number of years. It is not that there is not employer interest. It is just that several barriers have slowed down the progress. First, it was a lack of industry experience with regard to pricing that made many insurers reluctant to sell individual LTC let alone the lower cost group version of the coverage. There was zero experience on covering a substantial amount of people under a master policy for this risk. There was no evidence about what the risk would be, as LTC needs were almost as prevalent for under-age-65-year-olds as age-65-and-over individuals. Second, there was a lack of tax clarification about the paying of employees' premium costs for the coverage for both employer tax deductibility and employee benefit taxation. This made employers gun-shy about adding this benefit to the employee portfolio.

The federal law HIPAA finally clarified the tax issue for the employer and insurers began to feel better about their pricing of policies and more experience is now under the belt. That does not mean group LTC sales have taken off. In 1998, there were 644,871 covered people in group plans, a 12.6% increase over 1997, and total group LTC premium revenue of $287.5 million, a 12.3% jump.[25] Group LTC consisted of many variations from true group LTC with a master contract to individual, voluntary plans with the premium paid entirely by the employee. In 1999, total number of lives covered expanded by 24% to 786,317 lives, with a corresponding 28% leap for premium revenue to $357 million. True group LTC represented a growing part of these numbers, jumping 121% in 1999 to $67.8 million in premium.[26] By the year 2000, enrolled members had increased to 928,770, a 19% hike, with revenue now up to $520 million, a 17% jump. In addition, associations covered another 122,088 and CALPERS (California Public Employee Retirement System) covered another 144,000,

"Employer awareness and government tax policy are central to expanding job-based long-term care insurance and avoid a looming national crisis in long-term health care financing, according to the Employee Benefit Research Institute. Less than one-half of 1% of American employers currently sponsor LTC insurance, even though the benefit is typically paid for entirely by the workers. Among the major reasons for non-sponsorship are the absence of tax incentives for large employers that have 'cafeteria'-type benefit plans, a lack of awareness of LTC insurance by both employers and workers, and, especially for smaller employers æ 'work' force barriers such as young and lower-paid employees."[27]

bringing the total group number of lives to 1.2 million people.[28] These results, at least, are encouraging.

Two large entries into the group LTC market in 2001 should increase these numbers significantly. The federal Office of Personnel Management will be adding long-term care to the Federal Employees Health Benefit Program in 2002 and began soliciting insurer bids beginning June 15, 2001. It has the potential to reach about 20 million people between the federal employees, military personnel, retirees and dependents. The U.S. Chamber of Commerce also enters the group long-term care market, with a potential to reach 100 million member employees, employees of member companies and their dependents. This could double group enrollments immediately and raise the profile of long-term care among other employer groups.[29] If Congress is finally able to forge passage of legislation allowing LTC into Section 125 plans, the market penetration rate should increase exponentially. All of this is conjecture, but the awareness level about a product is vital to its long-term survival and LTC needs a few success stories among employers to cover a greater amount of Americans with this critical funding assistance.

A survey revealed that 15% of Lucent employees currently have elder care issues and another 20% anticipate facing these issues in the future. In response, the company collaborated with the National Council on Aging to develop Internet software to help individuals assess the probability of their or a family member's need for long-term care and aid the user in making the right elder care choices.[30]

More Americans today are concerned about financing long term care than about paying for retirement, according to *American Demographics* magazine. In fact, 60% worry that their spouses will need long-term care. One insurer is promoting the importance of long-term care insurance by offering its own product to its 23,000 active employees and 6,000 retirees who are eligible for benefits. Employees' spouses, and domestic partners, retirees' spouses, parents, step-parents, parents-in-law, step-parents-in-law, and grandparents can all be covered.[32]

It will be equally important to reach out to the dependents of employees to consider purchasing LTC through the employer-sponsored group program. Lost productivity to the employer is based more on losing an employee who has to render care to a dependent adult than the loss of that employee. Currently, about 80% of employers that sponsor group LTC make the coverage available to the employees' parents while 18% allow employees' grandparents to apply for coverage. Employee participation in the typical voluntary LTC plan is less than 10%. Sales to parents represented a small fraction of that already small fraction.[31] This needs to improve to accomplish the objectives group LTC was created to address.

There are some considerations about the use of a trust or a conventional group insurance policy to insure under group LTC. The same questions that arose (and still do) over group health trusts are valid here. The trust generally reduces the number of state filings that must be done as the "situs" state where the policy is issued to the group trustee policyholder typically has jurisdiction over the policy, meaning its laws and regulations apply. But there is a catch with long-term care insurance. About 30 states have claimed extraterritorial jurisdiction over LTC insurance issued to their residents. This requires filing the documents with each of these additional states, in essence defeating one of the main purposes of the trust – simplification.[33] It is very likely we will not have the same trust issues that still permeate the group health insurance market.

ALTERNATIVE DISTRIBUTION

If the traditional financial planners, advisors and insurance agents do not bring the long-term care insurance solution to those that would benefit from it, there are other distribution channels ready, willing and able to take over this crusade.

Banks

About 40% of 407 U.S. banks that participated in a study on insurance sales through this outlet said they would like to be selling long-term care insurance by the end of 2001. This does not necessarily mean it will happen or sell particularly well. The Financial Services Modernization Act made this possible, but whether banks can take advantage of a customer base that is mostly in need of this type of product is still to be known. The complexity of the product has made it difficult to train all of the necessary personnel that see consumers face to face on a daily basis. The banks usually sell LTC coverage through a time-consuming financial planning system that is targeted at wealthier clients, yet there is a great need for this product in Middle America.[34]

A bank's existing customers should be its primary source for LTC sales. However, three additional audiences are primary targets. Members of senior citizen programs offered by the bank (senior clubs), bank employees and the employees of a bank's corporate clients are all ready-made audiences for a product run through the bank's distribution channel.[35] Banks have a long way to go to penetrate this market, but they are not short of good prospects. If they can ever solve the training issues, large volumes of long-term care will be sold through this outlet.

AARP

This organization has undergone a personal facelift in an effort to woo the Baby Boomers to its membership ranks. Like any member-driven organization, it offers benefits to its dues-paying subscribers. It has marketed long-term care insurance with some moderate success over the years. AARP changed carriers beginning in January 1998 and MetLife now carries the banner. Its mailings appeal separately to both 50-64 year-olds (the cost of waiting) and 65-79 year-olds (it is not too late to buy). It invites members to send for information after answering three short questions:

1.   Are you in reasonably good health?

2.   Do you have at least $30,000 in assets (besides your home and car) to protect?

3.   Can you afford to spend at least $40/month for a long-term care insurance plan?

Get over this hurdle and a packet will be sent to you.

Let's face it. AARP has a substantial membership base and certainly there are people buying this policy because it has the AARP stamp on it. This does not mean it is a good or bad policy, but if this is an easy way to buy it, consumers may well take advantage of it. At least they will be among the LTC insured in this country, something that has the potential to benefit all of us.

"The agent is in his office one day when Mary calls on the telephone. Knowing the call is coming from Mary, and not Jack, is immediate cause for concern. Hearing the tone of her voice, the agent is sure something bad happened. He tries the usual pleasantries by asking how everyone is. Mary immediately sets the tone of the conversation. Mary tells the agent that a few months after the agent's last visit Jack began acting a little strange. It was kind of humorous at first; misplaced keys, forgotten appointments, repetition of comments made, forgetting birthdays. These little mistakes he attributed to pressure at the office, getting into his 'golden years,' nothing to worry about. Unfortunately, the little mistakes became big ones to the extent that a visit to a neurologist was deemed appropriate. After a series of extensive tests, this intelligent, kind, professional, loving father and husband was diagnosed with Alzheimer's Disease. Mary begins to break down as she relates that she is doing her best to care for her ever-increasingly dependent husband, but there's more to caring for him than she can handle. She needs help in her home, and to make matters even more horrible, if Jack gets much worse, he'll get to a point where he can't stay home. He may eventually need care in a long-term care facility. Mary then says something that tears into [the agent's] heart. She says, 'Thank God you've been there to give us the proper protection. What would we have done before, and now, without your advice?' The next words [the agent] says will have the most profound effects on Mary and her family, and the most profound effect on [him]. Hopefully, [the] response will be, 'Mary, my heart goes out to you, Jack, and your children. I thank God that two years ago we addressed this terrible possibility and you and Jack enrolled in comprehensive long-term care insurance that will support your need for home care for Jack. And if things really get bad, this plan will provide ample benefits in whatever setting is deemed appropriate. I'll stop by tomorrow and help you begin the process of applying for Jack's benefits.' Will that be [the] response? Or will it be, 'Mary, my heart goes out to you, Jack and your family, but the insurance I've obtained for you over the years is not designed to help in this dreadful situation.... Anyone who is an insurance professional must, in most situations, suggest long-term care to their clients...particularly their long-standing clients."[36]

Footnotes

1.   Jeff Kunerth, "Florida Slow to Embrace Less Costly Options," *Orlando Sentinel*, March 7, 2001, pp. A1, A13.

2.   Hal Stucker, "LTC Insurance Is Still a Tough Sell Despite Many New Features," *National Underwriter*, Life & Health/Financial Services Edition, May 10, 1999, p. 7.

3.   Jean Chatzky, " Is the Security Worth the Cost?" *USA Weekend*, July 28-30, 2000, p. 4.

4.   Allison Bell, "GE Financial to Acquire Travelers LTC Unit," *National Underwriter*, Life & Health/Financial Services Edition, April 24, 2000, p. 3.

5.   Allison Bell, "LTC Sales Rebounded in Second Half of 1999," *National Underwriter*, Life & Health/Financial Services Edition, March 13, 2000, p. 3.

6.   Trevor Thomas, "Growth of LTC Insurance Will be Strong: S&P," *National Underwriter*, Life & Health/Financial Services Edition, January 10, 2000, p. 6.

7.   Gary L. Corliss, "LTCI: Merging and Still Emerging," *National LTC Network Update* (April, 2000), p. 1.

8.   Mark Ameigh, "HIPAA's Dampening Effect on LTC Product Development," *National Underwriter*, Life & Health/Financial Services Edition, November 29, 1999, p. 11.

9.   Richard J. Bergstrom, "Buyer Beware," *Journal of Accountancy* (August, 1999), pp. 27, 30.

10. Ross Schriftman, "LTCI: Tax-Qualified or Not? It's not Our Decision to Make," *Health Insurance Underwriter* (October, 2000), pp. 12, 13.

11. Jane Bryant Quinn, "Insurers Marketing Long-Term Care," *Daytona Beach Sunday News-Journal*, April 22, 2001, p. 1E.

12. Allison Bell, "Mass Gives Go Ahead to Hybrid Products," *National Underwriter*, Life & Health/Financial Services Edition, March 13, 2000, p. 5.

13. Linda Koco, "Hancock Debuts Its First VUL/LTC," *National Underwriter*, Life & Health/Financial Services Edition, July 3, 2000, p. 23.

14. Cary Lakenbach, "Integrated VL/LTCs Pose Some Challenges," *National Underwriter*, Life & Health/Financial Services Edition, February 21, 2000, p. 10.

15. Donald Jay Korn, "Healthy, Wealthy and Wise," *Financial Planning* (September, 2000), pp. 176, 179.

16. "Accelerated Death Benefits' Popularity Doubles, New ACLI-LIMRA Survey Shows," *PR Newswire*, April 12, 1999.

17. Cary Lakenbach, "Keep an Eye on Annuity/LTC Combos," *National Underwriter*, January 15, 2001, p. 16.

18. Norse N. Blazzard and Judith A. Hasenauer, "Taxing Annuity Charges for LTC Riders Is not Sound Social Policy," *National Underwriter*, Life & Health/Financial Services Edition, January 15, 2001, p. 20.

19. "Hancock Offers Customers Easy, New LTC Payment Plan; Fixed Annuity Income Automatically Funds Long-Term Care Insurance Premiums," *Business Wire*, May 8, 2001.

20. Jeremy Alexander, "Annuity Nursing Home Waivers Vary a Lot," *National Underwriter*, Life & Health/Financial Services Edition, May 10, 1999, p. 18.

21. "Golden Rule Introduces Immediate Care ...," *PR Newswire*, June 5, 2001.

22. Allison Bell, "LTC Insurance Gap in Health Plans Seen," *National Underwriter*, Life & Health/Financial Services Edition, January 10, 2000, p. 6.

23. Gary L. Busack, "An Overlooked Opportunity: Selling LTC Via HMOs and PPOs," *National Underwriter*, Life & Health/Financial Services Edition, January 15, 2001, p. 10.

24. "Hartford Life Introduces Ability Plus℠ for Long-Term Disability," *Florida Broker News* (February, 2001), p. 9.

25. Allison Bell, "New Group LTC Sales Take a Breather," *National Underwriter*, Life & Health/Financial Services Edition, May 3, 1999, p. 3.

26. Allison Bell, "Group LTC Sales Jumped 121% Last Year," *National Underwriter*, Life & Health/Financial Services Edition, May 1, 2000, p. 5.

27. Allison Bell, "NEW EBRI Research: Employer Awareness, Tax Policy Central to Expanding Long-Term Care Insurance," *PR Newswire*, April 7, 2000.

28. Allison Bell, "Group LTC Plans Cover 1.2 Million," *National Underwriter*, Life & Health/Financial Services Edition, May 21, 2001, p. 5.

29. Allison Bell, "Group LTC Insurance Poised to Take Off," *National Underwriter*, Life & Health/Financial Services Edition, May 21, 2001, p. 4.

30. "Elder Care Issues," *Employee Benefit Plan Review* (November, 2000), p. 38.

31. M. Christian Murray, "Worksite LTC Sales for Parents Still Rare," *National Underwriter*, Life & Health/Financial Services Edition, May 1, 2000, p. S-14.

32. "Hartford Financial Services Group, Inc. to Offer Its Long Term Care Plan to Employees," *PR Newswire*, April 29, 1999.

33. Timothy P. Cassidy, "Looking to Enter Group LTC? Answer These Questions First," *National Underwriter*, Life & Health/Financial Services Edition, May 21, 2001, p. 6.

34. Allison Bell, "Forty Percent of Banks Want LTC on Shelf," *National Underwriter*, Life & Health/Financial Services Edition, November 15, 1999, p. 11.

35. Margie Barrie, "LTC Insurance May Mean Long-Term Cash," *National Underwriter*, Life & Health/Financial Services Edition, April 19, 1999, pp. 12, 16.

36. Paul S. Bunkin, "Due Diligence and Long-Term Care Insurance," *Health Insurance Underwriter* (September, 1999), pp. 37, 38.

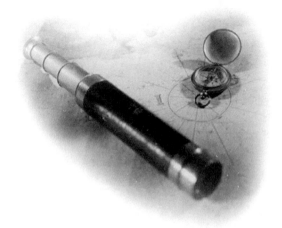

PART FOUR:
KNOWLEDGE IS POWER

"The illiterate of the 21st Century will not be those who cannot read or write, but those who cannot learn, unlearn and relearn."

– Alvin Toffler

There is an extraordinary amount of information about long-term care that one can learn in the hopes that this knowledge might ultimately benefit that person or another. This section of the book deals with that additional education that may come in handy one day. From general information about retirement goals to current state tax laws about long term care to partnership programs to viatical settlements to nursing home problems to medical breakthroughs, all of this data can be stored as a resource and used whenever needed. The information contained herein is loosely organized by general categories, but represents no specific order of importance.

OTHER FINANCING OPTIONS
State Partnership Programs

State partnership programs began in Connecticut in 1992, one of four states to ultimately put a program in place – with California, Indiana and New York – before Congress shelved the idea. Developed in part from grants by the Robert Wood Johnson Foundation, Connecticut set up a "working partnership" with long-term care insurers to market private policies that met the state's standards. In return for buying partnership policies, individuals who exhaust their private benefits are sheltered from having to use up their assets before they qualify for Medicaid. Partnership policies cost no more than similar policies sold outside the partnership.[1]

There are two partnership models: dollar-for-dollar and total asset protection. In the dollar-for-dollar model, beneficiaries are able to keep personal assets *equal* to the benefits paid by the policy. In the total-asset model, *all* assets are protected after a threshold for years of coverage has been crossed, typically three or four years. States that have these programs are expected to realize Medicaid savings since they are the last payer, not the first. See Figure 4.1.

So, why did Congress clamp down on this idea just as it started to take off several years ago? The chief objection to opening this option to everyone is the notion that it disproportionately favors more affluent Americans. This is a rather hollow argument. Rather than involve themselves in a potentially cumbersome Medicaid bureaucracy subject to a re-determination at least every 36 months, more affluent Americans are likely to rely on their income via interest on investments to pay for any long-term care costs. If left to do so, most Americans would not grant the government sole authority to maintain their health coverage at the expense of independence and choice.[2] Long-term care partnership programs give people more choices in terms of long-term care funding and help save the states critical dollars for their budgets. See Figure 4.2. As the nation ages over the first part of this century, these savings will only become more important.

Figure 4.1

PARTNERSHIP PROGRAM
RESULTS TO DATE:[3]

California (December 31, 2000)

Applications processed: 30,843

Applications approved: 24,549

Applications still in force: 21,345

Total asset protection earned of all policyholders who
have received policy benefits: $3,815,666

Number of policyholders qualified to receive benefits: 300

Number of policyholders who exhausted benefits and went on Medicaid: 2

Connecticut (December 31, 2000)

Number of policies purchased: 18,041

Policies still active: 14,725

Number of policyholders qualified to receive benefits: 97

Number of policyholders who exhausted benefits and went on Medicaid: 7

Total asset protection earned by all policyholders: $2,923,087

Indiana (September 30, 2000)

Number of policies purchased: 12,641

Total policies still in force: 10,830

Number of policyholders qualified to receive benefits: 58

Number of policyholders who exhausted benefits and went on Medicaid: 4

Asset protection earned by policyholders who exhausted benefits: ...$315,831.04

New York

Total applications approved: 35,181

Total policies still active: 27,903

Policyholders presently receiving Medicaid benefits: 15

Figure 4.2

STATE RESOLUTIONS, PASSED LEGISLATION, AND PUBLIC LAWS REGARDING LTC PARTNERSHIPS[4]

Iowa: Recently implemented its program that was based on a Medicaid State Plan amendment that the state legislature rushed through prior to 5/14/93.

Illinois: Public Act 89-525. Established a public/private Long-Term Care Insurance program that is pending, subject to lifting of moratorium on partnership creation.

Maryland: House Joint Resolution 11 – 2000 Maryland regular session. For the purposes of urging Congress to amend the Social Security Act to allow assets exempted under a long-term care partnership to be excluded from Medicaid estate recoveries.

Nevada: SB 370 – 1999 session. This law provides asset protection to seniors who exhaust private long-term care insurance. Implementation of the law has been delayed.

North Dakota: SB 2046 – 1999 session. Repeals chapter 26.1-45.1 of the North Dakota Century Code, relating to the partnership for long-term care program, repealing all prior legislation regarding the institution and funding of a partnership.

Oregon: SB 527 – 1999 session. Created new provisions relating to LTC Partnership program.

Pennsylvania: Senate Resolution No. 8 – 2001 session. (See Figure 4.3.) For the purposes of urging Congress to amend the Social Security Act to allow assets exempted under a long-term care partnership program to be excluded from Medicaid estate recoveries.

Vermont: HB 714 – 1999-2000 session. Established the Vermont partnership for long-term care services and provides Medicaid extended coverage to patients receiving long-term care services under a long-term care health plan.

Virginia: Senate Joint Resolution No.365 – 1996-97 session. Appeals to Congress to repeal section 13612(a)(C) of the Omnibus Budget Reconciliation Act of 1993 that discouraged states from implementing public/private long-term care partnerships.

Figure 4.3

PENNSYLVANIA
SENATE RESOLUTION 8[5]

Adopted April 2, 2001

Memorializing Congress to repeal a statutory impediment to state long-term care partnerships.

WHEREAS, costs borne by the taxpayers of this Commonwealth for long-term care under Medicaid exceed more than $500 million for a fiscal year; and

WHEREAS, skyrocketing costs of providing care to persons who need assistance to meet daily needs have hit the middle class especially hard. The national average cost for nursing homes is $38,000 per year and is significantly higher in metropolitan areas, such as Philadelphia, where the annual cost is approximately $50,000; and

WHEREAS, costs to the Commonwealth will increase on account of increased demands for services as our population ages; and

WHEREAS, the concept of long-term care partnerships promote personal responsibility and encourages the purchase of private long-term care insurance as the primary source of funds for long-term care services; and

WHEREAS, a partnership program allows participants to shelter assets from Medicaid "spend down" equal to the benefits paid by a long-term care insurance policy under the program or protect all assets when participants purchase a more significant policy; and

WHEREAS, the concept of long-term care partnerships results in private insurance paying first and government paying last; and

WHEREAS, the experience of the four states that have had partnership plans for almost a decade has resulted in significant savings to taxpayers as demonstrated by recent program reports listed below:

Number of Participants

State	Policies in Force	on Medicaid
New York	26,774	15
Connecticut	15,349	6
Indiana	6,998	2
California	17,762	1

Figure 4.3 (continued)

And;

WHEREAS, American citizens in 46 States, the District of Columbia and territories of the United States are being discriminated against by not being able to enjoy the benefits provided by long-term care partnership plans due to a restriction placed on Federal law in 1993 that has prevented additional states from enacting long-term care partnership programs.

RESOLVED, that the Senate of Pennsylvania memorialize the Congress of the United States to enact H.R. 1041 that amends Section 1917(b)(1)(C) of the Social Security Act (42 U.S.C. 1396p(b)(1)(C) by deleting the date of May 14, 1993 for states to have long-term care partnership plans approved affording states throughout the nation the ability to give their citizens the same rights to participate in these types of programs.

RESOLVED, that copies of this resolution be transmitted to the presiding officers of each house of Congress and to each member of Congress from Pennsylvania.

Viatical and Life Settlements

"Finance is the art of passing money from hand to hand until it finally disappears."

–Robert W. Sarnoff

Sarah Lorenti and Scott Ericsson have never met, yet the two are locked in a deal to the death. In early 1997, Lorenti and her husband, Raymond, then living in Naples, Florida, invested $50,000 to purchase a 22% share of Ericsson's $256,000 life insurance policy. According to the papers they received from the Fort Lauderdale viatical settlement company that brokered the deal, Ericsson (not his real name) had "advanced HIV disease" with a 6 to 12 month life expectancy. Under the viatical settlement arrangement, he would get a percentage of the policy for his immediate use. After he died and the insurance company paid off, investors would receive their share of the claim. In the Lorenti's case, that would be $56,320, a solid 12.6% return. Lorenti said the salesman advised that viaticals were better than CDs or stocks. Ericsson, a postal worker from the Midwest is still alive, and Lorenti is still waiting for the payoff. Though she continues to receive letters from the viatical company reporting that Ericsson's condition remains terminal, Lorenti (whose husband has since passed away), now wants the funds to meet her own needs and she worries that she'll never collect.[6]

The word "viatical" is derived from a Latin word meaning provisions for a journey. A viatical settlement is the sale of a terminally ill individual's life insurance policy at a discount to a third party, the purchaser. This purchaser may own all or a portion of the policy proceeds, depending upon whether other purchasers have also contributed money to acquire the policy. At the death of the insured (the viator), the purchasers (now beneficiaries) receive their portion of the death benefit.

To keep the policy in force while the viator is still living, the viatical settlement company who organized the purchase, sets aside enough money to make the premium payments. This same organization must notify the insurer upon the viator's death.

Viatical settlements provide needed funds for terminally ill individuals, who may need the money to pay for mounting medical expenses and living needs as other income sources, including active wages, may no longer be available to the dying person. Individuals in this medical condition are extremely vulnerable and should be careful about the type of deal they strike just to get their hands on some necessary dollars. And, even if it is a decent deal for those that are ill, it may have mixed results for those willing to invest in a policy through a viatical company, as evidenced in the case above.

Viaticals were introduced in the mid-1980s to primarily address the needs of people with AIDS, the majority of whom had already lost their jobs and benefits and would have died in poverty without this opportunity to cash in a life insurance policy that was doing them no particular good while they were alive. The Health Insurance Portability and Accountability Act of 1996 exempted viators from paying federal income tax on the proceeds if specific criteria were met. CBS aired a segment on viatical settlements in 1995. According to industry sources, common fixed returns in the viatical settlement business are tied to life expectancy: 12 months – 10-12% return; 24 months – 24-28% return; 36 months – 36-42%; and 48 months – 48 to 58%.[7]

Americans age 65 and older are the most affluent and one of the fastest-growing segments of the population. People in this demographic hold more than $492 billion in life insurance in force – a huge potential market for the viatical industry, according to a report compiled by Conning and Company.[8]

For seniors with long-term chronic conditions who have made no other arrangements for reimbursement of long-term care expenses, life settlements may represent the source of financing they need for the foreseeable future. Long-term care treatments are likely more worthy of need than continuing to pay for a life insurance policy.

The amount of money a policyholder receives for the policy is based on the insured's age and table rating (if any), and the policy's expected future premiums and cash surrender value. It is generally a better alternative than surrendering the policy. Even reinsurers are exploring this market for an opportunity, perhaps paying off within a certain timeframe following life expectancy.

From a flyer published by the Medical Escrow Society

You now have the opportunity to help your clients obtain immediate cash for a traditionally dormant asset – Life Insurance. This asset, that usually lapses or is surrendered over 80% of the time before any economic value is realized, can now be saved and redeemed at a discount through Life Settlements. Until now, policyholders' options were either letting their policies lapse or taking any surrender value when their policies became unwanted or unaffordable. The Life Settlement option allows redemption over surrender. It's been a financial tragedy for seniors too long and it's our responsibility to let them know there is a new solution.

A 2001 report issued by the Life Office Management Association (LOMA) said that the life settlement process for the affluent and elderly is fraught with difficulties. "The problems of the settlement industry arise in part because of the large sums of investor money that are flowing into an environment that remains marginally regulated, said the report's author. These sums attract both the honest and the dishonest, and the dishonest have major incentives for fraud. The report concluded that unless greater disclosure was required in the future, problems will grow rather than diminish.[9]

In 1999, Florida introduced new viatical terminology and better defined how the industry transacts business. Any person who wishes to solicit viatical settlement purchasers in the state must first obtain licensure as a life insurance agent from the Florida Department of Insurance.[10]

Viaticals and its adjunct – life or senior settlements (those sold by elderly who are not chronically or terminally ill) – will still have to battle through a plethora of bad publicity in their efforts to attain a legitimate foothold in the financial services business. Witness the following samples:

Florida Moves Against Another Viatical Company

August 23, 1999 – Florida Treasurer and Insurance Commissioner Bill Nelson has filed an administrative complaint against an Orlando-based viatical company for allegedly violating its licensing agreement. Mr. Nelson has vowed to "clean up" Florida's viatical industry, and at least five of the eight firms licensed in the state are under review. They include a group accused of selling bogus viatical policies, and two others accused of hiding terminal medical conditions from life insurers in order to obtain coverage.[11] This latter practice is called "cleansheeting" where viatical companies solicit patients with life-threatening or terminal conditions to lie about their health and apply for life insurance policies that are then resold to investors.

Long Warns North Carolinians of Viatical Settlement Schemes

Spring, 2000 – Insurance Commissioner Jim Long is applauding the combined efforts of the North Carolina Department of Insurance and the Federal Bureau of Investigation that resulted in the first conviction in the United States specifically for viatical settlement fraud, while warning consumers to be cautious of illegal viatical settlement schemes.

Ronald Patrick MacDonald was sentenced in January 2000 for mail fraud in which insurance policies were obtained under false pretenses. He was sentenced to two years in federal prison. McDonald misrepresented his health status on applications for life insurance and later sold his policies to a viatical settlement company for profit. "This case is only the tip of the iceberg in illegal viatical settlement schemes both in North Carolina and nationwide." Viatical settlements have been a good remedy for the terminally ill who are in need of cash, but criminal involvement has resulted in murder, extortion, criminal conspiracy, money laundering and investment fraud.[12]

In Florida, Anti-Fraud Plans Now Apply

Spring, 2001 – By December 1, 2000, every licensed viatical settlement provider and viatical settlement broker must have adopted an anti-fraud plan and filed it with the Department of Insurance, Division of Insurance Fraud. The anti-fraud plan should include the following:

1.   A description of the procedures for detecting and investigating possible fraudulent insurance acts and procedures for resolving material inconsistencies between medical records and insurance applications.

2.   A description of the procedures for the mandatory reporting of possible fraudulent insurance acts to the Division of Insurance Fraud.

3.   A description of the plan for anti-fraud education and training of underwriters and other personnel.

4.   A written description or chart outlining the organizational arrangement of the anti-fraud personnel who are responsible for the investigation and reporting of possible fraudulent insurance acts and investigating unresolved material inconsistencies between medical records and insurance applications.[13]

A viatical industry trade group that is worth checking if you intend to involve yourself or any client in a viatical or life settlement is the Viatical and Life Settlement Association (www.viatical.org).

Reverse Mortgages

Reverse mortgages have provided seniors with another source of income – the ability to tap into home equity without actually having to sell or leave the home. Unlike a traditional mortgage where one would borrow a specific loan amount and make payments until the loan balance is paid back, the reverse mortgage allows a senior homeowner the chance to borrow against the available equity in the home, remaining in the home without the burden of payments and with an income stream. The homeowner still retains the title to the property, and also continues to be responsible for taxes, maintenance and homeowner's insurance. The FHA (Federal Housing Authority) has a formal reverse mortgage program that is available in most states. The amount of money that can be borrowed is generally affected by the age of the borrower (youngest must be at least 62), the value of the home and current interest rates.

"The typical borrower has been about 75 years old, generally a woman and often a widow, whose home is worth more than the average for someone in her circumstances and her income is less," reports AARP's home equity information center. This is the type of individual who would seek a reverse mortgage that provides for a monthly payment or line of credit one can draw on as needed. Some retirees are taking reverse mortgages out to use the proceeds to pay off existing mortgages or home-equity loans. This eliminates their outstanding debt, along with the need to make monthly loan payments, and frees up cash for other spending needs.[14]

When the home is ultimately sold, that money borrowed through the reverse mortgage will have to be paid back with interest. But it serves the purpose for which it was intended.

BIG PICTURE

Retirement and Other Surveys

Forget the 85+ year-olds. The "Zoomers" are taking over. The new 2000 Census confirmed that the age group 45-54 has now become the fastest growing age group in the country. The new Census figures also revealed that the growth of the age 65+ population, now around 35 million, had slowed due to a relatively low number of births in the late 1920s and early 1930s. The only groups to decline were the Xers – age brackets 20-24 and 25-34 – despite a wave of immigration that is usually dominated by 20-something people. The 2000 Census also showed that single women raising children grew five times faster than married couples raising children.[15] Let's not forget the age 55+ Zoomers. This is the leading edge of the group barreling towards retirement. An estimated 3.2 million Zoomers turn age 55 in 2001, making them eligible to live in age-restricted communities. Over the next five years, another 17 million will celebrate a 55th birthday.[16]

Here's a look at where most seniors are moving:[17]	
"Big" Markets	Fast Risers
Phoenix/Tucson	Chicago
Las Vegas	Sacramento
South Florida	Denver
Central Florida	Charlotte
Ocean County, NJ	Dallas/Houston/Austin

These numbers have great implications for long-term care planning. Not only are the Zoomers closing in on the time they need to seriously consider this estate planning tool, but the number of potential younger caregivers is decreasing, making the possible dependence on outside (the family) help for long-term care needs much more of a likelihood.

Half of all Zoomers say they'd like to *retire* by age 55, but only one in five expects to be financially secure enough to do so, according to a new national survey commissioned by Aetna Financial. Nearly half of affluent Zoomers say they spend one hour or less on financial planning activities related to retirement in a typical month, while the average American, by contrast, spends 120 hours per month watching TV. One in five who have changed jobs said they cashed out the money in their former employer's retirement plan, a step experts strongly advise against. The survey's sponsors noted, "By most indicators, retirement by age 60 is not a very realistic prospect for most people. We're talking about a serious disconnect here between the golf course and the grindstone."[18] When you add in the potential long-term care expense factor, even fewer people are adequately prepared for retirement.

> **Beyond 50: A Report to the Nation on Economic Security – from AARP[19]**
>
> Americans older than 50 are better off than 20 years ago but many are ill-prepared for old age, with only a third having private pensions, and Social Security amounting to more than half of their retirement income after age 65. Social Security was a particularly important source of retirement income for women, without which more than half of all elderly women would be living in poverty. Social Security was the sole source of retirement income for 17% of those over age 65. The rise in health care costs means that America's elderly face out-of-pocket costs amounting to an average 19% of income for those over age 65.

There is even more evidence of most people being unprepared for retirement: A national survey of defined contribution plan participants conducted by John Hancock Financial Services indicated that most participants in a 401(k) retirement plan or similar vehicle remained "fundamentally unprepared" to manage their retirement portfolios. The problem has been hidden over the past decade by the booming economy and surging stock market. The do-it-yourself approach to managing one's own finances appeals to American ideals of thrift, self-reliance and individual initiative, but whether it is practical or even a good idea remains an open question, concluded the study's authors. According to the study,

- only 50% of respondents said they had determined how much money they will need for a financially secure retirement,

- 60% think they cannot lose money in a government bond fund,

- 65% didn't know they can lose money in any bond fund,

- 80% didn't know the best time to invest in a bond fund (best answer: when interest rates are expected to decrease), and

- 20% did not realize they could lose money in stocks.[20]

There is a long way to go in the retirement education of those in pre-retirement planning to avoid some of the financial disasters that may befall the naïve and the innocent.

Adding further confusion to retirement planning: Even though planning for income in retirement is the number one financial planning concern for America's most successful, well-educated professionals, most admit they aren't aware of all their retirement and financial planning options, according to a study conducted for Nationwide Financial. The study's sponsor said "This lack of knowledge comes at a pivotal point in retirement history, with a volatile market and Americans having to shoulder more of the burden themselves for their incomes during retirement." As expected, most successful professionals said they did understand their 401(k) plan (71%), their stocks (58%) and their mutual funds (61%). However, just 18% reported a high level of knowledge of variable universal life, variable annuities or long-term care insurance.[22] These recent sur-

In a 2001 survey, it was revealed that few people understand long-term care financing.[21]

- 9% do not understand long-term care insurance

- People who consider themselves as fairly knowledgeable on issues relating to investing and financial products over-estimate long-term care insurance premiums by as much as 500%.

- 50% of respondents believe that their spouse will be there to take care of them, while 22% indicated private insurance would provide help, and 12% cited their children in this role.

veys all seem to confirm that there is a tremendous lack of knowledge about wealth accumulation and wealth protection in the marketplace and part of the advisor's or planner's job is to educate prospects and clients about these vital planning concerns. The alternative is not likely to be very promising for the country's financial future.

Tax Issues

"The only thing that saves us from the bureaucracy is its inefficiency."

– Eugene McCarthy

As this book has documented, government has had a somewhat spotty record when it comes to addressing long-term care issues. First, there was the long-awaited clarification of the taxation of long-term care insurance in the Health Insurance Portability and Accountability Act of 1996 (HIPAA). While it did confirm the belief that long-term care insurance payouts would not be a taxable event for a policyholder, the legislation directed this tax favorability at only certain types of long-term care policies, taking (for all practical purposes) the most competitive long-term care insurance policy available at that time out of circulation. In addition, HIPAA failed to reopen the door on more states developing partnership programs. It also made it clear that long-term care insurance was not to be made a part of the popular Section 125 plans. Most planners and insurers said thanks for nothing.

The feds followed that up with the Balanced Budget Act a year later, a bill that literally sunk the home health care flagship that many Medicare beneficiaries were sailing. Cutbacks deep-sixed an incredible number of home health care agencies who were unable to maintain profitability on the meager allowances coming out of the notorious low-paying Health Care Financing Administration.

What could the federal government do for an encore? President Clinton took one last swipe at it, signing into law in September 2000 the Long Term Care Security Act, that added long-term care insurance to the Federal Employees Health Benefit Program beginning in

October 2002; coverage that will also be made available to veterans. In Congress' session in 2001, two bills hit the floor running – House Bill 831 (co-sponsored by Nancy Johnson (R-Conn.) and Karen Thurman (D-FL.) and Senate Bill 627 (co-sponsored by Charles Grassley (R-Iowa) and Bob Graham (D-FL.) – that have a lot of bipartisan support and a chance of passing. The primary highlights include:[23]

1. A phased-in, above-the-line tax deduction (no itemization necessary) for premiums paid for a tax-qualified long-term care policy.

2. Inclusion of long-term care insurance in employer Section 125 cafeteria plans and flexible spending accounts.

3. A $3,000 tax credit for people with long-term care needs or their family caregiver.

The phase-in for the tax deduction is based on the length of time a long-term care policy is in force, beginning in 2001. Of course, the 2001 Congress has already passed the Economic Growth and Tax Relief Reconciliation Act of 2001 that gives new meaning to the term "phase-in". So – stay tuned: phase-in language in the LTC bill could change before passage. In any event, the personal deduction for premium would extend to many more people then can take advantage of the HIPAA provision that requires the taxpayer to itemize. The Section 125 part of the bill would make long-term care insurance even more attractive to employers and, more important, their employees. There was a significant amount of revenue utilized for the tax bill and Democrats now control the Senate agenda, but there is still much bipartisan impetus to make this bill law. Congressional members have been hearing from their constituents about the importance of long-term care and feel inclined to put something in place, while still able to duck the larger question of taxation of non-qualified long-term care policies. It is much more significant legislation than President Clinton's $1,000 caregiver tax credit offered up in 1999.

Most Significant Legislation in a Generation to be Signed by President Bush Today

WASHINGTON, June 7, 2001 – A major effort by lawmakers, life insurers, plan providers and others to enhance the financial security of tomorrow's retirees becomes a reality today, when President Bush signs tax legislation containing crucial pension reforms and retirement savings incentives. The American Council of Life Insurers called the Economic Growth and Tax Relief Reconciliation Act of 2001 perhaps the most significant retirement security legislation in a generation, referring to laws enacted in the late 1970s that created 401(k) plans and legislation in the early 1980s that introduced IRAs.[25] Highlights include:

1. raises the limits on 401(k) contributions to $15,000 by 2006;

2. increases the limit on IRA contributions from $2,000 (limit established in 1981) to $5,000 by 2008;

3. indexes the contribution limits for both 401(k)-style plans and IRAs for inflation after they are fully phased in;

4. allows individuals age 50 and older to make additional annual contributions up to $5,000 in 401(k) plans and up to $1,000 in IRAs to help "catch up" with retirement planning; and

5. reduces the "red tape" that small businesses face in setting up and maintaining retirement plans by reforming parts of the tax code that were too complex and acted as more of a discouragement rather than an incentive to make these types of plans available.

Like all tax laws, this one will take some time to shake out. Even then, the final results may not be certain as this law also gradually reduces the estate tax rates and raises the exemption equivalent of the estate tax unified credit, and repeals the estate tax for one year in 2010. If no action is taken by Congress, the above mentioned retirement plan provisions and the estate tax provisions revert to pre-EGTRRA status. This could only make sense to the U.S. Congress.

If Congress were to pass the long-term care bill as outlined above, the combination of the two bills could be most beneficial to those preparing for and nearing retirement. The potential will certainly be there to make substantial progress in wealth accumulation and wealth protection planning.

A Tax Credit to Care for Mom Wouldn't Have Helped My Sisters[24]

"When the Clinton administration first announced a $5.5 billion plan to help millions of Americans who need long-term care – and to assist the relatives who take care of them – my first reaction was to wonder what that would have meant to our family had the program been in effect during the four years my mother lay in bed, incapacitated by the ravages of Parkinson's disease. My three sisters – Mariana, Dora and Carmen – made my mother's care in her own home their mission from the time she became seriously ill to that quiet New Year's Day when she died in her own bed. My other two sisters and brother and I were only able to contribute financial help as we did not live in the same town as my mother.

"Carmen, who did not have a job outside the home, was in charge of supervising my mother's care during the daytime… we were able to hire part-time help to sit with my mother half a day while Carmen went home long enough to take care of her husband and children. When the women we hired couldn't make it, Carmen had to spend the entire day at my mother's home. She did not get to go home until Mariana or Dora, who had worked all day at their jobs, arrived in the evening to spend the night with my mother. They, too, had husbands and school-age kids whose needs went unmet every other night for those four years.

"… They never had the luxury of a full night's sleep because they had to get up every hour or so to remove the phlegm that periodically threatened to choke her. Her throat muscles had been rendered useless by the Parkinson's. If one of them had to go out of town for a few days that meant the others had to put in double-shifts. Only when Maria Luisa and Delfina, my two other sisters, came to visit – not more than twice a year each – would the three get time off.…

"But my mother wanted to be at home… So all this is what I was thinking about when I read of the administration's proposal, and its principal feature, the $1,000-a-year tax credit – an insult, almost – when you take into consideration the time, hard work and heartache that is involved in taking care of the ailing elderly. …a profound sadness overwhelmed me. I was struck by how little we value both our elderly and those who take care of them."

State Issues

How to care for a growing population of people over age 65 has preoccupied state legislatures of late; they are spending considerable time and money researching how best to use their health and housing resources to care for this expanding population. Although tax deductibility of premium remains elusive for many on a federal level, states have done their level best to offer either a tax credit or a deduction for long-term care insurance plans. There are 23 states that have passed this type of law through the year 2000. They are: Alabama, California, Colorado, Hawaii, Illinois, Indiana, Iowa, Kentucky, Maine, Maryland, Minnesota, Missouri, Montana, New Mexico, New York, North Carolina, North Dakota, Ohio, Oregon, Utah, Virginia, West Virginia and Wisconsin. Maine offers both a credit and a deduction.[26]

Maryland Passes Tax Credit Law

In 2000, the state of Maryland gave first time buyers of long-term care insurance a credit against their Maryland state income tax, effective July 1, 2001. The credit is limited to the lesser of $500 or 100% of their annual premium. An individual who purchases a policy for parents or children is also entitled to the tax credit.[13] Currently, total expenditures on nursing home care in Maryland exceeds $1 billion. By 2030, total nursing home expenditures in Maryland are expected to rise to $5.8 billion. Medicaid nursing home spending is expected to rise from $385.4 million to $1.9 billion by the year 2030.[28]

Also in 2000, 17 states enacted 42 new laws on assisted living issues. Assisted living is currently the least regulated of all health care services, according to the American Health Care Association. The laws, in general, require facilities to be regulated by states and that alternative ways to finance assisted living be explored (including use of Medicaid waivers, which continue to be popular with lawmakers). By July 2000, 29 states and the District of Columbia had created regulations or statutes specifically for assisted living. Four other states – Arkansas, Illinois, New Hampshire and Vermont – were in the process of creating new regulations for assisted living in the year 2000. The remainder regulates ALFs under terms like adult homes, rest homes, congregate care, residential care facilities and elderly or senior housing.[29]

Other Government-Related Information

"Hell hath no fury like a bureaucrat scorned."
                                              – Milton Freedman

Law: Nursing Homes Can't Evict Medicaid Patients

WASHINGTON, March 25, 1999 – President Clinton signed into law today a bill that would protect nursing home residents from being evicted or forced to move solely because they rely on Medicaid to pay their bills. "This law closes a legal loophole that allows nursing homes to evict their most vulnerable residents. It puts patients ahead of profits," said Mike Bilirakis (R-FL.), a sponsor of the bipartisan legislation. The impetus for the bill came from the highly publicized 1998 attempt by one of the nation's largest nursing home operators, Vencor, Inc., to remove Medicaid patients from some of its homes in several states. While public criticism and pressure from government regulators caused Vencor to reconsider, lawmakers wanted legislation that would prevent any such actions by nursing home operators in the future.[30]

Law Curbs Nursing Home Evictions

WASHINGTON, March 26, 1999 – The new law would not force nursing homes to accept Medicaid patients. However, homes that choose to stop taking new Medicaid patients would be barred from evicting or transferring those Medicaid patients they already have. For the first time, homes that choose not to accept Medicaid patients would have to notify any new residents initially able to pay their own way that they might have to move if they eventually run out of money and need to rely on Medicaid. Senator Bob Graham (D-FL.), a sponsor of the legislation, said the bipartisan bill would ensure that the elderly wouldn't be forced to live like nomads in their retirement years. He called it an "American affirmation of its commitment to its older citizens."[31]

Hawaii Launches Innovative Long Term Care Plan

The state of Hawaii has launched a new long-term care insurance program for its public employees. The plan is unique because it offers participants the maximum amount of flexibility – they can buy whatever level of coverage they can afford now and can increase the coverage in later years. The plan also guarantees that benefits will be paid to survivors upon the participant's death. Hawaii's voluntary, self-pay LTC plan is available to more than 250,000 residents of the state, which is 25% of the adult population. The plan covers all eligible active and retired state employees and their spouses, parents, parents-in-law, grandparents, grandparents-in-law, and surviving spouses of deceased employees.[32]

AHCA Urges Creation of National Commission on Long-Term Care Financing Reform

WASHINGTON, March 23, 1999 – The American Health Care Association (AHCA) called today for the creation of a national commission to reform the current long-term care financing system. Linda Keegan, Vice President of AHCA said, "We need to educate Baby Boomers and encourage them to plan now for their long-term care needs. As Baby Boomers age and need long-term care, the demand for services will quadruple – and push Medicaid to the breaking point. Congress and the Administration must look at all aspects of how long-term care is paid for. A federal commission, similar to the Medicare Commission, should be convened to explore issues related to long-term care financing in the 21st Century."[33]

Coalition Calls for National Policy to Fund Long-Term Care

WASHINGTON, April 16, 2001 – Citizens for Long-Term Care (CLTC) called for a new national policy for the financing of long-term care today. There must be "a clear national commitment" to finance long-term care based on principles of social and private insurance, said the CLTC, a coalition of 63 long-term care providers, consumers, insurers and workers. CLTC said the coalition agrees that there must be a new social insurance benefit that finances a minimum floor of financial protection combined with a program of incentives for the early acquisition of private insurance. One CLTC board member said, "Clearly, the statistics show there is a need for both private sector and public sector solutions to the LTC financing dilemma."[34]

HUD Awards Help the Elderly, Disabled Live at Home

February, 2001 – A new program generated out of $29.3 million in grants recently announced by the U.S. Department of Housing and Urban Development will furnish "service coordinators" to help more than 35,000 low-income elderly and physically incapacitated residents in federally supported housing identify and receive health care, meals and other critical support services they need to remain living independently. The grants go to the owners of private housing developments in 39 states, Puerto Rico and the District of Columbia, who receive money from HUD to house low-income individuals. The owners or their management companies then will either hire or enter into a contract arrangement for service coordinators, who have backgrounds in providing social services, especially to the frail elderly and people with disabilities. HUD Secretary Andrew Cuomo said, "Too many older and disabled Americans who struggle to get by on fixed incomes just don't have the money to pay for housing and needed support services. HUD is helping them get both the housing they need and the services that will enable them to remain in their apartments, connected to their communities, families and friends." Part of the grant money will go to converting existing HUD-subsidized apartments into assisted living facilities.[35]

As Retirees' Needs Grow, So Will Services

Dear Readers: The retired population of America is growing faster than changes can be made to accommodate it. That means hardship for retirees needing the changes now. But it fits our economic model of supply and demand – and fits our political model of reacting to great social need rather than anticipating it. Most building blocks of today's golden years – pension and Social Security, Medicare and long-term care insurance – came about because of consumer

demand or human need that was established years and even generations earlier. In the interim, the time between the beginning of the
demand/need and the time it was satisfied, people suffered a little or
a lot. And so it is today – with several demands/needs of America's
retirees. Business is trying to satisfy the demands and make a profit in
the process. Government is trying to satisfy social needs and not bust
the budget in the process. Older people need tax breaks to pay for
their growing health-care costs. And retirees need programs that help
them stay in their own homes, hopefully forever. There are a few such
tax breaks and programs, but not nearly enough. The demand/need
is obvious, but the solution lags behind. These and other
demands/needs of American retirees will likely be met over time. The
growing number of retirees will generate great attention from private
enterprise and generate great debate from government. The time lag
from the onset of the demand/need to the satisfying of it will be
shortened by political activism.[36]

Long Term Care Facilities

*"My mother used to say that there are no strangers,
only friends you haven't met yet. She's now in a maximum security twilight home in Australia."*
                              –Dame Edna Everage

Nursing Homes in Crisis
The modern nursing home industry was born in the mid-1960s
with Medicare and Medicaid. Nearly 40 years later, these treatment
facilities are in danger of near-extinction in a time when demands for
this type of care are on a meteoric rise for a number of reasons having
to do with demographics and government cost controls. These problems are affecting all types of long-term care arrangements, but are
perhaps most noticeable today in the plight of skilled nursing facilities.

Nursing Homes Filing for Bankruptcy

CARSON CITY, Nev., April 5, 2000 – Just two days before
Christmas, 95-year-old Lily Coffman began packing up her belong-

ings to move to a new nursing home because her old one was closing abruptly. The move by Coffman and about 60 fellow nursing home residents is one that is repeating itself around the nation. More than 1,600 of the nation's 17,000 nursing homes have filed for bankruptcy since last fall as they struggle with federal funding cuts, a lack of state or local money, increased insurance costs and tougher quality-care standards. For some, the bankruptcy filings have resulted from bad business decisions, heavy debt loads and claims of defrauding government health care programs.

In Nevada and New Mexico, nearly half the homes owned by big chains and affiliated with the American Health Care Association (AHCA) filed for bankruptcy protection – the highest rates in the nation. The AHCA, which represents nearly two-thirds of the nation's nursing homes, says Medicare funding cuts in 1997 could total over $15 billion over several years, even though Congress last year restored $2.7 billion for patients needing skilled nursing care.[37]

Nursing Home Resident Complaints[38]

The five states with the most complaints, per bed:

Nevada:	4,250 beds	1.68 complaints
New Mexico	7,376 beds	1.24 complaints
Colorado	19,876 beds	0.39 complaints
South Dakota	2,171 beds	0.25 complaints
Wyoming	3,116 beds	0.24 complaints

Nursing-Home Residents Buffeted by Bankruptcies

TALLAHASSEE, May, 2000 – In Florida, over 16,000 of the 82,000 nursing home beds are owned by companies currently in bankruptcy proceedings. The problem in Florida is exacerbated by huge liability insurance premium increases brought on by a rising tide of court judgments against nursing homes for poor care. Nursing-home attorneys say that because Florida law does not limit punitive damages against homes, insurance premiums for these facilities in this state is eight times the national average.[39]

Quick Aid Unlikely for Nursing Homes

TALLAHASSEE, May 25, 2000 – More than one in seven nursing homes in the state have signaled that they soon could close because of skyrocketing insurance premiums or canceled policies. Heavy debt, rising insurance premiums and unfavorable changes in government reimbursement rules threaten the existence of the institutions housing Florida's oldest and frailest residents.[40]

Nursing Shortage Leads to Long Hours, Frustration

June 1, 2001 – It was a scenario that nurse Linda Warino had come to dread: Too many patients. Not enough nurses. No volunteers to work overtime. About once a week – and she works only three days a week – she said she was required to work beyond her 12-hour shift. It led her and her colleagues in Youngstown, Ohio to walk off their hospital jobs in a demand for better conditions and pay. They have been on strike now for 31 days.

Warino, a nurse for 28 years, said it wasn't just the long hours or salary issues that prompted the 770 nurses at Youngstown's Forum Health hospital system to act. They feared patient care was suffering. "Let's be real," she said. "In your 14th or 15th hour, you are not as good as you are in your first, second or third hour."

Dissatisfaction with pay and increasingly stressful working conditions, aggravated by a shortage of nurses at hospitals across the country is spurring job actions and the formation of nurses' unions at more hospitals. There have been seven nursing strikes across the country in 2001. There were 10 in 2000 and 21 in 1999. By comparison, there were only four strikes in 1995. Last year, 19% of the country's 1.3 million hospital nurses were unionized, up from 17% in 1999. United American Nurses is now campaigning to unionize in 18 more hospital systems. The increased union activity is coming at a time when hospital finances are being squeezed by lower reimbursements from both private and government insurers. A third of all hospitals operate at a loss, according to the American Hospital Association.[41]

Nursing Shortage is Raising Worries on Patients' Care

April 8, 2001 – The vacancy rate for nursing positions at 73 hospitals in New York, Westchester and Long Island is averaging 8%, up sharply from 5.5% in 1999, the Greater New York Hospital Association said last week. The shortage is even worse in California: vacancies in the 470 hospitals there averaged 20% in December 2000, according to the California Healthcare Association. At Westchester Medical Center in Valhalla, New York, the largest and busiest hospital between New York City and Albany, more than 25% of the positions for operating-room nurses were unfilled as of late last year. Surgeries backed up and some were postponed, often for several days.[42]

Care for Elderly Suffers from Severe Nursing Assistant Shortage

TALLAHASSEE, May 6, 2001 – State lawmakers in Tallahassee may not know Trish Anderson by name. But they've been talking about her for months. Anderson is a CNA – certified nursing assistant. And she's at the crux of what lots of people, including members of the Florida legislature, have been calling a crisis in the state's nursing homes.

It's not her fault. The problem – at least one of the problems – is that there aren't enough Trish Andersons to go around. And the shortage of employees opens the door to insufficient care, neglect or worse for the state's large population of frail elderly people. Which leads to the other big problem facing nursing homes: lawsuits. People in the industry say lawsuits and malpractice insurance drain their resources and cause some nursing homes to go bankrupt.

According to a recent federal study, every nursing home resident needs at least 2.9 hours of care from a CNA each day. If not, they're being neglected, according to federal health regulators. In Florida, some nursing home residents are lucky to get 1.7 hours of care, which had been the minimum established by state law.

After months of debate, Florida legislature passed a law [on May 4, 2001] – the last day of the session – upping that requirement to 2.3 hours a day by 2002 and 2.9 hours per day by 2004, and allocating more than $70 million to help pay for more staff. The government-supported Medicaid program pays the bills for the vast majority of Florida's nursing home residents. The Legislature also appeased the nursing home industry by *placing caps on punitive damages* paid out in lawsuits.[43]

Nevada Nursing Home Crisis – Elderly Abuse

LAS VEGAS, June 5, 2001 – The Nursing Home Justice Center today announced the opening of its office in Las Vegas. Their focus is on patient negligence and abuse cases for residents of nursing home and assisted living facilities. The firm consists of experienced trial attorneys representing victims of nursing home negligence and abuse, with a unique team approach in its representation of its clients. The Nursing Home Justice Center is committed to protecting the rights of residents in nursing homes and assisted living facilities, as well as making efforts to prevent neglect and abuse from occurring. A Managing Partner of the Center said "our staff has made itself available to nursing homes and other senior residential facilities, at no cost to the facility, to discuss measures and steps they can implement to help prevent future neglect and abuse." The Center is conducting seminars and speaking engagements to heighten public awareness regarding the level of care the elderly are receiving in nursing homes, assisted living facilities and group homes in the state of Nevada and across the nation.[44]

Government Pushes Nursing Home Rules

WASHINGTON, July 23, 2000 – Federal health officials have concluded that most nursing homes are understaffed to the point that patients may be endangered. For the first time, the government is recommending strict new rules that would require thousands of homes to hire more nurses and health aides. In a report to Congress, encouragement was for rules that would require nursing homes to have enough registered nurses to provide at least 12 minutes a day of care to each resident, on the average. But, it pointed out, 31% of nursing homes do not meet that standard.[45]

Drug Errors Hit Nursing Home Patients, Report Says

BOSTON, August 10, 2000 – About 150,000 nursing home patients suffer adverse drug reactions each year – sometimes fatal ones – because of staff errors in prescribing and monitoring their medications, the *Boston Globe* reported, quoting a study by Massachusetts researchers. The study, by the University of Massachusetts Medical School and Brigham and Women's Hospital found 546 medication-related injuries at 18 Massachusetts nursing homes over a year. The report included one death and 31 injuries that were life threatening. About half of the incidents could have been prevented.[46]

More Citations, More Litigation

ORLANDO, March 5, 2001 – Nursing homes with high numbers of quality-of-care violations in state inspections tend to be sued more often. The average number of lawsuits from 1996 to 2000:[47]

Homes with 40 to 80 violations .5.72 lawsuits
Homes with 30 to 40 violations .4.37 lawsuits
Homes with 19 to 30 violations .3.75 lawsuits
Homes with 18 or fewer violations . . . . .1.63 lawsuits

For-profit homes: . .average violations 32.2 . . .average lawsuits 4.41
Nonprofit homes: . .average violations 21.2 . . .average lawsuits 2.20
Government: . . . . . .average violations 31.8 . . .average lawsuits 1.80

Numbers are for 241 nursing homes in South and Central Florida, including 53 nonprofit, 182 for-profit and 6 government facilities.

Sources: Health Care Financing Administration, county court records, Florida Agency for Health Care Administration

Lax State Regulation Lets Nursing Homes Sidestep Rules

PALM BEACH, March 12, 2001 – When Luella Hearn's son recalls her last days at the Darcy Hall Nursing Center in West Palm Beach, he sees a woman suffering from dehydration, bedsores, bruises and broken bones from 20 falls in less than two years. Two weeks after the 93-year-old woman died on October 26, 1997, state inspectors cited Darcy Hall for 15 violations of state nursing home standards. Last year, the nursing home paid $265,000 to Hearn's son to settle a wrongful death lawsuit.

And how much did the state agency responsible for enforcing nursing home standards fine Darcy Hall for its transgressions? Not one penny.[48]

Record Number of Nursing Home Closures Putting Seniors at Risk

INDIANAPOLIS, April 3, 2001 – Indiana's dramatic rise in nursing home closures could be a warning sign to the nation's long-term health care providers, according to the Indiana Health Care Association. So far [through March, 2001], 10 nursing homes have either closed their doors or announced their impending shutdown in 2001, compared with 11 closings statewide all last year. Closures seem to be more pervasive in states such as Indiana, Michigan and Minnesota, where reimbursement rates are lower than average. Indiana's average Medicaid daily reimbursement is $94 per Medicaid patient, meaning the care of most Medicaid patients is subsidized by private-pay patients at about $5 each day, per patient.[49]

Nursing Facilities Not Up to Code

LOS ANGELES, April 20, 2001 – An investigation into nursing home abuses across California revealed numerous problems, including embezzlement and patient neglect, the state attorney general said. He added, "For elderly and dependent Californians in these facilities, [surprise annual inspections] means run-down and unsafe nursing home buildings are being fixed, improvements are being made in the quality of care they receive and attention is being given to their dignity." According to a report of the findings, the serious infractions included nurses failing to cover the open wounds of a resident infected with hepatitis B and staffers at another facility not getting the proper signatures before making purchases from patients' trust accounts.[50]

Study Finds Nurses Dissatisfied

PHILADELPHIA, May 7, 2001 – One of every three U.S. nurses surveyed under age 30 planned to leave their jobs within the next year, according to a *Health Affairs* published study. More than 43% scored high on a "burnout inventory" used to measure emotional exhaustion and the extent to which they felt overwhelmed by their work. More than half said they had been subject to verbal abuse. The director of the study said these feelings were said to be the equivalent of "ward rage."[51]

Assisted Living Facilities Experience Growth, Problems

"Americans will put up with anything providing it doesn't block traffic."

–Dan Rather

Letter to the Editor, *National Underwriter,* **March 20, 2000**[52]

"...Assisted Living is another potential trap for consumers. This is a congregate living arrangement without any common definitions in most states. Some states don't even license these living arrangements, while others license or regulate them using different terminology. Insurance policy definitions of assisted living facilities don't reflect the multitude of living arrangements sold in a particular community, state, or neighboring state as an assisted living arrangement. A February article entitled 'Assisted Living Benefits Are Not Uniform" was a good summary of a lurking time bomb for the unwary consumer, and perhaps for the selling agent who may fail to understand the relationship between policy definitions and retirement homes advertising assisted living care. The definitional problems are one issue, but eligibility thresholds are another in a setting that is apt to be more like a group home than an institution. I have handled several of these cases in California, and while I am happy to say those claims were eventually paid, I often wonder about the ones I didn't hear about.

- Bonnie Burns, Education Director
California Health Advocates

Assisted living facilities (ALFs) have been in a period of incredible growth, the "low-cost alternative" to nursing homes. After the negative avalanche of publicity accorded nursing homes in the last few years, combined with a person's own innate fear of these facilities, it's no wonder that ALFs have taken over in many consumers' minds as the best place to acquire long-term care services.

But growth is often accompanied by problems and ALFs have not been immune to this pattern. Even as building of these new residences explodes, regulators and insurers have their hands full trying to monitor care and the quality of the treatment one might receive. It is a monumental task, given the aging of the population and the growing demand for this type of health-related housing.

Assisted living facilities provide a generally more desirable option for those that dread leaving their home. ALFs are home-like settings and they still allow the resident some independence and privacy. Where people 20 years ago might leave their house for a rest home, ALFs have built a more enticing environment.

This does not mean ALFs are immune from some of the same problems plaguing the nursing home industry. Remember that ALFs are loosely regulated in many jurisdictions. Recently, the nation's largest chain of assisted living centers, including about 150 residences for people with Alzheimer's disease, came under scrutiny by state regulators over care quality and safety. In at least five states, the Alterra Health Corporation was reported as having inadequate or untrained staffs, failing to give residents needed medicines or failing to protect their safety. Alterra executives said these were isolated incidents. Regulators were also looking into other ALF centers run by other providers.[53]

Promise Versus Reality[54]

Assisted living entrepreneurs emphasize that their facilities don't look, feel or smell like nursing homes. Yet some practically offer nursing home care, with little government oversight, while others provide so little care that families must hire home attendants to meet their relative's needs. As one facility manager noted, "What sells the family are safety and security, value for price, the food and a homelike environment." And so facilities appeal to the aesthetics of residents and their adult children. Some facilities sport features like old-fashioned ice cream parlors and 1940s-style jukeboxes.

A long-term care ombudsman from Colorado warns that "the critical consideration is the philosophy of the place and how the staff carries it out." A fancy front room with Georgian-style furniture does not guarantee that a resident needing help with a bath every day will get it, or that the facility will accommodate a resident's declining eyesight with appropriate help and activities.

A Brandeis University study in the mid-1990s of 396 residents in ALFs found that although many experienced fairly independent and autonomous lives, they also had unmet health and long-term care needs. The study concluded that those facilities that offered residents more autonomy had more avoidable negative health outcomes than facilities that offered less choice.

Therein lies the crux of assisted living: autonomy versus supervision. Balancing a resident's desire for autonomy with his or her need for assistance is no easy task.

Insurance Rates Ignite a Crisis Among ALFs

ORLANDO, December 24, 2000 – Insurance rates for assisted living facilities suddenly are going through the roof, as carriers hedge against the high legal awards they have seen levied against nursing homes under Florida's liberal patient-rights laws. The cycle of high awards leading to skyrocketing insurance rates hit the nursing home industry last year. Now operators of the facilities are being told their premiums will quadruple, quintuple – or more, if they carry licenses allowing them to take patients with more advanced medical needs. Some companies simply won't issue any liability policies for them.

Florida's Agency for Health Care Administration that regulates nursing homes and assisted living facilities, recently notified 29 of the facilities statewide that their licenses would be revoked if they did not show proof of insurance within 21 days. One Florida surplus lines insurance brokerage firm said last year he had 15 to 20 companies actively writing new assisted living policies. Now he has none. Essentially, what happened to nursing homes is now passing down to ALFs as insurers having difficulty assessing their actual liability risk are either not issuing coverage at all or writing it at incredibly high rates.[55]

ALFs Now in Spotlight

February, 2000 – Governor Jeb Bush announced last month that he put $52.4 million in his proposed budget to help elderly residents go to assisted living facilities, or stay at home with outside help, rather than move into nursing homes. This comes at a time when huge increases in liability insurance costs are forcing many of the state's ALFs to scale down occupancy, scale back on levels of care, and in some cases, shut their doors.

A well-known Tampa-area attorney, nationally known for his litigation efforts in nursing home cases said that fewer than 1% of his cases involve ALFs. Sixty percent of the state's ALFs have fewer than 16 beds and are usually privately run. Still, these facility owners talk about liability rates going from $800 to $5,000 for a 6-bed facility.

Another issue involves covering increased levels of care. Some owners get licenses to offer more extensive medical services. This can put them into a risk category comparable to a nursing home and raise rates from $6,500 to $66,000 annually, as in an example from a 22-bed South Florida facility. One broker noted that the threat for insurers is that residents or their families can file suit under residents' rights laws rather than medical malpractice guidelines, and suits can be filed up to four years after an incident.[56]

Liability troubles have stymied growth in ALFs in recent months. In Florida, the number of assisted living facilities grew by more than 50% since 1992, but the pace of assisted living licenses granted by the state has slowed since January 2000. Forty-one licenses were awarded in the first three months of 2001 versus 85 for the same period in 2000.[57] It remains to be seen what this shakeout will mean for ALFs and long-term care services in general.

State Must Do More to Ensure Quality of Home Health Care

PITTSBURGH, October 27, 1999 – From July 1, 1996 to April 20, 1999, Pennsylvania conducted its first-ever performance audit of its home health care system. In this state, nearly 400,000 adults and children who live in their own homes require some type of nursing services for short-term acute needs or long-term chronic conditions; nearly 250,000 receive services paid for with government dollars. Half of the agencies were cited for deficiencies and in one case, a young girl died while in the care of a home health nurse. The severity of the deficiencies found at 28 agencies varied, ranging from patients' records lacking skilled nursing assessments to plans of care or doctors' orders not being followed. In the case of one agency with 10 deficiencies, a nurse repeatedly failed to follow acceptable infection control procedures. No sanctions were imposed in *any* of these cases, and no one from the state conducted on-site visits to verify that corrections had been made accordingly.[59]

Where does all this leave the long-term care insurance industry? While this type of coverage gives the policyholder a wide range of care and facility options – a choice that is becoming more important as varying facilities battle their own difficulties – one can be sure that consumers will not necessarily feel confident that good care and facilities will be available when needed in the future. Advisors should understand this will be a challenge when presenting long-term care insurance as a funding alternative.

Even as the number of elderly is growing, home health agencies are having greater difficulty finding aides. And although financial constraints are forcing home health agencies out of business – 203 of 590 agencies and their branches have closed in Florida in recent years – the surviving agencies are having trouble luring their former competitors' aides.[58]

Small Picture
LTC Insurance Rate Stability

"If you want a guarantee, buy a toaster."
–Clint Eastwood

> "Four years ago, Camille and Virdon Strey thought they had hit on a perfect way to avoid being shunted to a nursing home. A new kind of insurance called long-term care coverage promised to provide them with help from home-health aides in the comfort of their [California home]. And the relatively modest premiums wouldn't go up because of age or illness, marketing materials pledged. Late last year, though, the couple abruptly canceled their insurance. Premiums on Mr. Strey's policy ... had shot up 41.6%. His wife's bill (from another insurer) had risen 20%. When the Streys told their agent they could no longer afford the coverage, she said it would be fruitless to look elsewhere. By then, Mrs. Strey had severe osteoarthritis and Mr. Strey was tethered to an oxygen tank. 'They were totally uninsurable,' said [their agent], who felt 'betrayed' by the companies' rosy representations. The 82-year-old Mr. Strey adds bitterly, 'I'd been suckered.'"[60]

The above story was a centerpiece for a June 2000 *Wall Street Journal* front page story that blasted the insurance industry for attracting customers to long-term care through low rates and then using their renewal privilege to raise the rates for a "class" of business – the entire block that was sold in this manner. This followed a 1999 Jane Bryant Quinn story warning of low-priced LTC policies. While she pointed out again that LTC insurance seemed to be the best solution for people who don't want to spend their own savings on long-term care, she also warned of a scandal brewing as some insurers would practice the art of squeezing the policyholder out through high premium rate increases before any significant claims might occur. Often, these policies are rich in benefits – and in agent commissions – and low in price, while accepting unhealthy as well as healthy risks. A couple of years after issue, the rate increases start coming and soon the person can't afford to pay for the benefits. The healthy customers in this situation will switch to something newer and cheaper. The others – the older and sicker – will file claims justifying even more rate increases until one-by-one, most of these older policyholders will have to drop the coverage because they cannot afford it. Their old age protection is gone.[61]

We've seen this before – with health insurance. Insurers would lure a group of policyholders in with low rates, banking on the fact that people are constantly shopping their health insurance looking for a better deal. Once this block is solidified, insurers collect premium for a couple of years, ever so slightly raising the premiums until three or four years in, the rates skyrocket. Healthy and younger people leave their policies or that *same insurer* offers them a better policy. Why

> Tom Foley, a life and health actuary with the Kansas insurance department: There is evidence that "a significant number of companies are marketing products that offer tremendously rich benefits, have low prices and sloppy underwriting. This is fraud on consumers. We can't take a consumer's money for 10 years and then run.[62]

lose the healthy people if you don't have to? The only ones left in this "class" of business are the ones that are not insurable or too old to find a much better premium rate. The block of business deteriorates due to high claims experience and the insurer keeps the price increases up until the individuals left insured are only dollar-trading with the company. It's an abominable practice and the possibility that it could be used in the long-term care field is of grave concern to anyone in this market. The industry does not need any more "black eyes."

In North Dakota, consumer action followed a series of alarming rate increases on long-term care policies issued by Acceleration Life and Commonwealth Life for policies originally purchased in the 1980s. Large rate increases drove out policyholders in numbers, including people like Harold Hanson, who bought his level-premium policy in 1987 for around $1,094 annually. Nine years later, his premium costs had increased to $3,603, which he could not afford to pay. Another, Nellie McIlroy, 93, saw her premiums leap from about $830 in 1987 to $6,638 in 1999. She now has Alzheimer's disease and is paying the high premium because she knows she needs the coverage. Of more than 2,000 people who bought these policies in North Dakota, fewer than 130 are still insured.[63]

The case, *Harold Hanson, et al. vs. Acceleration Life Insurance Company et al.*(Civil #3-97cd-152) drew the attention of everyone in the insurance industry in addition to a wave of consumer groups and

The willingness of state regulators to raise rates could be waning. Florida, Georgia, Kansas, Iowa, North Dakota, South Dakota and Virginia are denying rate increase requests more often. Some states limit rate increases. Delaware limits increases to 20% per calendar year. Kentucky, Maryland and Oklahoma limit them to 15% during any 12-month period. New Mexico imposes a three-year initial rate guarantee. New York last approved a rate increase for a long-term care policy in 1994. Wisconsin imposes a three-year initial rate guarantee and a two-year rate guarantee on subsequent rate increases and rate increases cannot exceed 10% for insureds over age 75 with policies in force for more than 10 years.[64]

Source: Larson LTC Group, LLC

insurance regulators. The average cost of the long-term care insurance policies cited in the case rose from under $1,300 annually when purchased in the mid-1980s to over $9,000 a year.[65]

The case went to trial in October 1999 and a settlement was reached shortly thereafter. The settlement was national for $12.6 million in cash and $2.1 million in rate freezes and reductions. The rollback would bring rate increases back to 1993 levels, effective November 1, 1999. One example showed that for premiums that had gone to $7,000 from $1,000 annually, the rollback would reduce the rate back down to $3,500. The insurer alleged no wrongdoing and advised it was only settling to avoid the high cost of continued litigation.[66]

Shortly after this settlement, the NAIC assembled a committee to study and make recommendations on a LTC rate stability model. They felt this problem was just beginning, but they could head off future problems by taking some proactive steps as soon as possible before the level of LTC industry business activity started to really take off. The task force was headed by Kansas Insurance Department director of the health and accident division – Tom Foley. Kansas was already working to require insurers to submit a disk prepared by the Insurance Department that would detail items including assumptions used in determining the need for a rate increase. Regulators can then match up these assumptions to the previous filings to see why a rate increase was being applied for. It would certainly tell much more about a carrier's initial and subsequent rate filing then the Department was currently able to obtain.[67] The eventual draft model had as its centerpiece the premise that loss ratios should be removed up front because they encourage premium increases. In return, the model provided for stiff loss ratio requirements if a carrier returns to a regulator requesting a rate increase. The loss ratio on the initial earned premium would be 58% and 85% on new premiums.[68]

There was one more hurdle to cross for the NAIC's Rate Stability Model. This involved a discussion over the Model's "white knight" provision. This dealt with rate increase disclosure requirements for an insurer that acquires a "sick" block of individual LTC business from another insurer. The draft regulation required that most insurers give applicants information about any history of rate increases, so the applicants would be aware of the possibility that the policy could be subject to future increases. But the white knight provision allowed insurers acquiring a "sick" block of business to file rate increases in the 24-month period following acquisition and they would *not* be required to disclose that rate increase activity to a prospective consumer under the Model Law. Drafters of the Model did not want to discourage insurers from taking over blocks of business that may need rate adjustment for future handling.[70]

"The concept of 'insurability' requires that a relatively small percentage of insureds will be on claim. If a large percentage of insureds are on claim, then ... we have a prepayment plan, not an insurance plan.... [W]ith average annual claim payments of $40,000 or more, a prepayment plan for LTC is not economically feasible. Viable LTCs can't be all things to all people, but they can provide much needed funds for the relatively small percentage of insureds with significant, severe needs." Liberal policy benefits at low prices will create future rate problems for an insured. Therefore, in choosing a policy, it is critical for consumers to understand the forces that provide upward pressure on their LTC premiums.[69]

It's safe to say that rate stability will continue to be a concern for consumers, agents and advisors, insurers, and regulators. Adequate pricing for reasonable insurable events should be fine going forward, but the agent will have to continue to help research the insurer for a previous history of rate increases in addition to identifying those plans ripe for increases – significantly lower premiums than the com-

petition for the same or even better benefits, significantly higher commission payouts than the competition, and loose underwriting that
takes on more questionably insurable risks than they should.

Underwriting

As experience in long-term care underwriting and claims
evolves, the tracking of data becomes more important. At this point,
experience monitoring by age and by duration is critical for the product. Experience is also being measured by tracking a liberal versus
conservative underwriting approach. Liberal underwriting consists of
a haphazard use of underwriting tools, a lack of checking the veraci-
ty of application answers, and irregular ordering of medical records
and face-to-face assessments. By contrast, conservative underwriters
will want medical records and face-to-face assessments on virtually
every application. Figure 4.4 shows some potential experience differences divided by the two approaches.[71]

Benefit Period Selection

In designing a long-term care insurance plan, the benefit period
is one of the elections made by the applicant. The longer the benefit
period selected, the greater the total benefits *and* the premium
amount charged for the plan. Since the average stay in a nursing facility is about 2.5 years, many agents recommend a three or four-year
benefit period. The benefit period is often the selection that is modified based on the budget constraints of the buyer. When altering this
design component, it is best to keep in mind the following data.

The average length-of-stay calculation is dependent on how the
stay is defined. For example, the average length of stay for all stays of
one day or longer is only 521 days, or about 17 months. This 1.5 years
figure used to be the most commonly quoted average stay. On the
other hand, the average stay for all stays longer than one year is 6.2
years. The current quoted 2.5 years is based on all stays of 90 days or
longer.

The primary consideration, though, should be the risk of a catastrophic stay. The purchase of a four-year-benefit means that bene-

Figure 4.4

HYPOTHETICAL LOSS RATIOS

Policy Year	Liberal Underwriting	Conservative Underwriting
1	.25%	13%
3	.44%	36%
5	.64%	60%
7	.78%	78%
Lifetime	.60%	60%

ACTUAL DURATIONAL LOSS RATIOS ESTIMATED SELECTION WEAROFF **

Policy Year*	Liberal Underwriting	Conservative Underwriting	Liberal Underwriting	Conservative Underwriting
1	.24%	.11%	.52%	.39%
2	.38%	.16%	.77%	.55%
3	.49%	.25%	.92%	.76%
4	.57%	.32%	.97%	.92%
5	.64%	.38%	.100%	.100%

*Policy year results estimated from calendar year data provided in NAIC Exhibits

**Selection factors estimated by removing 8.75% per year aging from policy year loss ratios. All durations were taken as ratios to policy year 5, the latest year separately available in the NAIC Exhibits.

Source: Milliman & Robertson

fits could expire while the patient is still receiving long-term care services. Since there is more than a 10% risk of a confinement lasting longer than four years, individuals should at least review the longer benefit options like lifetime, before they settle for anything less.[72]

Conning & Company Study of LTC Pricing

There have been many concerns about the adequacy of the policy pricing in long-term care insurance in light of the minimal claims experience available to estimate expected losses and prepare rate filings. As noted previously in this book, due to the nature of this disability-related type of insurance, it will take several years to fully measure the premiums charged versus experience results to gauge the success (or not) of a block of LTC business.

In 1999, Conning and Company did a study of 1997 business results to measure actual losses versus expected losses used in the pricing of the policy. As evidenced in Figure 4.5, the actual cumulative loss experience at that point in time was surprisingly close to expected and that LTC pricing has been adequate – so far.[73]

Medical Information

Impact of Cognitive Testing on LTC Insurance Profitability

According to a 1999 survey of 18 of the largest LTC insurers conducted by LifePlans, Inc., dementia was listed as the number one cause of claims, as well as the number one reason for contestable claims. The cognitively impaired are difficult to identify, since fewer than 25% of medical records make mention of a severe impairment when it exists, and only about 4% when it is mild or moderate. The stigma attached to a cognitive impairment often leads applicants and their families to deny the early warning signs. Compounding the identification problem is that a person in the early stages of cognitive impairment may appear "sharp" and normal one day, and disoriented the next.[74]

Given the importance of measuring an applicant's cognitive ability in light of the claims experience to date, the use of a cognitive

Figure 4.5

TOP 15 COMPANIES

Duration (Years)	Loss Ratio Actual	Expected	Ratio of Actual to Expected
0	11.2%	14.7%	76.8%
1	20.1%	21.6%	93.1%
2	29.9%	29.3%	101.9%
3	40.0%	43.0%	92.9%
4	47.0%	46.4%	101.2%
5-9	61.6%	61.5%	100.1%
10+	69.3%	87.2%	79.4%
TOTAL	**32.4%**	**33.5%**	**96.7%**

TOTAL INDUSTRY

Duration (Years)	Loss Ratio Actual	Expected	Ratio of Actual to Expected
0	11.6%	15.6%	74.2%
1	20.8%	22.5%	92.4%
2	31.2%	30.6%	102.1%
3	41.4%	43.7%	94.8%
4	49.3%	47.8%	103.0%
5-9	64.6%	63.5%	101.9%
10+	71.6%	87.9%	81.4%
TOTAL	**33.5%**	**34.6%**	**96.8%**

Source: Conning & Company, Hartford, Conn.

screen is generally of more value than a doctor's records can be in this regard. The balance to be struck is in cost – how to find a reliable screener that can be used for most applicants without driving up the administrative expenses so high that it has a negative impact on policy pricing. The information needs to be sought – the question is how best to do that. This text has previously referred to some cognitive screeners. One, the Minnesota Cognitive Acuity Screen (MCAS), a telephonic screen for cognitive impairment, has been measured for value (see Figure 4.6).[75]

As we know, medicine is not an exact science. An applicant's present cognitive condition is important information for an underwriter to have. Obtaining it in the least intrusive yet most economical way can yield positive results that benefit all concerned. As agents, you should be aware of these various types of tests not only to advise your client that someone will be in touch to ask various questions, but also to understand its overall importance in keeping claims – and, thus, premiums – reasonable. Whether companies switch to using the Minnesota test or not, they will be using some type of cognitive screener to ensure the best underwriting results.

Cancer Self-Advocacy

Sixty percent of all cancers occur in people age 65 and older, with two in every 100 Americans in this group diagnosed with cancer each year, including breast, prostate, colon and lung. According to an Institute of Medicine Report of the Cancer Policy Board, while most individuals diagnosed with cancer are elderly, they often do not receive appropriate cancer care despite evidence that the elderly can tolerate and benefit from newer, effective treatment. For example, older women with breast cancer are less likely to get breast conservation surgery and less likely to receive adjuvant chemotherapy (additional treatment that may complement standard chemotherapy) than younger women. In addition, physicians tend to deviate more often from recommended or standard staging, diagnostic work-ups and treatment regimens for their older patients.[76]

This means it will be important for older individuals to advocate for themselves. The National Coalition for Cancer Survivorship has a

Figure 4.6

FINANCIAL RESULTS BY COGNITIVE SCREEN

Description	Number of Applicants Issued Policies (1)	Present Value of Future Premiums	Present Value of Future Claims	Loss Ratio (2)	Change in Contribution in Moving to MCAS (3)
Loosely managed Underwriting	80,770	$544,459,730	$351,688,654	64.6%	$43,463,907
MCAS	79,584	540,211,236	303,976,253	56.3%	-0-
Mini-Mental State Examination	77,510	525,476,906	304,383,493	57.9%	15,141,570
Short Portable Mental Status Questionnaire	75,8065	13,872,913	298,353,034	58.1%	20,715,104
Cognitive Capacity Screening Exam	74,532	503,051,692	318,545,670	63.3%	51,728,961
Delayed Word Recall	80,146	543,864,626	308,182,523	56.7%	552,879
Neurobehavioral Cognitive Status Exam	61,994	421,030,621	234,037,610	55.6%	49,241,972
Mattis Dementia Rating Scale	67,965	456,985,219	306,562,067	67.1%	85,811,830
Telephone Interview For Cognitive Screening	80,191	543,322,055	316,640,838	58.3%	9,553,765
7-Minute Screen	78,873	534,755,247	309,249,284	57.8%	10,729,020

(1)   Assumes an original cohort of 100,000 applicants
(2)   Present Value of Future Claims/Present Value of Future Premiums
(3)   Present Value of Future Premiums Less Present Value of Future
        Claims for the MCAS, minus the Present Value of Future Premiums
        less the Present Value of Future Claims for other cognitive tests

Source: Milliman & Robertson

self-advocacy tool that includes, among other items, discussions of specific issues faced by the older cancer survivor, such as paying for outpatient care and medicines not covered by insurance and Medicare. Long-term care insurance can be an important funding element for the cancer survivor.

Adapting to Chronic Health Conditions

The University of California, Los Angeles School of Medicine, received a grant from the AARP Andrus Foundation to look at a group of men and women ages 70 to 79 and follow them for two-and-one-half years to see how lifestyle factors, social relationships, and psychological characteristics affected their perceptions of successful aging in the face of such chronic conditions as heart disease and cancer. The study found that older adults who were functioning best, and thus less likely to show declines in functioning over the next several years, were those engaged in regular physical activity, had a strong sense of self-efficacy or received regular social support from friends or family, and had few symptoms of psychological distress. Even in older adults with one or more chronic health conditions, there are significant differences in functional status and different levels of change in functioning over time. This suggests the value of promoting interventions to increase physical and cognitive functioning in older adults with health problems, since both physical and psychological status can be improved.[77]

Medicine in the 21st Century

"Sylvia Elam, a Virginia coal miner's daughter, lay on an operating table at the Pittsburgh Medical Center. The tiny 65-year-old stroke victim was wrapped like a mummy, her head attached by four screws to the sides of a metal box called a stereotactic frame. Men in blue, all eyes and masked mouths, milled around rows of syringes, scalpels, and vials filled with human neurons.

"… She was about to become one of the first 12 patients in history to have neuronal cells, created in a lab from stem cells, implanted in her brain. And they came from a highly unusual source: a cancerous tumor removed from an adult. Partially paralyzed by a stroke in 1993, she had watched her life since, unable to live it, wheelchair bound at her husband

Ira's side as he ran their autoparts store. [That day], the resident drilled a quarter-size hole into her skull. A syringe, guided by the stereotactic frame, was pushed through her cortex, and six million neuronal cells were shot deep into her damaged brain.

"Two months later, Elam was walking again. Despite a second stroke, unrelated to the operation, she says she would like to receive more cells.... Six of the initial 12 patients had improved brain activity."[78]

New treatments are being explored for nearly every dominant chronic condition. Many will involve some type of continued long-term care treatment. This is why many LTC policies specifically state that newer treatments not known about today would be covered out into the future if adopted for use in a long-term care situation. It's another important part of a policy that recognizes that the length of time the coverage would be in force will likely see many new types of treatments (and facilities) not yet identified, but for which the policy is ultimately intended.

I Want A New Drug (Part 2)

Out-of-pocket spending on prescription drugs is another reason additional uncovered medical expenses in the form of long-term care can severely alter the financial circumstances of an individual and family. With dollars stretched in retirement simply due to longevity today, any ongoing financial liability is going to set back many today. One such ongoing liability would seem to be prescription drugs.

U.S. spending on prescription medications is believed likely to double over the next five years. Driving this latest increased forecast are two categories of drugs: cardiovascular medicines (controlling cholesterol and blood pressure levels) and central nervous system drugs (depression, pain and arthritis).[79]

As Congress continues to debate a prescription drug benefit for the elderly, the average price of the top 50 medicines most often prescribed to the elderly rose 6.1 % in 2000, according to a report by

Families USA. The 50 medicines in the report were ranked by number of prescriptions issued in the Pennsylvania Pharmaceutical Assistance Contract for the Elderly, reportedly the largest U.S. outpatient drug program for older Americans. This 6.1% rise contrasts with the year 2000 inflation rate, calculated as 2.4%.[80]

> "Annie Ryman, a retired nurse in Bay City, Texas, won't shop for cheap drugs in Mexico. Her doctor told her not to because some of her medicines have very precise formulations. So she copes with the high cost of prescription drugs by skimping on medicines. She cuts some pills in half and ends up taking only half the prescribed dose. "I've cut down on my gifts to grandchildren. I've cut down on everything to pay for my prescription drugs," says Ryman, 72, who has a monthly income from Social Security and her pension of $1,440 and a $250 a month drug bill. The high cost of prescription drugs has forced millions of Americans, especially the elderly, to make difficult choices.[81] Will LTC costs force them to do the same?

A 2001 study by *Consumer Reports* concluded that one of the reasons drug bills have been so high for such ailments as allergies, anxiety, heartburn or high blood pressure is that cheaper generic equivalents have not made it to the marketplace as early as they could have after expiration of the typical 20-year drug patent. They paint a

> "Why does the world's best-selling drug, the heartburn medicine Prilosec, cost $3.30 a pill in the United States but only $1.47 in Canada? Why does the allergy drug Claritin cost almost $2 a pill in the United States but only 41 cents in Great Britain and 48 cents in Australia? Why does a year's supply of Rilutek, the only drug approved to treat Lou Gehrig's disease, cost $9,000 in the United States, but only $5,000 in France? Why does the United States have the highest drug prices in the world?... Every industrialized country – except the United States – imposes some form of price controls on prescription drugs. As the lone holdout, the United States pays the price, literally. U.S. consumers subsidize research and development for the world as well as the pharmaceutical industry's substantial profits. *Fortune* magazine has ranked the pharmaceutical business as the most profitable of all industries when measured by returns on equity, sales and assets. ...calculates that Americans overpaid $16 billion in 1998 on a total drug bill of $120 billion.... But the pharmaceutical industry says lowering prices to international levels would devastate research and development.[82]

picture of pharmaceutical industry collusion and note that the Bush Administration has recently given the green light to the FTC to begin an industry-wide investigation focusing on the business relationships between brand-name and generic-drug manufacturers.[83]

MORE LTC NEWS

Letter to the 'Condo Living' Column

Question: I live in a 335-unit condominium and am beginning to see a problem, which could impact our daily lives. We have recently noted a number of children with elderly parents purchasing a condominium and putting their aged parents in them, living alone. In many cases, the individuals are not capable of taking care of themselves and have to depend on their neighbors to help them with shopping, cooking, transportation to health care providers and various other chores. Some of the residents don't dress properly. Some cook, forget what they are doing, and burn whatever is on the stove, setting off the fire alarm? What legal recourse do we have?

Answer: I am well aware of this problem that I refer to as "Elder Dumping." The high cost of assisted living facilities has forced some families who are in search of alternatives to do exactly as you suggest – place their aged parents in a Florida condominium where they wrongly assume they will be better off than living with family up north. It reminds me of the Inuit Eskimos, who placed their dying relatives on ice flows where they spent the waning moments of their lives. Only, in this case, the elderly wander unattended around the condominium property, often disheveled and disoriented. Some have caused fires, flooded condominiums and other disturbances, while their families ignore the situation. Although the [condo] association has no legal obligation to the "dumped" elder, it does have a duty to protect the unit owners from threats of physical harm and the condominium property from damage. To this extent, the association may find it necessary to initiate steps to have an owner committed to a state mental facility under the Baker Act, or to contact the state Department of Elderly Affairs for assistance. Today, there are also programs, such as Easy Living, a privately operated company that specifically designs packages for home health and concierge-type assisted living services. [These packages] can include such items as meals, transportation, house cleaning, handyman, home improvements, shopping, social activities, laundry and other custodial services, as well as nursing companions, homemakers and other home health services.[84]

IMSA and Long-Term Care

The Insurance Marketplace Standards Association (IMSA) has added long-term care products to its assessment of ethical business practices. IMSA is a voluntary association of insurers that has reviewed the insurers' marketing practices to meet prescribed market conduct standards. Initially, it focused on life and annuity products. IMSA has become a routine compliance function and LTC insurers are reviewing their own practices to be sure they fall in line with IMSA standards. This supervision and monitoring is in effect regardless of whether the insurer distributes products through captive agents or independent entities, such as broker-dealers and banks. So, if a company markets LTC through an independent network of brokers, the standards of supervising and monitoring are applicable. This will ultimately benefit the senior market for long-term care, life and annuity sales.[85]

The Granny Tax

Remember the nanny tax? This was failure to keep accurate tax records for the babysitter, the lack of which caused Zoe Baird to forego the Attorney General nomination back in 1993. The tax was complex and expensive, increasing the cost of child care considerably – the reason that many chose to ignore it.

But there's "a whole new wave of unsuspecting taxpayers – those that hire home health care workers. Yvonne Edwards, 50, a San Francisco psychotherapist, has no children but she does have an 87-year-old mother with Parkinson's disease. Four years ago Edwards had hired an aide to care for her mother in her Honolulu home. The employment agency she used informed her she'd owe the nanny tax, or should we say, granny tax. Edwards had to farm out the tax work to an accounting service due to its complexity and her fear she'd make a mistake in computing it.[86]

How do you know if you have to pay it? If you provide the place and tools for work (your house, medical supplies) and you have the right to control how the work is performed (make sure aide takes mother shopping), the IRS considers you an employer. It makes no difference what you call your worker (employee or independent contractor) or whether this person is employed full or part time, paid hourly, daily or weekly. Unless you find an agency that employs the home health care worker, you're likely on the hook for this tax. Hire the worker privately and the taxes and record keeping are all yours. The taxes include Social Security, Medicare, and state and federal unemployment taxes. You must also get an employer ID number from the IRS, among other requirements.[87]

The New Grandparents
How to be a grandparent today, courtesy of a recent AARP study: Be generous. Seven in ten bought a gift for a grandchild within the month prior to the survey. The subset of grandparents most likely to spoil the kids were young grandmothers, ages 50-59. In overall cash outlays on grandchildren, grandfathers dig deeper than grandmothers ($562 per year versus $453). The median amount spent by individual grandparents – both genders combined – is $489 per year. Grandparents with only one grandchild spend about $500. Spending per child drops to about $200 when the total number of grandchildren reaches three. Lower income grandparents (less than $25,000 per year) spend $239 on grandchildren. Middle-income grandparents ($25,000 – $50,000) spend $627 per year, and higher income (over $50,000 per year) spend $840.[88]

You can be sure this generosity would be significantly impacted by a long-term care event with no funding alternatives.

Geriatric Specialists in Short Supply
Although people are healthier and living longer, they're also experiencing chronic conditions associated with aging, thereby flood-

ing the health-care system and presenting a clinical challenge for medical practitioners. Among the remedies, experts say, would be more trained geriatricians to oversee their care.

But a Rand Corporation study estimates that the United States should have at least 20,000 physicians trained in geriatric care. Currently, there are just 7,000. Geriatrics as a specialty has been declining for years. Young physicians see geriatrics as depressing and not as well-paying as other specialties. Geriatricians have to think beyond the treatment of disease to the issues of promoting function, preventing decline and preserving independence. The result is that due to the shortage of geriatric specialists, elderly people often receive substandard care.

Physicians with elderly patients were being encouraged to reorient their treatment methods more towards care of chronic conditions.[89]

HCFA Name a Thing of the Past

We won't have the Health Care Financing Administration (HCFA) to kick around any more, at least not under the HCFA name. The Bush Administration has officially renamed it – the Centers for Medicare and Medicaid Services. And they are about to launch a new $35 million public information campaign to help seniors and other participants navigate its complex territory. Changes are the watchword here. This fall, there will be a 24-hour customer service line where representatives will be taking calls. The new Centers are also developing a rating service for nursing homes, dialysis centers and other health care providers. The Centers will have three distinct divisions. One would be solely for Medicare. Another would be focused on programs for poor children and families and other projects. The third would involve consumer education, grievances, appeals, and other concerns about the Medicare HMO project.

Health and Human Services Secretary Tommy Thompson advised that he hoped this new look and name would mean a fresh start from its previous image as a department only a bureaucrat could love. Thompson also intends to ask Congress to reduce the number of private health insurance companies that process claims.[90]

LTC and Privacy Regulations

Many of you may have seen the abundance of privacy notifications issued from virtually every insurer in the United States lately. This is a long-awaited fall-out from the Health Insurance Portability and Accountability Act of 1996 (HIPAA). It will also affect long-term care insurers.

The first impact felt will be on applications in the underwriting process. There will be severe limitations on the amount of information about the applicant that can be disclosed to an agent. Those used to receiving regular, detailed underwriting updates or specific reasons for a decline or modification of the coverage applied for can forget those in the future, unless the agent is able to get specific authorization from the applicant.

The larger change in underwriting will involve the authorization form that is part of the application. Prior to these new rules, one authorization fit all requests for medical records. No longer. It's very likely that separate authorizations will be required for each physician from whom records are being sought. This makes the field underwriting process more meaningful in terms of obtaining accurate physician information. Leave out a physician and/or a specific signed authorization for that doctor and it will delay the underwriting process until you can re-visit with the applicant to obtain the properly signed form.

Producers will also have to sign a document called a Business Associate Contract. These will subject the agent to many of the same requirements with which insurers must comply.

These laws were effective April 14, 2001 and compliance will be required by April 14, 2003.[91]

Internet Resources

"There is much pleasure to be gained from useless knowledge."

–Bertrand Russell

There are a substantial number of resource outlets for additional long-term care related information. The Internet especially has opened up the subject to a wide variety of educational opportunities. The difficulty is in measuring their value in terms of accuracy and usefulness. The following list is not intended to be an all-inclusive one, nor is it in any specific order, but it will offer a number of places to go for specific information.

- **TLChoices.com** – Total Living Choices.com – offers seniors resource information on elder care assisted living, long-term care facilities and retirement communities. Total Living Choices is dedicated to seniors and their families who need to make a change in a senior's living situation. It provides the information and resources needed to match the senior's needs with the best available senior living options. It includes 360-degree virtual tours and toll-free phone numbers.

- **Healthgrades.com** – HealthGrades helps assess and improve the quality of healthcare nationwide. With its proprietary objective provider ratings and expert advisory services, HealthGrades' goal is to establish a standard of healthcare quality. HealthGrades works with all parties to the healthcare agreement – including providers, employers, payers and patients – to offer targeted solutions to ensure quality healthcare. HealthGrades offers consumers free ratings to evaluate and select providers, works with providers to assess and enhance their care and helps employers and payors lower healthcare costs by improving quality overall. They offer report card ratings for approximately 7,800 Medicare-certified home health agencies.

- **Seniorhousing.net** – a partner of American Association of Homes and Services for the Aging. Here, you can search Senior Housing Net's comprehensive guide to retirement communities, assisted living residences, Alzheimer's facilities, and nursing homes nationwide. The website includes: 1) an "Evaluation Tool" to determine what type of housing or care may be most suitable; (2) guides to options for different types of housing and care; (3) checklists to review what's important when evaluating a senior community or care facility; and (4) links to information about Alzheimer's disease and other health care topics.

- **Quotesmith.com** – Unsure of where to go for long-term care insurance proposals? You can get quotes from numerous LTC companies here with LTCompare. They provide the widest number of quotes in one place that can speed up the research process.

- **The ElderCare Connection, Inc.** – eldercare_con@msn.com – There are a number of organizations around the country that provide geriatric care management, professional guardianship and even assist with Medicaid applications and eligibility. This firm happens to be in Fort Lauderdale, but there are probably others closer to your location. For those that may need a knowledgeable individual acting on their behalf, this is the type of organization that can provide that.

- **Protect Our Families Coalition** – Comprised of individuals and organizations representing nursing home residents, their families and consumers, this group is based in Texas and lobbies the legislature there to pass legislation that protects the rights of some of the most vulnerable in the country – nursing home residents. Other similar organizations are located in other states and attempt to accomplish much the same thing.

- **Americans For Long-Term Care Security** – ltcweb.org – ALTCS works to educate the public and policy makers about the importance of long-term care as an intricate part of life planning and advocates public and private sector financing options.

- **Extendedcare.com** – Extended Care Information Network (ECIN) offers Internet solutions and resources that connect hospitals and consumers with extended-care providers, including nursing homes, assisted-living and other senior-living residences, and home health care agencies. Founded by healthcare professionals, ECIN's products and services improve the discharge-planning process for hospitals, enhance the admissions process and improve business efficiencies for extended-care providers, and assists consumers in finding extended-care providers and information on senior-health issues through its web site, http://www.extendedcare.com.

- **Center for Disability and Long Term Care Insurance** – An offshoot of HIAA, located in Washington, D.C., the Center focuses on policy development and public advocacy for disability and long-term care insurance and tracks emerging issues related to these areas. Their staff also works to educate the public about both disability and long-term care insurance and the advantages of each to consumers, businesses and the economy.

- **Agenet.com** – This site provides health and drug information specific to seniors including online senior drugs reviews of commonly prescribed drugs for the elderly. Marketed under *"Solutions For Better Aging,"* AgeNet's current product and service offering includes medical and personal care supplies, durable medical equipment, emergency monitoring, medication assessments, housing assessments and placement, home modification equipment, wills and advanced directives, long-term care insurance referrals, viatical life insurance settlement referrals, and reverse mortgage placement.

- **Alfa.org** – Assisted Living Federation of America, founded in 1990, represents over 7000 not-for and for-profit facilities that provide for assisted living, continuing care, independent living and other types of housing and services.

- **AAHSA.org** – American Association of Homes and Services for the Aging – represents not-for-profit organizations dedicated to providing high-quality health care, housing and services to the nation's elderly. Its membership consists of over 5,600 not-for-profit nursing homes, continuing care retirement communities, senior housing facilities, assisted living and community services. AAHSA organizations serve more than one million older persons of all income levels, creed and races. AAHSA serves its members by representing the concerns of not-for-profit organizations that serve the elderly through interaction with Congress and federal agencies. It also strives to enhance the professionalism of practitioners and facilities through the Certification Program for Retirement Housing Professionals, the Continuing Care Accreditation Commission, conferences and programs offered by the AAHSA Professional Development Institute and publications representing current thinking in the long-term care and retirement housing fields. AAHSA also seeks to enhance its members' financial strength through group purchasing and insurance programs. The AAHSA Development Corporation, an AAHSA subsidiary, helps members expand their mission of service by increasing their access to cost-effective capital and assisting with the development.

- **Thirdage.com** – serving interests and needs of first-wave baby boomers, adults in their mid-40s through 50s. Helps consumers locate free caregiving classes or seminars, usually given at a local hospital.

- **Benefitscheckup.org** – A free, easy-to-use service that identifies federal and state assistance programs for older Americans. The BenefitsCheck*Up* is the nation's first 50-state (including the District of Columbia) online service to help seniors, their families and caregivers find the right benefit programs to meet their needs. BenefitsCheck*Up* is the brainchild of the National Council on the Aging (NCOA).

- **Eldercare Locator** – a way to find community assistance for seniors – 1-800-677-1116 – The Eldercare Locator is a public service of the Administration on Aging, U.S. Department of Health and Human Services and is administered by the National Association of Area Agencies on Aging and the National Association of State Units on Aging.

- **Nfcacares.org** – National Families Caregivers Association Web site allows caregivers to share experiences and swap information. Also provides information on caregiving in general.

- **Ncoa.org** – National Council on the Aging – the nation's first association of organizations and professionals dedicated to promoting the dignity, self-determination, well-being, and contributions of older persons.

- **Elderweb.com** – ElderWeb was created by a CPA with years of experience in long term care, finance, and technology. Over its seven years of existence, ElderWeb has grown to include over 6,000 reviewed links to long term care information, as well as an expanding library of articles and reports, news, and events. It is designed to be a research site for both professionals and family members looking for information on eldercare and long term care, and includes links to information on legal, financial, medical, and housing issues, as well as policy, research, and statistics.

- **Seniorimpact.com** – Resource guide/handbook for senior citizens and family caregivers. Includes preview table of contents and online ordering.

- **Seniors.gov** –Members of the public can go to one comprehensive website to help them find the particular agency(ies) to satisfy their needs. It is one of several projects created at the direction of the National Partnership for Reinventing Government (NPRG). The Social Security Administration (SSA) agreed to create, host and maintain FirstGov for Seniors as a service especially geared toward senior citizens.

- **Healthcare Intelligence Network** – hin.com – is an electronic publishing company providing information on the business of healthcare. In one place, healthcare executives can receive exclusive, customized up-to-the minute information from more than 50 of the nation's leading healthcare publications in five key areas: the healthcare and managed care industry, hospital and health system management, health law and regulation, behavioral healthcare, and long-term care.

- **Carequestplus.com** – *CareQuest®* / *HealthChoice*™ operates primarily as a long-term care and eldercare Care Planning & Resource Program for employees of state and local government agencies and now private sector businesses. They claim to maintain the largest database of care services and providers in the country (i.e. home health care, assisted living, nursing homes, home chore and repair, etc.). Unlike many Information & Referral (I & R) assistance programs, they do not accept or require payment from care providers to be listed or referred.

- **NAELA.ORG** – National Academy of Elder Law Attorneys, Inc. is a non-profit association that assists lawyers, bar organizations and others who work with older clients and

their families. Established in 1987, the Academy provides a
resource of information, education, networking and assistance to those who must deal with the many specialized
issues involved with legal services to the elderly and disabled.

- **Caremanager.org** – The National Association of
Professional Geriatric Care Managers is a non-profit, professional organization of practitioners whose goal is the
advancement of dignified care for the elderly and their
families. With more than 1,000 members, GCM is committed to maximizing the independence and autonomy of elders while striving to ensure that the highest quality and
most cost-effective health and human services are used
when and where appropriate.

- **Unclaimed.org** – NAUPA – National Association of
Unclaimed Property Administrators – information on the
most current trends and information affecting unclaimed
property, including forgotten property titles, bank and brokerage accounts, pension claims, and other assets. Often
children are unfamiliar with their parents' finances and,
especially in Alzheimer's cases, it may be necessary to use a
service like this to locate personal resources that the patient
has but can't remember.

- **Children of Aging Parents** – Children of Aging Parents
(CAPS) was founded in 1977 to assist caregivers of the elderly. It was incorporated as a non-profit, charitable organization in 1980 and today has a national mission to provide the 22.4 million family caregivers with reliable information and referrals, a network of support groups, and
publications and programs that promote public awareness
of the value and the needs of caregivers. CAPS provides
phone numbers and names of nursing homes, retirement
communities, elder law attorneys, day care centers, medical in-home services, respite care, assisted living centers,

state and county agencies and more. CAPS will also write, collect, and distribute fact sheets on various caregiving-related topics.

- **aarplifeanswers.com** – This site has articles, links, chats and information related to elder care. It covers a wide variety of subjects and is exclusive for AARP members.

- **Andrus.org** – Another AARP related site committed to making a positive difference in the lives of older adults through the funding of age-related research. A number of study results are available here.

- **estateplanningdigest.com** – A newsletter designed exclusively for estate tax attorneys and financial planners. This may come in handy in deciphering the new tax law passed in 2001 by Congress.

- **Ceridian.com** – offers LifeWorks Online, a resource that provides a self-help approach to obtaining information and resources on a wide variety of personal and business issues – from elder care to planning for retirement.

- **National Senior Service Corps** – 800-424-8867 – They provide assistance and visits to elderly individuals, helping with simple chores and transportation to medical appointments.

Footnotes

1. "Few Claims Made on Connecticut Partnership's LTC Policies," *Best's Review* (March, 2001), p. 84.

2. Representative John E. Peterson (R-PA), "A Common Sense Approach to Long-Term Care: Medicaid-Private Insurance Partnerships," *Health Insurance Underwriter* (December, 2000), p. 72.

3. LTC Partnership Statistics provided by the NAHU Long-Term Care Working Group, 2001.

4. "State Resolutions, Passed Legislation and Public Laws Regarding LTC Partnerships," provided by the NAHU Long-Term Care Working Group, 2001.

5. "Long Term Care Partnership Resolution," courtesy of Ross Schriftman and the NAHU Long-Term Care Working Group, 2001.

6.   "Betting on Death," *Consumer Reports* (February, 2001), p. 37.

7.   Mark Ruttenberg, "Educate Yourself About Viatical Sales," *Life Insurance Selling* (February, 1999), pp. 132, 136.

8.   Joseph D'Allegro, "Study: Seniors Will Fuel Viatical Growth," *National Underwriter*, Life & Health/Financial Servcies Edition, January 10, 2000, p. 13.

9.   "Viaticals Evolving into Burgeoning Securitization Market," *Advisor Today* (March, 2001), p. 30.

10.   "Thinking About Selling Viaticals? Read this First," *Florida Broker News* (April, 2000), p. 1.

11.   Joseph D'Allegro, "Florida Moves Against Another Viatical Company," *National Underwriter*, Life & Health/Financial Servcies Edition, August 23, 1999, p. 14.

12.   "Long Warns North Carolinians of Viatical Settlement Schemes," *Insurance Newsletter* (Spring, 2000), p. 9.

13.   "Viatical Settlements and the Reporting of Fraud," *The Intercom* (Spring, 2001), p. 9.

14.   Eileen Alt Powell, "House Rich Elders Get Help," *Associated Press*, February 22, 2001.

15.   Jef Kunerth, "We're not Just Getting Older; We're Booming," *Orlando Sentinel*, May 15, 2001, pp. A1, A4.

16.   Cecily Fraser, "Extending the Limits of 55-Plus," *CBS MarketWatch.com*, May 25, 2001.

17.   Ibid.

18.   "ING Aetna Financial Services Study Reveals Baby Boomers' Retirement Dreams Are Unrealistic," *Business Wire*, May 31, 2001.

19.   Sue Pleming, "Report: Most Retirees Rely on Social Security for Income," *Reuters*, May 23, 2001.

20.   Catherine Arnold, "Survey Finds Workers Are Unprepared for Retirement Planning," *National Underwriter*, Life & Health/Financial Servcies Edition, May 7, 2001, p. 74.

21.   "Survey Reveals That Few People Understand Long Term Care Financing," *LTC Sales & Marketing Insight* (March, 2001), p. 6.

22.   "Confused About Retirement and Financial Planning Options?," *PR Newswire*, May 29, 2001.

23.   "ALTCS Likes Grassley/Graham LTC Bill," *Florida Agent* (April, 2001), p. 43.

24.   Juan R. Paloma, "A Tax Credit to Care for Mom Wouldn't Have Helped My Sisters," *USA Today*, March 8, 1999, p. 13A.

25.   "Most Significant Retirement Security Legislation in a Generation to be Signed by President Bush Today," *PR Newswire*, June 7, 2001.

26.   "Major Health Care Policies: Fifty State Profiles, 2000," *Health Policy Tracking Service*, National Conference of State Legislatures.

27.   "New Tax Credit Available Through Senior Insurance Services for First-Time Buyers of Long-Term Care Insurance," *PR Newswire*, May 19, 2000.

28.   "ACLI Applauds Maryland's Approval of Long-Term Care Insurance Tax Credit," *PR Newswire*, May 11, 2000.

29.   "Major Health Care Policies: Fifty State Profiles, 2000," *Health Policy Tracking Service*, National Conference of State Legislatures.

30.   Alice Ann Love, "Law: Nursing Homes Can't Evict Medicaid Patients," *Daytona Beach News-Journal*, March 26, 1999, p. 6A.

31.   Alice Ann Love, "Law Curbs Nursing Home Evictions," *Associated Press*, March 25, 1999.

32. "Hawaii Launches Innovative Long-Term Care Plan," *Employee Benefit Plan Review* (November, 2000), p. 24.

33. "AHCA Urges Creation of National Commission on Long-Term Care Financing Reform," *PR Newswire*, March 23, 1999.

34. Mary Jane Fisher, "Coalition Calls for National Policy to Fund Long-Term Care," *National Underwriter*, Life & Health/Financial Servcies Edition, April 16, 2001, p. 30.

35. "HUD Awards Help the Elderly, Disabled to Live at Home," *Florida Broker News* (February, 2001), p. 9.

36. Kent S. Collins, "As Retirees' Needs Grow, So Will Services," *Orlando Sentinel*, February 18, 2001, p. K7.

37. Brendan Riley, "Nursing Homes Filing for Bankruptcy," *Associated Press*, April 5, 2000.

38. "Nursing Home Videos Could Hasten Sorely Needed Reforms," *USA Today*, September 21, 1999, p. 18A.

39. "Nursing-Home Residents Buffeted by Bankruptcies," *AARP Bulletin*, May 2000, pp. 9, 10.

40. Mark Hollis, "Quick Aid Unlikely for Nursing Homes," *Orlando Sentinel*, May 25, 2000, pp. D1, D6.

41. Theresa Agovino, "Nursing Shortage Leads to Long Hours, Frustration," *Associated Press*, June 1, 2001.

42. Milt Freudenheim and Linda Villarosa, "Nursing Shortage Is Raising Worries on Patient Care," *The New York Times*, as reprinted from their web site, April 8, 2001.

43. Donna Callea, "Care for Elderly Suffers from Severe Nursing Assistant Shortage," *Daytona Beach News-Journal.online*, May 6, 2001.

44. "Nevada Nursing Homes Crisis – Elderly Abuse," *Business Wire*, June 5, 2001.

45. "Government Pushes Nursing Home Rules," *Daytona Beach Sunday News-Journal*, July 23, 2000, p. 8A.

46. "Drug Errors Hit Nursing Home Patients, Report Says," *Reuters*, August 10, 2000.

47. "Problem Homes Are Most Sued," *Orlando Sentinel*, March 5, 2001, p. A1.

48. Gary Kane and Scott Hiaasen, "Lax State Regulation Lets Nursing Homes Sidestep Rules," *Palm Beach Post*, March 12, 2001, p. 1A.

49. "Record Number of Nursing Home Closures Putting Seniors at Risk," *PR Newswire*, April 3, 2001.

50. "Nursing Facilities Not Up to Code," *Associated Press*, April 20, 2001.

51. Bill Bergstrom, "Study Finds Nurses Dissatisfied," *Associated Press*, May 7, 2001.

52. "Letters: LTC and HIPAA," *National Underwriter*, Life & Health/Financial Servcies Edition, March 20, 2000, pp. 51, 52.

53. Barry Meier, "Assisted Living Provider Draws States' Scrutiny," *Daytona Beach Sunday News-Journal*, November 26, 2000, p. 3A.

54. "Is Assisted Living the Right Choice?" *Consumer Reports* (January, 2001), pp. 26, 27.

55. Diane C. Lade, "Insurance Rates Ignite a Crisis Among Assisted Living Facilities," *Orlando Sentinel*, December 24, 2000, p. B3.

56. "ALFs Now in Spotlight," *Florida Underwriter* (February, 2001), p. 25.

57. Greg Groeller, "Assisted Living Industry Puts on Brakes," *Orlando Sentinel*, April 8, 2001, p. H1.

58.   Tom Berson, "Caregivers," *Daytona Beach News-Journal*, February 16, 2000, p. 1C.

59.   "Pennsylvania Auditor General Casey: State Must Do More to Ensure Quality of Home Health Care," *PR Newswire*, October 27, 1999.

60.   Ann Davis, "Shaky Policy: Unexpected Rate Rises Jolt Elders Insured for Long Term Care," *Wall Street Journal*, June 22, 2000, p. 1.

61.   Jane Bryant Quinn, "Is a Backlash Brewing in LTC?" *Newsweek*, August 30, 1999, p. 39.

62.   Jim Connolly, "NAIC Says Industry Broke LTC Promises," *National Underwriter*, Life & Health/Financial Servcies Edition, June 14, 1999, p. 1.

63.   Jane Bryant Quinn, "Is a Backlash Brewing in LTC?" *Newsweek*, August 30, 1999, p. 39.

64.   Ron Panko, "Good for the Long Term?" *Best's Review* (March, 2000), pp. 97, 100.

65.   Allison Bell, "LTC Rate Increases Create Long-Term Challenges," *National Underwriter*, Life & Health/Financial Servcies Edition, August 16, 1999, p. 7.

66.   Jim Connolly, "N. Dakota Suit Gets Court OK to Settle," *National Underwriter*, Life & Health/Financial Servcies Edition, November 1, 1999, pp. 1, 38.

67.   Jim Connolly, "LTC Rate Stability Initiative Gains Ground," *National Underwriter*, Life & Health/Financial Servcies Edition, October 11, 1999, p. 5.

68.   Jim Connolly, "Progress Seen on LTC Rate Stability Model," *National Underwriter*, Life & Health/Financial Servcies Edition, March 20, 2000, p. 5.

69.   Tom Foley, "LTC Rate Stability Linked to Design," *National Underwriter*, Life & Health/Financial Servcies Edition, August 14, 2000, pp. 7, 24.

70.   Jim Connolly, "LTC Rate Model Survives Disclosure Dispute," *National Underwriter*, Life & Health/Financial Servcies Edition, June 26, 2000, p. 5.

71.   Dawn E. Helwig, "Underwriting Individual Long Term Care Insurance," *Disability Newsletter* (September, 1999), pp. 1, 8.

72.   James M. Glickman, "A Long-Term Care Commitment," *Best's Review* (October, 2000), pp. 137, 138.

73.   Linda Koco, "Conning Study Finds Overall LTC Pricing 'Adequate,'" *National Underwriter*, Life & Health/Financial Servcies Edition, August 30, 1999, p. 19.

74.   "Impact of Cognitive Testing on Long Term Care Insurance Profitability," from Milliman & Robertson, Inc. report, published September 7, 1999.

75.   Ibid.

76.   "High Cancer Rate in Elderly Calls for Strong Self-Advocacy Skills," *BW Health Wire*, November 22, 1999.

77.   "Adapting to Chronic Health Conditions," as reprinted from the Andrus.org Web site, May 6, 2001.

78.   Cynthia Fox, "Why Stem Cells Will Transform Medicine," *Fortune*, June 11, 2001, pp. 159, 164.

79.   Linda A. Johnson, "Report: U.S. Prescription Drug Spending to Double," *Associated Press*, June 6, 2001.

80.   Anjetta McQueen, "Prices for Seniors' Drugs Said Up," *Associated Press*, June 12, 2001.

81.   Dennis Cauchon, "High Prices Force Tough Decisions," *USA Today*, November 10, 1999, p. 10A.

82.   Dennis Cauchon, "Americans Pay More: Here's Why," *USA Today*, November 10, 1999, p. 1A.

83.   "Generic Drugs: The Stalling Game," *Consumer Reports* (July, 2001), p. 36.

84.   Gary Poliakoff, "Elder Dumping Is Not Illegal, But Yet a Problem," *Daytona Beach Sunday News-Journal*, July 4, 1999, p. 4F.

85.   Douglas I. Friedman, "IMSA's LTC Move Is Getting Underway Now," *National Underwriter*, Life & Health/Financial Servcies Edition, May 1, 2000, p. 8.

86.   Carolyn T. Geer, "Remember the Nanny Tax? Now It's the Granny Tax," *Fortune*, January 10, 2000, p. 218.

87.   Ibid.

88.   Glen Waggoner, "The New Grandparents," *Modern Maturity* (March/April, 2000), p. 85.

89.   "Geriatric Specialists in Short Supply, and Problem's Getting Worse," *Palm Beach Post*, March 12, 2001, p. 5E.

90.   Gina Holland, "Medicare Agency Gets New Name," *Associated Press*, June 15, 2001.

91.   Andrew L. Black, "Privacy Regs Will Affect LTC Producers," *National Underwriter*, Life & Health/Financial Servcies Edition, May 28, 2001, p. 21.

GLOSSARY

AARP. This organization has undergone a facelift in an attempt to keep both segments of members and potential members – the-over-age-65 and the age 50-65 group. It is now known only by the acronym AARP. They currently offer a long-term care insurance program for their members.

accelerated death benefit. An option in a life insurance policy that will pay all or part of the policy face amount prior to death. This benefit can pay the cost associated with catastrophic medical conditions, which can include the need for nursing home confinement.

activities of daily living. Functional routines that relate to one's ability to live independently. These activities consist of bathing, dressing, feeding, toileting, continence and mobility.

adult congregate living facility. Residential or apartment housing for people which can include a minimum amount of assistance with the activities of daily living.

adult day care facility. An institution designated to provide custodial and/or minimum health care assistance to individuals unable to remain alone, usually during working hours when the caregiver is employed.

adult day care. Services provided to individuals who cannot remain alone, including health and custodial care and other related support. This care is rendered in specified centers on a less-than-24-hour basis.

alternate plan of care. A long term care insurance policy feature that allows for substantial flexibility in designing a recovery and/or maintenance program for a claimant, using as many types of long term care assistance as needed on a reasonable cost basis, delivered in an agreed-upon setting.

annuity-based LTC. A combination product whereby an individual buys both an annuity and long-term care rider and the policy can function as either or both, depending on the insured's future needs.

asset spend-down. Procedure where an individual's income and assets are diminished in order to attain the minimum required levels of the various states' eligibility requirements for Medicaid assistance.

assisted living facility. Residence for long term care patients on a less expensive basis that offers some long term care services.

Balanced Budget Act of 1997. This federal legislation made several changes to control spending, provide incentives to agencies to deliver care more effectively, and rein in the use of home health care to trim spending.

benefit period. The length of time for which benefits under a long term care insurance contract will be paid (e.g., four years or lifetime).

bereavement counseling. A support service designed to assist family members of terminally ill patients to cope with their grief. This service is often available under a hospice care program and a benefit may be payable under a long term care insurance policy.

cap states (also known as income states). In Medicaid, if a person's monthly income exceeds a cap, eligibility for Medicaid benefits is denied regardless of health or need. There are about 20 income states.

care coordinator. A person designated by an insurer to organize a plan of care at claim time between the insured, medical providers and family members.

caregiver. A person providing assistance to a dependent person due to medical reasons or the inability to conduct routine activities of daily living.

Centers for Medicare and Medicaid Services. The new name for the Health Care Financing Administration, this organization, under the supervision of the Department of Health and Human Services, administers the Medicare and Medicaid programs.

chronically ill. This is the definition under which an individual qualifies for favorable tax treatment for long term care expenses, whether self-insured or reimbursed by an insurance company. To be chronically ill, the person must be either unable to perform two of six activities of daily living for at least 90 days or suffer a severe cognitive impairment.

cognitive impairment. One of the measurements used to determine eligibility for long term care benefits in a policy, it is the deterioration or loss of one's intellectual capacity, confirmed by clinical evidence and standardized tests, in the areas of: (1) short and long term memory; (2) orientation as to person, place and time; and (3) deductive or abstract reasoning.

community-based care. Catch-all name for long-term care services that are administered outside of a facility such as home care, adult day care, respite care and other services.

comprehensive benefits. A long term care insurance plan that offers a wide variety of coverage for long term care insurance services. This plan was modeled after the NAIC model policy in 1988. These policies could be both tax-qualified and non-qualified plans.

continuing care retirement communities. This campus-type environment offers houses, apartments, communal dining facilities, a nursing facility, recreation, a library and other services. An entry fee and a stipulated monthly payment is required.

custodial care facility. Licensed by the state to provide custodial care and assistance with activities of daily living and a nursing staff to oversee the administering of medication.

custodial care. The most common type of long term care service rendered, it provides assistance with activities of daily living and generally is performed by a trained aide in a variety of settings, most often in the home.

daily benefit amount. The specified amount of benefit payable for long term care services. The dollar amount may vary by service such as $100 a day payable for a nursing home confinement and $75 a day payable for home health care.

elimination period. In a long term care insurance policy, this is a period of time during which no benefits are payable and is sometimes referred to as a deductible. Examples of elimination periods are 15 and 100 days.

employer-sponsored plans. This is group long term care insurance first introduced in 1987. These earlier plans were voluntary, portable products with benefits and premiums similar to individual long term care coverage. Development of true group long term care insurance plans is currently underway.

estate recovery acts. Established by OBRA '93, each state developed its own version of legislation that allows it to recover Medicaid costs from heirs who received assets transferred to them by a Medicaid beneficiary, following that beneficiary's (and spouse's) death.

expenses-incurred. A method under which daily benefit amounts are paid based on the actual expenses incurred for the necessary long-term care service.

family member rule. Nineteenth century legal principle holds that family members shouldn't be paid for services to each other.

geriatric case manager. An individual assigned to handle the various needs of a person unable to do for themselves. This qualified individual can coordinate every aspect of an aging adult's care from interviewing and hiring household help to paying bills and often serves as the eyes and ears of other family members not located in the immediate area.

granny tax. Requirement that those employing a private duty nurse or companion for someone have to act as an employer, deducting FICA and Federal taxes, contributing to unemployment compensation and other payroll-related functions.

guaranteed renewable. The renewal provision of a long term care insurance policy, ensuring that the policy cannot be canceled by the insurer nor can policy provisions be changed without the insured's consent. Policy premiums, however, may be adjusted upward based on the company's experience for an entire class of business.

Health Care Financing Administration. Former name of the administrator for the Medicare and Medicaid programs.

health care surrogate. An individual designated by a medical durable power of attorney to make medical decisions on behalf of another person.

Health Insurance Portability and Accountability Act (HIPAA). This federal legislation, passed in 1996, clarified the tax treatment of long term care insurance, defining when benefits and expenses are received tax-free.

home care. This is a type of long term care service, provided in the home, that generally consists of activities of daily living assistance and is rendered by a trained aide.

home health care agency. An organization providing home health care or home care, state licensed or accredited as required, keeping clinical records of all patients, and supervised by a qualified physician or registered nurse.

home health care. A program of professional, paraprofessional and skilled care usually provided through a home health care agency to a person at home. This care is often prescribed by a physician as medically necessary and can include nursing services and physical, speech, respiratory, and occupational therapy.

hospice care. A coordinated program for control of pain and symptoms for the terminally ill which may also provide support services to family members.

indemnity. See *per diem.*

inflation protection benefit. This optional benefit is designed to help preserve the value of the daily benefit amount. It automatically increases the daily benefit annually on a simple or compounded basis, either by a stipulated percentage amount or an index measurement.

instrumental activities of daily living (IADLs). These are primarily homemaker services such as preparing meals, shopping, managing money, using the telephone, doing housework and taking medication.

intermediate care facility. An institution licensed by the state to provide patient care for those requiring constant availability and support, but very little in the way of skilled care. This facility may also provide custodial care services.

intermediate care. Occasional nursing services, preventive or rehabilitative, performed under the supervision of skilled medical personnel.

life insurance-based long term care insurance. This is a form of long term care coverage where benefits are wrapped inside a life insurance policy. Benefits can be provided for both long term care insurance and death, with cash values also available for withdrawal.

life settlements. The purchase, on a reduced basis, of a life insurance policy owned by an individual willing to sell the policy. This person need not be terminally ill. It may help to provide necessary cash during retirement that may carry a higher priority than the policy face amount at death.

liquid assets. Assets that can be more easily cashed in to help pay for long-term care services if an individual has no alternative funding source.

long distance caregiving. A difficult position in caring for a family member while located in another area and not available for day to day assistance.

long term care insurance. A specific type of insurance policy designed to offer financial support in paying for necessary long term care services rendered in a variety of settings.

long term care rider. This is an optional benefit that can be added to a life insurance, annuity or disability income policy to provide benefits for long term care.

Long Term Care Security Act of 2000. Legislation that allows long-term care coverage to be offered to federal employees (and their family and extended family members) effective October, 2002. In addition, veterans will also be able to access this coverage.

managed care. A type of claims management system for long term care insurance policies using pre-selected providers who have agreed to treat insurance company claimants on a reduced cost basis.

Medicaid. The joint federal and state welfare program administered by the states to provide payment for health care services, including long term care, for those meeting minimum asset and income requirements.

Medical Information Bureau. Clearinghouse of data specific to medical conditions that an underwriter can access to learn more about an applicant for long-term care during the underwriting process.

medically needy states. In Medicaid, a state where a person can qualify for medical care, including long-term care, if one's assets are below a specified amount and who agrees to pay monthly income in excess of a specified amount to the custodial provider.

Medicare Catastrophic Act. Federal legislation enacted January 1, 1989, it expanded long term care benefit payments provided under Medicaid and also changed some Medicaid requirements. The Medicare changes in the Act were repealed that same year effective January 1, 1990. The Medicaid changes stayed intact.

Medicare, Medicaid and SCHIP Benefits Improvement Act of 2000. This federal legislation helped to restore some funding to skilled nursing facilities and home health care agencies that was cut back by the Balanced Budget Act of 1997.

Medicare. Federal program organized under the Health Insurance for the Aged Act, Title XVIII of the Social Security Amendments of 1965, it provides hospital and medical expense benefits, including long term care services, for those individuals over age 65 or over or those meeting specific disability standards.

Miller Trust. Trust established by law that can be used to shelter income and may still qualify a patient for Medicaid services as long as the trust meets certain requirements.

NAIC Model Policy. Recommended minimum policy standards as designated by the insurance industry watchdog, the National Association of Insurance Commissioners (NAIC), originally established in 1988 and amended thereafter, states have the choice to adopt part, all or none of the standards for their own regulation. HIPAA legislation, passed by Congress in 1996, re-defined some of the provisions of the model policy.

90-day ADL certification. A new requirement under HIPAA which requires certification by a licensed health professional that the loss of at least two of six activities of daily living will last a minimum of 90 days. The certification must be made to facilitate insurer claim payments.

nonforfeiture benefits. This long term care insurance policy feature enables the insured to continue long term care coverage in some form after the insured has ceased making premium payments. A cash return, a paid-up policy or an extended term feature are typical non-forfeiture benefits.

non-qualified plans. This term refers to all long term care insurance policies being sold that do not meet the required definitions under HIPAA federal legislation. There could be adverse tax consequences for these plans sold from January 1, 1997 forward.

NORC. Naturally occurring retirement community, a new suburban phenomenon that lets people age in place, as many cities and towns offer incentives to keep older adults in a community rather than have them move to a "retirement community."

partnerships. A joint public and private sector program that allows residents of a state to buy an approved long term care insurance policy that would pay benefits during a long term care claim and enable these residents to conserve some assets that would otherwise have to be spent down to access Medicaid. States introducing partnerships so far are Connecticut, New York, Indiana and California, with Iowa ready to go and others waiting for an amendment to OBRA '93 legislation that froze the implementation of these programs.

per diem. A method for paying the daily benefit amount that is based on an elected amount and not on the actual expenses incurred. Long term care insurance policies that are tax-qualified have capped the $175 tax-free per diem amount that may be elected for 1997. This maximum is increased annually. The 2001 per diem tax-free limit is $200.

pool of money. Under a long term care insurance program, this is a variation on the typical benefit period. Rather than designate a period of time over which benefits can be payable, this concept creates a lump sum of money to be used as needed during a long term care claim. The claim ceases when services are no longer needed or the lump sum of money runs out.

pre-existing condition. A diagnosed injury or sickness for which medical advice or treatment was sought prior to the effective date of the long term care insurance contract.

respite care. Services provided for caregivers to permit temporary periods of relief or rest in caring for a person. These services can be provided by a home health care agency or other state licensed facility and may be reimbursable under a long term care insurance policy.

restoration of benefits. Long-term care policy feature whereby an insured could access benefits, recover for a specified period of time, and have the total benefits restored to their original amount as if the previous claim never happened.

return of premium. An optional benefit under a long term care insurance policy that provides a return of all or a portion of premiums paid less claims paid, either on a specified policy anniversary, at policy surrender, or at death of the insured.

reverse mortgage. A way to utilize the equity in one's own home to create an income stream for an individual whose substantial assets may be tied up in his or her residence.

sandwich generation. This term was coined when describing individuals caring for both dependent children and an aging parent or relative.

skilled care. A professional type of nursing assistance performed by trained medical personnel under the supervision of a physician or other qualified medical personnel. It is the only type of care eligible for reimbursement in a skilled nursing facility under Medicare.

spousal impoverishment protection. Medicaid changes made as part of the Medicare Catastrophic Act of 1988 provided an income and shelter allowance for the at-home spouse whose partner is institutionally confined.

standby assistance. An individual is considered unable to perform an activity of daily living if someone must be in close proximity to him to help when he is attempting to perform the activity.

tax-qualified plans. These are long term care insurance policies that meet the definition required by HIPAA and, therefore, are eligible for favorable tax treatment.

transfers. In qualifying for Medicaid, transfers are moving assets to someone other than a spouse or to a trust for the purposes of qualifying for Medicaid. Transfers must be made 36 months before Medicaid application (or 60 months if a trust is involved). Transfers made specifically to avoid Medicaid spend-down could result in criminal penalties for the person that assisted with the transfer.

triple trigger. This is the designation for the three ways to be eligible for benefits under a long term care insurance policy including assistance with activities of daily living, cognitive impairment or medical necessity. This definition is not available in tax-qualified plans.

viatical settlements. The purchase, on a reduced basis, of a life insurance policy owned by a terminally ill person.

waiver of premium. A policy provision of a long term care insurance contract that suspends premium payment after a specified period of time during which the insured is receiving policy benefits for long term care services. The suspension continues until recovery at which resumption of premium payment is expected.

wealth accumulation. The process of creating and building assets and income for retirement.

wealth distribution. The process of taking money out of various funding vehicles in the most efficient and effective manner to avoid attrition of dollars.

wealth protection. The process of protecting assets and income from the costs of an illness or injury.

wealth transfer. The process of moving assets around to take advantage of tax-favorability and protection from creditors. This process can occur both before and after death occurs.

Zoomers. Today's Baby Boomers, hurtling toward retirement, and in need of planning for this fast-approaching future.

INDEX

A

D

E

F

G

H

I

L

M

N

O

P

R

S

Z

To order, call **1-800-543-0874** and ask for operator BB or fax your order to **1-800-874-1916**, or visit our online catalog at www.nationalunderwriter.com.

PAYMENT INFORMATION

Add shipping & handling charges to all orders as indicated. If your order exceeds total amount listed in chart, call 1-800-543-0874 for shipping & handling charge. Any order of 10 or more items or $250.00 and over will be billed for shipping by actual weight, plus a handling fee. Unconditional 30 day guarantee.

SHIPPING & HANDLING *(Additional)*

Order Total	Shipping & handling
$20.00 to $39.99	$6.00
40.00 to 59.99	7.00
60.00 to 79.99	9.00
80.00 to 109.99	10.00
110.00 to 149.99	12.00
150.00 to 199.99	13.00
200.00 to 249.99	15.50

Shipping and handling rates for the continental U.S. only. Call 1-800-543-0874 for overseas rates.

SALES TAX
(Additional)

Sales tax is required for residents of the following states:

CA, DC, FL, GA, IL, KY, NJ, NY, OH, PA, WA.

The
NATIONAL
UNDERWRITER
Company
PROFESSIONAL PUBLISHING GROUP

The National Underwriter Co. • Orders Dept #2-BB
P.O. Box 14448 • Cincinnati, OH 45250-9786
1-800-543-0874

2-BB

_____ Copies of ***How to Sell Long Term Care Insurance:*** *Your Guide to Becoming a Top Producer in an Untapped Market* (#5010000) $29.95

_____ Copies of ***Long Term Care Sales Power Kit***
(includes a copy of How to Sell Long Term Care Insurance) (#4710002) $69.95

❑ Check enclosed*   ❑ Charge my VISA/MC/AmEx (circle one)   ❑ Bill me

*Make check payable to The National Underwriter Company. Please include the appropriate shipping & handling charges and any applicable sales tax (see charts above).

Card # _____ Exp. Date _____

Signature _____

Name _____ Title _____

Company _____

Street Address _____

City _____ State _____ Zip _____

Business Phone (_____) _____ Fax (_____) _____

E-mail_____

The
NATIONAL
UNDERWRITER
Company
PROFESSIONAL PUBLISHING GROUP

The National Underwriter Co. • Orders Dept #2-BB
P.O. Box 14448 • Cincinnati, OH 45250-9786
1-800-543-0874

2-BB

_____ Copies of ***How to Sell Long Term Care Insurance:*** *Your Guide to Becoming a Top Producer in an Untapped Market* (#5010000) $29.95

_____ Copies of ***Long Term Care Sales Power Kit***
(includes a copy of How to Sell Long Term Care Insurance) (#4710002) $69.95

❑ Check enclosed*   ❑ Charge my VISA/MC/AmEx (circle one)   ❑ Bill me

*Make check payable to The National Underwriter Company. Please include the appropriate shipping & handling charges and any applicable sales tax (see charts above).

Card # _____ Exp. Date _____

Signature _____

Name _____ Title _____

Company _____

Street Address _____

City _____ State _____ Zip _____

Business Phone (_____) _____ Fax (_____) _____

E-mail_____

BUSINESS REPLY MAIL

FIRST CLASS MAIL   PERMIT NO 68   CINCINNATI, OH

POSTAGE WILL BE PAID BY ADDRESSEE

The National Underwriter Co.
Orders Department #2-BB
P.O. Box 14448
Cincinnati, OH 45250-9786

|ı|ıı|ı|ıııı|ı|ı|ı|ı|ı|ıı|ıı|ı|ıı|ııı|ıı|ı|ıı|ıı|ıı|ı|ıı|

BUSINESS REPLY MAIL

FIRST CLASS MAIL   PERMIT NO 68   CINCINNATI, OH

POSTAGE WILL BE PAID BY ADDRESSEE

The National Underwriter Co.
Orders Department #2-BB
P.O. Box 14448
Cincinnati, OH 45250-9786

|ı|ıı|ı|ıııı|ı|ı|ı|ı|ı|ıı|ıı|ı|ıı|ııı|ıı|ı|ıı|ıı|ıı|ı|ıı|